# WRESTLING WITH GOD:

## JOB DEFENDS HIS INTEGRITY

# Also by James A. Colaiaco

*Frederick Douglass and the Fourth of July*
(Palgrave Macmillan)

*Socrates Against Athens: Philosophy on Trial*
(Routledge)

*Martin Luther King, Jr.: Apostle of Militant Nonviolence*
(St. Martin's Press)

*James Fitzjames Stephen: The Crisis of Victorian Thought*
(St. Martin's Press)

# WRESTLING WITH GOD:

## JOB DEFENDS HIS INTEGRITY

### JAMES A. COLAIACO

WRESTLING WITH GOD: JOB DEFENDS HIS INTEGRITY

ISBN- 13    978-1514396742

ISBN- 10    1514396742

*For Nancy, my kindred spirit*

# Acknowledgements

I am deeply grateful to my wife, Nancy Ruggeri Colaiaco, to whom this book is dedicated, for her support and insightful readings of the manuscript. I am blessed to have her as my partner in our life journey. I am also sustained by the memory of my parents and first teachers, Helen and Alfred Colaiaco.

Cover Art: "Job and His Friends"
By Ilya Yefimovich Repin (1844-1930)

# CONTENTS

# DRAMATIS PERSONAE

Job

God (Yahweh)

Satan (the Adversary)

Job's Three Friends:

      Eliphaz the Temanite

      Bildad the Shuhite

      Zophar the Naamathite

Elihu the Buzite

Job's Wife

# INTRODUCTION:
# A REVOLUTIONARY BOOK

"Have you really read Job? Read him, read him again and again....because he is so human in every way."— Søren Kierkegaard[1]

"I think we ought to read only the kind of books that wound and stab us. If the book we are reading doesn't wake us up with a blow on the head, what are we reading it for?"— Franz Kafka[2]

"Job is the just man crushed by injustice. He is the victim of a cruel wager between Satan and God."— Primo Levi[3]

"I read the Book of Job last night—I don't think God comes well out of it."— Virginia Woolf[4]

"The integrity of the upright shall guide them." —*Proverbs* 11:4

WHY READ THE BOOK OF JOB? It is the greatest masterpiece of the Hebrew Bible and among the most renowned classics of world literature. Its poetry reaches sublime heights and the questions it raises continue to haunt us. Along with the Book of Proverbs and Ecclesiastes, the Book of Job belongs to the tradition of Israelite wisdom literature. No work of scripture provokes like the Book of Job. For many religious people, the story of Job is about the test of a virtuous man's faith when God subjects him to terrible suffering. But the book is more complex, calling into question the goodness and justice of the Judeo-Christian God. The book is less about faith than innocent suffering, and as much about the character of God as the character of Job. Indeed, the book reflects a fundamental transformation in the conception of God in the Hebrew Bible. The faith of ancient Israel was based on the doctrine of divine retribution, prevalent throughout the ancient Near East. The doctrine assumed a divinely-established moral order. Confronted by a hostile world, humans projected a God as the supreme lawgiver who rewards the virtuous and punishes the wicked without fail. If God is absolutely just, it is reasonable for humans to expect that their fate in life should correspond with their conduct.

The Book of Job was composed during what the German philosopher Karl Jaspers called the Axial Age.[5] Spanning the eighth to the second centuries BCE, the Axial Age was a seminal period in the development of human consciousness. The world's great religions are the product of this time. The place of human beings in the universe and the meaning of life became central questions. It was the age of the Upanishads and the Buddha in India, Confucius and Lao-tse in China, Zoroaster in Iran, Socrates and Aeschylus in Greece, and the Hebrew prophets in Palestine. To this list must be added the anonymous poet of the Book of Job. The great luminaries of the Axial Age challenged and overturned traditional wisdom and values, raising questions that still preoccupy us today. Indeed, the Job poet confronted the greatest problem for people of religious faith—the problem of innocent suffering in a world supposed to be under the care of a benevolent God.

The Job poet responded to a profound theological crisis among the ancient Israelites. Not until the Nazi Holocaust would Israel receive a more disturbing challenge to its faith. The fall of Jerusalem and destruction of the Temple of Solomon by the Babylonians under King Nebuchadnezzar in 586 BCE undermined the retribution theology. For the ancient Israelites, it was a period of great suffering. The doctrine of strict divine retribution was easy to hold during the period of national prosperity. But after the destruction of Judah and the Exile of Israelites to Babylonia as war prisoners, many questioned the traditional link between virtue and success. The majority of scholars believe that the prose framework of the Book of Job, consisting of a Prologue and an Epilogue, is pre-exilic in origin, while the poetic dialogue, which constitutes most of the book, was written either during or shortly after the Exile, sometime between the sixth and fourth centuries BCE. The Job poet might have been a survivor of the Babylonian Exile. Why did God permit his chosen people to suffer and die while their wicked Babylonian conquerors prospered? Israelites asked God: "Why do you tolerate those who deal treacherously, and keep silent when the wicked swallows up the man who is more righteous than he?"[6] According to the creed of divine retribution, promulgated in Deuteronomy and confirmed by the wisdom teaching in the Book of Proverbs, suffering is penal, the consequence of sin. Refusing to view all suffering as punishment for sin, many Israelites realized that their conception of God and the moral universe could not be sustained.

The Book of Job is the most philosophical work in the Bible. Indeed, much of the book can be characterized as philosophy in the form of a poetic dialogue. The problem of innocent suffering provoked the Job poet to raise profound questions that had been hitherto ignored. The tension between Job and the traditional understanding of God pervades the text. If God is just and good, why does he allow innocent suffering in the world? Why do the wicked prosper? The poet saw the need for a theological paradigm shift towards a more realistic conception of God, one that no longer sees the deity as a strict moral policeman.

Whether Job is a fictional character or based on a historically true person, the story strikes a responsive chord in all readers. Innocent suffering is integral to the human condition, raising what theologians and philosophers since the eighteenth century Enlightenment have called the theodicy problem. The word "theodicy" was coined by the German philosopher Gottfried Leibniz in 1710. A theodicy is an attempt to justify God. It derives from two Greek words: "theos," meaning God and "dikē," meaning justice. Witnessing the suffering of his people, the poet who composed the Book of Job might have himself experienced spiritual struggles not unlike Job. To try to make sense of innocent suffering, the poet had to write about it. In creating the Job character, the Bible's greatest dissenter, the poet challenges orthodox theology on the justice and goodness of God. Job is the prototype of the innocent sufferer, scripture's Everyman, wrestling with God to grant him justice.

The Job poet was probably an Israelite, but the characters of the book are Gentiles. The poet possessed superior learning and knowledge of Hebrew scripture and ancient Near Eastern culture. Although they are Gentiles, Job and his friends worship Yahweh, the personal God of Israel. Nevertheless, Job invokes God's holy name only once throughout the lengthy dialogue, possibly owing to a scribal error or alteration to the text.[7] The other characters in the story never mention Yahweh at all, but use instead more generic pre-Israelite names for the deity, most often Shaddai, "the Almighty," in addition to El, Eloah and Elohim. The book is not set in Israel and contains no reference to the Jewish nation and its history—the Exodus, Mount Sinai, Moses or the Promised Land—and no reference to the covenant between God and Israel. While it is true that non-Jewish characters help to universalize the story, for all humans suffer, the Job poet might have wished to protect himself from the critical reactions of fellow Israelites. For the Job character the poet created dares to blaspheme God.

Subjected to grievous suffering by God for no reason, Job refuses to remain silent in the face of divine injustice. If blasphemy is defined as abusive and contemptuous language against God, Job is guilty. Blasphemy includes cursing or reviling God. While generations of pious commentators have understated or ignored the vehemence of Job's language, his blasphemies against God are multiple, direct and explicit. According to the nineteenth-century French historian of religion, Ernest Renan, the Book of Job is "the most sublime expression" of a "cry of the soul. In it blasphemy approximates the hymn, or rather itself is a hymn, since it is only an appeal to God against the lacunae which conscience finds in the work of God."[8] The Hebrew Bible regards blasphemy as a capital crime.[9] Left unpunished, the entire community would suffer God's wrath. According to Leviticus, Yahweh, the Hebrew God, declared to Moses: "He who blasphemes Yahweh's name, he shall surely be put to death. All the congregation shall certainly stone him. The foreigner as well as the native-born, when he blasphemes the Name, shall be put to death."[10] Speaking from righteous indignation, Job goes as far as any mortal can in denouncing God without denying his existence.

The character Job is the poet's persona. Job's questions about God's justice are the poet's questions. Job's challenge to God's government of the universe is the poet's challenge. Job's blasphemies are the poet's blasphemies. Job speaks with oratorical brilliance and moving poetry as he confronts God. Job laments, curses, challenges, argues, rages, implores, mocks, attacks, parodies, defies, pleads and rebels. Magnificent poetry also comes from the mouth of the Hebrew God at the dramatic climax of the book. Indeed, Yahweh speaks more eloquently in the Book of Job than anywhere else in the Hebrew Bible. But God pales in comparison with Job, among the most courageous characters in world literature. Like the Greek Prometheus, Job challenges the divine.

The spoken word dominates the Book of Job, comprising two-thirds of its contents. There is relatively little narration, confined mostly to the prose of the Prologue and the Epilogue. Dialogue is a prominent feature of the Hebrew Bible, reflecting the fact that much of it originated as oral literature. With the literacy rate relatively low and texts expensive to reproduce, ancient people relied more upon the spoken than the written word. Texts were intended to be read aloud, usually to groups of people. Even when alone, one read aloud, not silently as we do today. The Book of Job is the quintessential dialogical work of the Bible, honoring human speech. Robert Alter observes: "Everything in the world of biblical narrative ultimately gravitates toward dialogue—perhaps…because to the ancient Hebrew writers, speech seemed the essential human faculty; by exercising the capacity of speech man demonstrated, however imperfectly, that he was made in the image of God."[11] The honor that the ancient Israelites bestowed upon the spoken word is reflected in Genesis, when the entire universe is created from God's word: "And God said."

The core of the Book of Job is organized around three cycles of dialogue between Job and his three friends. First Eliphaz the Temanite speaks and Job replies; then Bildad the Shuhite speaks and Job replies; finally, Zophar the Naamathite speaks and Job replies. The same sequence occurs in the second and third cycles, but Zophar has no speech in the third cycle, perhaps signaling that the dialogue has run its course. Overall, Job delivers nine speeches, Eliphaz and Bildad three each, and Zophar two. As the dialogue progresses, the speeches of the friends become shorter while those of Job become longer, his struggle with God intensifying. We imagine that the dialogue occupied several days. The dialogue format, with each character speaking and replying in turn, brings immediacy to the text.

Except for the Prologue and the Epilogue, the Book of Job contains no external action. Instead, the book is an extraordinary drama of the mind. The poet creates a battle of ideas through the dialogue. The book is a drama without a stage, without a curtain to rise and fall, and no spectators, apart from a young bystander named Elihu the Buzite who has much to say later, and the all-seeing God. The central scene of the book is not an academic forum but the narrow confines of a city ash-heap. Readers receive minimal guidance from an omniscient narrator, who presumably speaks for the poet.

The dialogue explores two conflicts simultaneously: one between Job and his friends, the other between Job and God. As the hero, Job engages in both conflicts at once. The Job poet creates a passionate debate between a dying man fighting to defend his integrity and three friends desperate to retain a moribund theology. The conflicts occur within the context of what is known as a lawsuit drama. Legal language is prominent in the Book of Job, and the poet shows a sophisticated knowledge of ancient legal procedure. Job knows that God is the cause of his suffering. But the testimony of his conscience, an innate sense of right and wrong, informs him that he is innocent of serious wrongdoing. To defend his integrity, he will seek to institute a lawsuit against God. At a dramatic moment in the dialogue, Job declares a solemn oath to his innocence designed to compel God to indict him with a list of charges.

The dialogue is not a strict debate with interlocutors systematically addressing each other's points. In linear thinking, one question is answered before proceeding to the next. The Book of Job does not strictly follow this pattern. The movement of the dialogue is more circular than linear. Instead of being developed by following a logical step-by-step process from beginning to end, arguments are often introduced, dropped and resumed later. As biblical scholar Samuel Terrien points out, the Job poet employed the "highly original" technique of "delayed reaction."[12] Job and his friends often reply to a point not made by the immediately previous speaker, but to an argument of an earlier speaker. Indeed, the speeches of the friends often kindle thoughts in Job that he will not address directly until later. Despite the lack of a strictly logical progression, Job's speeches reflect a development while the friends repeatedly revert to the traditional theology of retribution.

We cannot know the reaction of the original audience to the Book of Job. But we assume that, like Job and his friends, they believed that the universe reflects a moral order and that God is absolutely just in applying the principle of retribution. At the same time, the original audience must have had difficulty reconciling their conception of God with their own experience of innocent suffering and the apparent triumph of evil. In ancient times, the Book of Job was probably as provocative as it is today. Despite efforts of many commentators to mitigate its message to fit their belief system, the Book of Job is nothing less than subversive. Within the Hebrew sacred canon, the book is an anomaly, for Job challenges the fabric of established theology. While there is a biblical tradition of arguing with God, no character provokes like Job. His stance is nothing short of heroic; his language is nothing short of volatile. Abraham and Moses question God's justice, Jeremiah laments that God allows the wicked to prosper, but Job goes much further, attacking God as unjust and malevolent, morally unqualified to rule the universe.

We asked, why read the Book of Job? Given the profound questions it raises about justice and innocent suffering, the book compels us to examine critically the traditional conception of God. The Hebrew Bible is not divinely authored. It did not descend fully formed from heaven. It is the product of a multitude of human writers who projected their own views of divinity upon God. We regard the Book of Job as a magnificent work of literature. The God of the Job poet is a literary character. Indeed, modern critics such as Harold Bloom and Jack Miles have written about Yahweh, the God of Israel, as a fiction.[13] The God of the Book of Job is no more divine than the God of Milton's *Paradise Lost*. With this understanding, we offer an ethical reading of the Book of Job that does not ignore the moral deficiency of the God it portrays. We show how Job, a paragon of righteousness, wrestles an immoral God who murders and abuses with impunity. Reading the Book of Job critically demands close attention to its prose Prologue, for it provides incontrovertible facts necessary to judge both God and Job. Enlightened by the Prologue, readers know that Job is innocent, affirmed by an omniscient narrator and by God himself. Readers also know that God causes Job's innocent suffering. The facts provided by the Prologue cannot be ignored or divorced from the rest of the book.

Many religious commentators do the Book of Job a disservice by attempting to shift the blame from God to Job, his victim. They accuse Job either of sinful pride or self-pity. Indeed, one commentator goes to the extent of describing Job as mentally ill, that his suffering made him paranoid.[14] But such distortions of the text merely reveal the biases of the commentators and betray the character of Job. Job grieves over colossal losses unjustly inflicted upon him by God. Would these same commentators accuse victims of the Holocaust of pride, self-pity, and paranoid delusions because they challenge God's justice and goodness? Too often, commentators minimize the negative depiction of God in the Prologue in order to support tendentious dogmatic readings of the text. Only by ignoring the uncomfortable truths of the Prologue can they mitigate the revolutionary message of the Book of Job.

# PROLOGUE TO THE BOOK OF JOB
## Chapters 1-2

## God Betrays His Righteous Servant
Five scenes alternating between Earth and Heaven

*Scene One: Earth*

THE BOOK OF JOB COMMENCES with an ancient didactic folktale. An omniscient narrator briefly introduces the hero: "There was a man in the land of Uz, whose name was Job. That man was blameless and upright, and one who feared God, and turned away from evil." The location of Job's homeland of Uz is uncertain, but it is believed to be part of the territory of Edom, south of Israel, famous for its wisdom and wise men. Hence Job is not an Israelite, but a Gentile paragon of righteousness whose devotion to God and relationships with his fellow humans fulfill the ideal of moral perfection. "Blameless" refers to Job's integrity. "Integrity" is derived from a Latin word meaning "wholeness." "Upright" refers to Job's moral rectitude. In the biblical tradition, to "fear God" means to show great devotion, obeying God's word and acknowledging absolute dependence on him. Job's conduct reflects his moral values. He is honest, truthful, compassionate and just. Along with Noah and Daniel, Job is singled out by the prophet Ezekiel as the most righteous among men, heroes of virtue.[1]

According to the prevailing theology of divine retribution, God in his justice rewards the righteous and punishes the wicked. Because of his supreme righteousness, Job is richly rewarded by God. His prosperity equals his character: "There were born to him seven sons and three daughters. His possessions also were seven thousand sheep, three thousand camels, five hundred yoke of oxen, five hundred female donkeys, and a very great household." Job's family is ideal. Having ten children was regarded as a sign of perfection or completeness. Job is a great patriarch, whose wealth and wisdom make him revered throughout the land as the "greatest of all the children of the East."

The righteous Job is devoted to his family, solicitous toward their material and spiritual welfare. He is blessed with a happy household: "His sons went and held a feast in the house of each one on his birthday; and they sent and called for their three sisters to eat and drink with them. When the days of their feasting had run their course, Job sent [for his children] and sanctified them, and rose up early in the morning, and offered burnt offerings according to the number of them all. For Job said, 'It may be that my sons have sinned, and cursed God in their hearts.' Job did so continually." These words provide the first glimpse into Job's mind. He is anxious about the piety of his children. He fears that his sons, absorbed in the conviviality of the feasts, which he apparently does not attend, might sin, cursing God in thought if not in deed. The righteous Job seeks to protect them from God's wrath. As head of the family, he acts as a priest, offering animal sacrifices to God for atonement on behalf of his sons. Before making these offerings of sheep or bullock in expiation, Job has his sons purified, involving ritual washing and perhaps changing clothes.

How might Job's sons have cursed God in their hearts? To curse or blaspheme God in one's heart is to do so in one's mind. According to ancient Hebrew psychology, the heart is regarded more as the center of intellect and will than of emotion. Job fears that his children might have turned their thoughts against God in some way. He believes that God can peer into the minds of humans, revealing their secret sinful thoughts.

*Scene Two: Heaven*

The scene shifts abruptly, transporting us from earth to heaven. God is depicted like an earthly monarch, presiding over his heavenly council of angels, receiving their reports and giving assignments: "Now on the day when God's sons came to present themselves before Yahweh, Satan also came among them." We have noted that Job, while not an Israelite, worships the Hebrew God, Yahweh. God's sons are angels, regarded as his instruments in the moral government of the universe. The Satan is not the devil, the demonic arch-enemy of God. The devil does not appear in the Hebrew Bible, but is an invention of later Hebrew and Christian theology. The Satan is not an evil being but God's loyal servant. The Hebrew word used in the Prologue is "ha-satan," the Satan, with the definite article, meaning the adversary or accuser. Satan is not a proper name, but rather designates a title or function, akin to a legal prosecutor or an investigator. His divinely-designated function is to monitor the behavior of humans on earth, accusing sinners before God. He is especially vigilant in pointing out hypocrisy. He acts as God's eyes and ears and never independently of the divine will. The Satan is God's advocate, not his enemy.

With his heavenly entourage in rapt attention, God bids the Satan to report on his earthly activity: "Yahweh said to Satan, 'Where have you come from?' Then Satan answered Yahweh, and said 'From going back and forth in the earth, and walking up and down in it.'" Perhaps the Satan detected wrongdoing among God's faithful that needed to be addressed. But God is more interested in singling out his servant Job, the epitome of righteousness, for the Satan's attention: "Yahweh said to Satan, 'Have you considered my servant Job?'" With this simple question, God initiates the action that sets the plot of the Book of Job in motion. "Servant" was a privileged title bestowed only upon the great heroes of the Hebrew Bible such as Abraham, Moses, David and Isaiah. God then boasts about Job, endorsing the judgment of the omniscient narrator: "For there is no one like him in the earth, a blameless and an upright man, one who fears God and turns away from evil." No person is more devoted to God than Job. But the Satan takes his office seriously. He does not believe in disinterested faith. Many people may act according to

God's law without really loving God. The Satan questions whether Job's righteousness might not be unconditional, but stem from self-interest. Job's motives, not his righteous actions, are challenged. The perceptive Satan exploits the weakness in the wisdom theology of divine retribution. If God inevitably rewards the righteous and punishes the wicked, virtue might not be pure, but rational self interest. The Satan moves the focus from external action to internal motivation. Piety should be more than deeds. Motives and intentions are essential in evaluating virtuous actions. One can do the right thing for the wrong reason. Perhaps Job is righteous merely to receive God's rich rewards.

The skeptical Satan addresses God: "Does Job fear God for nothing? Have not you made a hedge around him, and around his house, and around all that he has, on every side?" In other words, does Job worship God freely? Is Job's virtue disinterested or dependent upon rewards? This is the crux of the entire Book of Job and most troubling to those whose faith has never been tested. It is not difficult to be righteous when one expects great rewards. The Satan's probing questions startle God. The Satan impugns not only Job's honor, but God's as well. Ancient cultures valued honor, and the possibility that Job's piety might be self-interested was a grave insult to God. Job might be virtuous merely because God protects his person, his family and his great material prosperity. The Satan raises the issue whether any human is capable of pursuing virtue simply because it is virtue and shunning evil simply because it is evil, regardless of the personal consequences. Is righteousness an intrinsic value for Job? The Satan knows the frailty of human nature.

Focusing on Job, the Satan avers, "You have blessed the work of his hands, and his substance is increased in the land." The Satan boldly challenges God's judgment of Job. What if God removes his protective hedge from his servant? The Satan believes that if Job is afflicted with great suffering instead of great blessing, his piety will be demonstrated to be false. Job will be proven to be a hypocrite, his faith only mercenary. The Satan is among the shrewdest of God's creations, for he has placed God in a "no-win" situation. If God rejects the Satan's challenge, he will never know whether Job's piety is unconditional. At the same time, if God accepts the Satan's challenge, he will violate justice by causing Job to suffer innocently. The Satan implicitly challenges God's character as well as Job's. Did God doubt the piety of his servant Job? The Satan reveals a troubling insecurity in God. God does not trust humans to revere him for his own sake, or to live righteously without expecting rewards. Can humans love God for his own sake? Does God inspire only selfish piety? If humans are always recompensed for virtue, God cannot tell whether their virtue is pure or self-interested. The only way for God to test the purity of Job's faith is to suspend the inexorable law of retribution in his case and subject him to undeserved suffering. God must sever the link between righteousness and prosperity. Indeed, a major objective of the Book of Job is to undermine the orthodox theology of divine retribution. The Satan is confident that if Job suddenly lost his prosperity, he would turn from God: "But stretch out your hand now, and touch all that he has, and he will curse you to your face." According to the Satan, if Job lost everything he possessed, he would curse God in his presence, directly and openly to his face.

Apparently, God could not look into Job's heart to perceive his motives. An omniscient God would not question the sincerity of Job's virtue. God has supported the narrator's judgment that Job is without serious sin. Yet the Satan seems wiser than God in distinguishing between a righteous action and a righteous state of mind. The Satan's challenge: "Does Job fear God for nothing?" troubles God. The question insinuates that Job is a hypocrite. The Satan is a projection of God's dark side, a dimension of the deity prevalent in the Hebrew Bible. The Satan's skepticism about Job reflects God's skepticism about all humans. We can see how easily the Satan, God's agent, would later be transmogrified into the diabolical character, wise in the ways of the world, who seduces the faithful.

Instead of consulting his own wisdom, God is manipulated into betraying Job, his most faithful servant. A double burden is placed upon unsuspecting Job. He must defend his own character as well as God's. If Job's faith proves to be mere rational self interest, God will learn that his servant is a hypocrite. And if God cannot inspire pure faith, he must concede that he is worshipped merely out of fear and expectation of rewards. God therefore accepts the Satan's challenge to test Job's character: "Behold, all that he has is in your power." Since God gave Job everything as a reward for his righteousness, the Satan is granted permission to take everything away. This will determine the sincerity of Job's righteousness. Having given freedom to humans, God must wait to see how Job meets the challenge. The stakes could not be higher. The honor of God, creator of the universe, depends upon the unsuspecting Job. God expects that Job will set a sterling example of faith, independent of external reward.

What is done to Job is done by God, for in the Bible God is the ultimate agent; the Satan is merely God's instrument. God permits Job to suffer not in order to strengthen his piety, which has already been established, but to ascertain his motives. God wants to prove the Satan wrong by demonstrating that Job's motives are as pure as his virtuous deeds. One limit is placed on the Satan's actions: Job's physical body must be spared. God enjoins: "Only on himself do not stretch out your hand." His assignment given, "then Satan went out from the presence of Yahweh."

*Scene Three: Earth*

In suspense we anticipate the dreadful fulfillment of God's intention. The floodgates of suffering suddenly open upon Job as the Satan does God's bidding. Within a single horrifying day, four disasters hit in successive waves, each coming so quickly that Job is unable to recover from the previous one. The first disaster strikes in the midst of happiness, as Job's children are enjoying their feast: "It fell on a day when his sons and his daughters were eating and drinking wine in their oldest brother's house, that there came a messenger to Job, and said, 'The oxen were plowing, and the donkeys were feeding beside them, and the Sabeans attacked, and took them away. They have killed the servants with the edge of the sword, and I alone have escaped to tell you.'" Job loses much of his livestock and his herdsmen are murdered, victims of nomads from Arabia. Before the first messenger finishes with his report, a second disaster strikes. The threefold repetition of the refrain, "while he was still speaking" accentuates the rapidity of the disasters striking Job. While the first messenger "was still speaking, there came another, and said, 'The fire of God fell from the sky, and has burned up the sheep and the servants, and consumed them, and I alone have escaped to tell you.'" Job lost more livestock and their herders were dead, struck suddenly by God's lightning. Before the stunned Job was able to absorb this shock, another disaster struck as the messenger spoke: "While he was still speaking, there came also another, and said, 'The Chaldeans made three bands, and swept down on the camels, and have taken them away, yes, and killed the servants with the edge of the sword; and I alone have escaped to tell you.'" Chaldeans marauders from Mesopotamia seized Job's camels and slew their drivers.

Next is the most horrific disaster to befall Job. Preoccupied with their feast, Job's children were not aware of the three previous disasters that day. Now it was their turn. As the previous messenger "was still speaking, there came also another, and said, 'Your sons and your daughters were eating and drinking wine in their oldest brother's house, and behold, there came a great wind from the wilderness, and struck the four corners of the house, and it fell, and they are dead. I alone have escaped to tell you.'" Job lost his seven sons and three daughters in one fell swoop. Having lost everything, would Job remain faithful to God? The test had been severe, more than almost any person could endure. With four swift blows, Job's entire world collapsed. According to God's will, Job had been hit by four disasters, two inflicted by human agents, now called moral evil, and two by the forces of nature, now called natural evil.

It is doubtful that Job fully grasped the magnitude of his misfortune. The economical prose of the Prologue leaves the reader to imagine Job's reaction to his terrible losses. As a patriarch, he had received each of the messengers while seated. Having lost his material possessions, Job is unmoved. But when he heard of the death of his children, Job "arose, and tore his robe, and shaved his head, and fell down on the ground and worshipped." These actions were ancient symbols of mourning. Job humbly prostrated himself, touching his forehead to the ground in solemn worship of God. Instead of denouncing God for having taken so much from him, Job adhered to his integrity. A model of serene detachment, he regards all he possesses, including his children, as gifts from God. He declares: "Naked I came out of my mother's womb, and naked I shall return there." What Job appears to value most in life are not material possessions, not even his children, but his relationship with God. Job owned nothing when he came into the world; he is willing to depart the world with nothing. Temporal goods are given to humans by God and taken away by God, according to his will. Job proclaims his absolute dependence upon Yahweh, the sovereign Hebrew God who gives and takes according to his will: "Yahweh gave, and Yahweh has taken away. Blessed be Yahweh's name."

The Danish philosopher Søren Kierkegaard celebrates Job's words as expressing true religious faith. The fact that Job first said "Yahweh gave," shows his gratitude for the many blessings God bestowed upon him. And when God removes these blessings, "Yahweh has taken away," Job remains faithful to God. With pious resignation, Job accepts the good and the evil that God has caused. There is no bitterness in Job's heart. His faith remains pure and unselfish as he submits completely to God's will. God was absolutely good when he gave; God was absolutely good when he took. What God gives is a free gift, which he can take away. Such religious faith, according to Kierkegaard, should fill us with trepidation. For no one knows when the God who gives will choose to take away.[2]

It seems that Job has met the Satan's challenge to God. Job has maintained his integrity in the face of sudden disaster. His piety appears to be selfless, motivated by pure love of God. Instead of cursing God, as the Satan said he would, Job praises God: "Blessed be Yahweh's name." To emphasize that Job does not curse God, the narrator concludes: "In all this, Job did not sin, nor charge God with wrongdoing." Job did not accuse God of injustice. Job did not challenge God's goodness. This is the patient Job of folklore, stoically resigned to his awful fate, steadfast in his piety. While Job, contrary to the Satan's prediction maintains the purity of his piety, his reaction is disturbing. Does he not realize what God has done to him? Job is not privy to the conversation in Heaven between God and the Satan, but he knows that the disasters are the will of God. One might admire Job's refraining from cursing God, but to bless God in the midst of such devastation is difficult to believe. Job does not charge God with any wrongdoing. But Job's testing has not ended. The Satan is not convinced that Job has met the challenge.

*Scene Four: Heaven*

How much time has elapsed since Job's first test is not clear, but the narrator presents the reader with another scene in heaven, with God presiding over his court. The opening three verses virtually repeat the three verses from the second scene: "Again, on the day when God's sons came to present themselves before Yahweh, Satan came also among them to present himself before Yahweh. Yahweh said to Satan, 'Where have you come from?'" The Satan answered as he did in the second scene, "From going back and forth in the earth, and from walking up and down in it." Gloating over the fact that Job has met the Satan's challenge, God again inquires whether he has noticed the righteous Job: "Have you considered my servant Job?" For the second time, God confirms Job's integrity: "There is no one like him in the earth, a blameless and an upright man, one who fears God, and turns away from evil." Emphasizing Job's enduring piety, God declares sarcastically: "He still maintains his integrity, although you incited me against him, to ruin him without cause." The cause, according to the Satan, is to demonstrate Job's selfish piety. God is proclaiming victory. The test had been unnecessary. The Satan's suspicion of Job's sincerity was groundless. Job had been afflicted for no reason.

Although Job's suffering was undeserved, he maintained his integrity and absolute trust in God. He did not curse God. Nevertheless, God's character is questionable, for he betrayed his most loyal servant, subjecting him to a gratuitous cruel test. The portrayal of God would later shock Rabbinic Judaism. As Rabbi Yochanan confessed in the *Babylonian Talmud*, "Were it not written in the Bible it would be impossible to say: God is like a man whom someone tries to incite and who is in the end incited."[3] But the reputed God of justice blames the Satan for inducing him to afflict Job. An all-too-human God has been seduced by the Satan's specious rhetoric. Given God's repeated praise of Job's integrity, confirmed by the omniscient narrator, it is clear that Job's suffering is not the result of sins he committed. This is essential for understanding the heart of the book in which Job will have to defend himself against accusations that he is a great sinner. By permitting Job to suffer innocently, God has undermined the link between virtue and prosperity fundamental to the wisdom tradition.

The Satan still believes that Job's piety is self-serving. He proposes a more severe test. One layer of God's protective hedge remained. The Satan suggests that God lift the ban on touching Job's body: "Skin for skin; all that a man has he will give for his life." A man's life is most important to him. He will easily sacrifice everything he owns to save his own skin. Take everything away from a man that is external to him, his wealth, his possessions, even his children, and he may remain faithful. But touch his skin, his body, threaten him with death, and he will really be tested. To save his life, a man will do or say anything. The Satan again presents the challenge: "But stretch out your hand now and touch his bone and his flesh, and he will curse you to your face." For the second time, the Satan alleges that Job will curse God directly to his face.

If God is omniscient, he would know that another test of Job would, like the first, be "without cause." Seeing into the heart of Job, he would have rejected the Satan's accusation from the outset. But God is again manipulated by the Satan. He grants the Satan's request, allowing Job's body to be assaulted, with one stipulation: "Behold, he is in your hand. Only spare his life." If Job were killed, the sincerity of his devotion to God could never be determined. Anxious to prove his case, the Satan immediately does God's will: "So Satan went out from the presence of Yahweh, and struck Job with painful sores from the sole of his foot to his head." Job's whole body is stricken with an inexplicable gruesome skin disease, possibly leprosy, similar to that which God threatened to inflict upon ancient Israelites who violated the covenant.[4] Having carried out his mission on behalf of God, the Satan abruptly disappears from the book.

Job's body has now been ravaged. What more could he suffer? The medieval Christian theologian Thomas Aquinas noted that the story of Job's suffering is presented in reverse order to that of his prosperity. The story began by focusing on Job, moving from him to his offspring, extensions of himself, and finally to his great possessions. In contrast, Job's suffering begins with what is most external to him, his material possessions, his herds and flocks, followed by the killing of his children, and finally with the affliction of his person. In order to undermine Job's piety, the Satan begins with the relatively smaller suffering, and moves increasingly closer to Job's self by killing his children, and finally striking Job's body. According to Aquinas, this gradual sequence enhanced Job's suffering, "for one who has been crushed by a greater adversity does not feel a smaller one, but after a smaller one a greater is felt all the more."[5]

*Scene Five: Earth*

Inflicted with severe physical pain, Job took a piece of broken pottery to scrape his skin and "sat among the ashes," an expression of grief. According to the traditional theology of divine retribution, Job's community viewed his suffering as evidence of a sinful life. A social pariah, the grieving Job exiles himself outside the city walls to the public ash-heap, where his fellow citizens take their trash to be burned. The ash-heap is the place for outcasts and victims of contagious diseases. Job also donned the coarse sackcloth, the apparel of those in mourning.

But Job is not the only victim of God's cruel test. Job's nameless wife also suffers, having lost her ten children, her material security and her reputation in the community. She suddenly breaks into the story. Where has she been through the tribulations of Job? She and her husband have buried their children, and Job now sits on the ash-heap, bereft of his dignity. True to the patriarchal culture of the day, the canonical Book of Job relegates her to a single ambiguous verse. She interrogates: "Do you still maintain your integrity?" She then exhorts: "Curse God and die." Her question and imperative have provoked much commentary. While her question unconsciously affirms God's judgment of Job's integrity, her poignant imperative recalls the Satan's prediction that Job will curse God. Saint Augustine characterizes Job's wife as *diabolic adjutrix*, Satan's helper, merely because she unknowingly took his position that Job would curse God. John Calvin dubbed her Satan's tool. Job's wife has also been compared to the Eve of *Genesis*, who induced Adam to sin.

But Job's wife's reaction can be interpreted in more than one way. Many argue that she is expressing her anger at God. Why continue to behave righteously, she might be saying to Job, when God afflicts you innocently? Curse the unjust God who has betrayed you and welcome death as an end to your misery. Another interpretation is that, speaking from the prevailing belief in divine retribution, she might have concluded that Job is being punished for some secret sin deserving death. If so, she is enjoining Job to abandon his pretended righteousness and call for the death his hypocrisy deserves. Alternatively, Job's wife may speak from compassion. Witnessing her husband's severe suffering, she might think that a quick death as punishment for cursing God would end his agony. Cursing God would be tantamount to suicide.

Regardless of his wife's intention, Job must feel the sting of her suggestion that he curse God. Yet Job's pain is not his alone. His wife's intense suffering is expressed in the later Greek translation of the Hebrew Bible, known as the Septuagint. The Septuagint humanizes Job's wife, allowing her to vent her anguish as a spouse and a mother. She says to Job: "How long will you endure and say, 'See, I will wait a bit longer, looking for the hope of my salvation?' Look, your memory is already blotted out from the earth, along with the sons and daughters, the travail and pangs of my womb, whom I reared in toil for nothing. And you, you sit in wormy decay, passing the nights in the open, while I roam and drudge from place to place, and from house to house, waiting for the sun to go down, so that I may rest from my toils and the griefs which now grip me." She concludes bitterly: "Now, say some word against the Lord, and die."[6] Each of the above interpretations of the reaction of Job's wife is plausible. Having suffered devastating losses, she is angry at God, angry at Job, and yet she feels compassion for her tormented husband.

The righteous Job summarily rejects his wife's impious counsel: "You speak as one of the foolish women would speak." In the wisdom tradition, impiety is folly. Job rebukes his wife for speaking like one who has turned from God. Frustrated, Job asks her: "Shall we receive good at the hand of God, and shall we not receive evil?" Job humbly accepts everything, his health and prosperity, as well as his suffering, as God's will. He does not curse God; nor does he question God's justice or goodness. The narrator declares that, despite his undeserved suffering, Job remains unwavering in his piety: "In all this, Job did not sin with his lips." Instead, Job submits to his fate with unbelievable stoicism.

Nevertheless, the question has been raised whether Job sinned in his heart if not with his lips. As we have seen, he recognized the possibility that his children might have "sinned and cursed God in their hearts." Significantly, while Job responded to his initial losses by blessing God, he does not bless God after his entire body is afflicted. The twelfth-century Jewish commentator Rashi, following the *Talmud*, alleged that although Job does not sin with his lips, he does so in his heart.[7] But this is to read into Job's mind what the text of the Prologue does not support. Job is presented as a person of impeccable virtue. Adhering to the purpose of the Prologue, it is unlikely that Job's view of God has now changed. The ancient Israelites believed that the lips express what is in the heart.[8] Moreover, the omniscient narrator, with access to Job's innermost thoughts, would express them. If we are skeptical of Job's integrity by the end of the Prologue, we should be equally skeptical of God and the omniscient narrator's affirmations of Job's integrity at the beginning. To call him a mental sinner at this point in the story is to read the Prologue through the lens of the remainder of the book, in which a more complex and irreverent Job appears.

Thus far in the story, Job has met the Satan's challenge. He demonstrates disinterested righteousness and pure devotion to God. According to the Prologue, suffering is inflicted upon the innocent as a trial of faith. One can imagine God nodding to the Satan in smug satisfaction, proud of his faithful servant, the embodiment of piety. The purpose of the didactic tale is to portray an outstanding example of faith, even in times of great adversity. But what kind of God would do such great harm to a righteous person? Job's innocent suffering is shocking, but what is more shocking is God's immoral conduct. No critical reader can excuse the behavior of God. Testing Job's integrity, God undermines his own. If the devout could wish a section of the Hebrew Bible never to have been written, it would be the Prologue to the Book of Job. Indeed the depiction of Yahweh, the Hebrew God, easily seduced by the Satan to afflict a righteous man, is nothing short of blasphemous. By the Prologue's conclusion, God's character is revealed. Afflicting Job innocently, God has perpetrated horrific evil. If Job, a person of impeccable integrity, is so easily betrayed by his Creator, whom among the righteous is safe?

The patient Job of the Prologue does not provide a realistic model for how most people cope with suffering. This Job is not true to human psychology. The original tale does not consider the anger directed at God by many people who suffer innocently. Few humans, if any, could emulate the patience of Job. Few humans could suffer the loss of their children and possessions and remain grateful to God, knowing him to be the cause. Yet the Prologue is indispensable to the canonical text and provides the frame for the poetic dialogue between Job and his friends. The Prologue also provides the dramatic irony that enriches the entire book. If the veil were lifted, allowing Job to see that his suffering was a malicious test of faith, the contest between God and the Satan would be suspended, making the rest of the story unnecessary. But having witnessed the words between God and the Satan in the Prologue, readers have knowledge hidden from Job. They know that Job is innocent and that his suffering is gratuitous. They will also know that Job's upcoming accusations against God's justice and goodness are true.

In the poet's creative hands, Job of the dialogue becomes an extraordinarily complex character, more true to life. The poet transforms the original naïve portrayal of faith into a probing exploration of innocent suffering and the justice of God. The cruel irony is that in order to test the strength of Job's faith, God afflicts him with suffering due the worst sinner. The test of Job's integrity becomes a test of God's integrity. Even though Job has met the Satan's challenge, his suffering does not end with the Prologue, but continues for another thirty-nine chapters, leaving readers in suspense, wondering whether Job will eventually curse God to his face.

Job's multifaceted character is reflected by the various suggestions given for the origin of his name, each presenting an aspect of Job that will be revealed in the remainder of the book. In Hebrew, the name "Job" (Iyyob) might denote "inveterate foe," (Oyeb) or the "hated or persecuted one." Indeed, Job will view God as his enemy, who torments him without reason. Another suggestion interprets the name to mean "where is my [Divine] father?" In the depth of despair over his suffering, Job will lament the absence of God, his divine father whose face is hidden. In the Arabic of the Koran, Job is characterized as one who is "pious," or a "penitent" returner to God. As we have seen, Job's piety is unequalled, but while many believe that he repents at the end of the book, the text does not necessarily support this interpretation.

At the conclusion of the prose Prologue, Job's friends arrive. This scene is the transition to the poetic dialogue that constitutes the vital core of the book. We do not know whether this transition was part of the folktale, slightly adapted by the poet, or his original creation. News of Job's calamities spread through his city, as the pitiful Job remains mourning on the ash-heap. When Job's friends— Eliphaz the Temanite, Bildad the Shuhite, and Zophar the Naamathite— hear about what has befallen him, they travel from their distant homes, meet together, and go to "sympathize with him and to comfort him." Because travel was slow in the ancient Near East, it took the friends a long time, weeks, perhaps even months, to reach him, crossing the desert by camel.[9] Like Job, his friends are Gentiles, probably his countrymen. We presume that, like Job, the friends were known for their wisdom, piety and prosperity. During this period, Job has ample time to reflect upon the magnitude of his devastation. Approaching Job, disfigured by his physical and emotional suffering, the friends "lifted up their eyes from a distance, and did not recognize him, they raised their voices and wept; they each tore his robe and sprinkled dust on their heads toward the sky." These are gestures of mourning. The suffering Job is virtually dead. The friends sit on the ground with him for seven days and seven nights, the traditional mourning period.[10] Their presence is meant to console Job. The Hebrew word "nud," to console, denotes shaking the head and rocking the body back and forth as an indication of sharing the grief of others. As Job says nothing, they think it best to support him in his silence. For words could not alleviate his suffering: "No one spoke a word to him, for they saw that his grief was very great." Yet in their silence, the friends could not help contemplating Job's precipitous fall. In the space of a single horrific day, Job had been reduced from a person favored by God with great prosperity and honor to a person afflicted by unbearable suffering.

What are Job and his friends thinking during the long silence? They are ignorant of the events in Heaven. They do not know that God decided to afflict Job even though he is innocent. The retribution doctrine, found in the Hebrew Bible and upheld throughout the ancient Near East, assumed that a perfectly just God unerringly rewards the righteous and punishes the wicked. The idea of divine retribution was applied first to the Israelite nation as a whole, as found in Deuteronomy and Leviticus.[11] Based upon the Mosaic covenant between the Hebrew God and the Israelites, whom he liberated from bondage in Egypt, the prophets taught that a just God rewards Israel for fulfilling his Law, and punishes Israel for sinful behavior. Israel reaped what it sowed. Peace and prosperity were regarded as signs of God's favor, while famine, pestilence, and defeat in war were regarded as signs of God's wrath. A virtuous Israel would survive in the wilderness; the sinful nation would be conquered by the Assyrians and the Babylonians. As long as the individual was subsumed in the nation, personal calamity could be explained as a result of the nation's sin. But the retribution theology was eventually applied to individuals as well as the nation. The Psalms, the prophets Jeremiah and Ezekiel, and the Book of Proverbs demonstrate a shift in focus from the relationship between God and the nation to God and the individual. Prosperity and misery were believed to be determined by individual character. When people suffered, it was assumed that they were guilty of sins and received the proper punishment. The friends will invoke the retribution doctrine to justify Job's suffering.

Neither Job nor his friends could attribute his suffering to any other source but God. Along with their contemporaries, they did not understand secondary causes.[12] God causes everything, the good as well as the evil. Living in a pre-scientific age, they had no knowledge of the unalterable laws of nature. Natural disasters such as earthquakes, famines, plagues and floods were thought to be directly caused by God. According to Job's contemporaries, to deny that God is the cause of everything is to deny his absolute sovereignty. There are no mitigating circumstances to relieve God from the responsibility for evil as well as good. When people behave rightly, God rewards them with prosperity; when they behave wickedly, God punishes them with suffering. Strict monotheists, the Israelites did not believe in a rival power, such as the later Christian Satan or devil, as a cause of evil and suffering. Speaking through his prophet, known as the second Isaiah, God proclaims: "I am Yahweh, and there is no one else. Besides me, there is no God. I form the light, and create darkness. I make peace and create calamity. I am Yahweh, who does all these things."[13] The prophet Amos declared: "Does evil happen to a city and Yahweh has not done it?"[14] The Book of Lamentations affirms: "Does not evil and good come out the mouth of the Most High?"[15] We recall that Job himself saw no other cause of his suffering than God: "Shall we receive good at the hand of God, and shall we not receive evil?"[16]

The work of Elisabeth Kübler-Ross sheds light on Job's emotional plight. In her book, *On Death and Dying,*[17] she outlines five now well-known stages of death experienced by many of the terminally ill: denial and isolation, anger, bargaining, depression, and acceptance. These stages are not to be viewed as a rigid sequence. Indeed, some persons do not experience every stage; others experience them in a different sequence; and others may fluctuate between one stage and another. The stages are a mere framework to assist in comprehending the various emotional reactions of a person with a terminal illness. Relating the framework to Job, we see that he undergoes each stage of the grief cycle. In the Prologue, he is compelled to face his imminent death. Unaware that God ordered the Satan to spare his life, Job believes that he has a terminal illness.[18] His entire world has been shattered. In modern times, Job's loathsome skin disease would have a psychological effect similar to cancer or AIDS. Throughout the dialogue with his friends, Job is obsessed with death, wavering between wishing for death and fearing that he will die before being vindicated. He experiences many changes in mood, oscillating like a pendulum between anger, despair, and hope. His mistreatment by God and his friends arouses his indignation. Believing that God caused his suffering gives rise to despair. At the same time, Job's firm conviction of his integrity gives him hope in ultimate vindication. The Job poet displays a penetrating knowledge of human psychology, portraying a character grieving over the prospect of his death.

Throughout the Prologue, Job is in a state of denial. Having lost so much, he responds stoically, with complete equanimity, humbly accepting his suffering as God's will. Although Job mourns, his initial submissive response is puzzling. Has he forgotten his ten dead children? The Prologue says nothing of the painful experience of Job and his wife as they buried their children. Does not Job realize that he has lost all material necessities? Does not Job feel for his wife, mother of his children who shares his suffering? Does he not realize that his adversity stigmatizes him as a grave sinner? In shock, Job is psychologically unable to absorb the gravity of what happened to him so suddenly. Never having experienced great suffering, he is overwhelmed. Denial is a natural early emotional defense when a person confronts extreme calamity. Job might have thought that, given his righteousness, the God who took away would soon give back.

Relegated to the ash-heap, Job sat alone until his friends arrived. As they sit with him for seven days and nights in absolute silence,

Job's friends attempt to justify his suffering in their minds. Sitting across from Job, covered with sores from head to foot, they cannot believe their eyes. Why does Job have to endure such suffering? According to the creed of divine retribution, innocent suffering does not exist. In the Book of Job, the friends are spokespersons for orthodox theology. The conception of retribution is inseparable from their conception of God. God afflicts only the sinner. Despite their compassion, they cannot ignore their disturbing thoughts about Job's condition. They conclude reluctantly that they do not know the real Job. He cannot be a person of integrity. Beneath his righteous exterior, Job must have sinned. The God of justice would not afflict Job innocently. Only because he remains alive do his friends have hope that they might persuade him to repent and be restored to God's favor. While the friends initially sympathize with Job, they have little understanding of his spiritual and emotional plight. Their limitations as counselors merely augment his anguish. Believing that suffering is the consequence of sin, and severe suffering the consequence of severe sin, the friends will counter Job's every plea for relief with traditional moral platitudes, exhorting him to seek God's forgiveness. They will insist that Job must atone for his guilt. Job's isolation pervades the book. He is abandoned by God, maligned by his friends, and ostracized by society.

Like his friends, Job believes in retributive justice. He assumes that his prosperity and his honorable reputation were his recompense for a life of the utmost integrity, showing great reverence for God and adhering to a strict moral code in his behavior. But now Job's anguish is extreme. Physically transformed almost beyond recognition, Job is even more transformed emotionally and psychologically. His children are dead, his property destroyed, and his body is wasting away from a painful disease. His suffering having stigmatized him as a great sinner, Job is no longer the greatest man of the East. He is now impoverished, bereft of his children, rejected by his community as a sinner, and relegated to the burned rubbish beyond the city gate. He also suffers spiritually, for he believes that God has abandoned him. The Psalmist lamented, "My God, my God, why have you forsaken me?"[19] What did Job do to deserve such adversity? His relationship with God had changed. Job now realizes that an innocent person like himself can suffer. He is unaware that, according to the sinister plan of heaven, his suffering is not punishment but a test of his faith, engineered by God and executed by the Satan. According to the prevailing theology, God is the cause of his suffering. But only the wicked are supposed to suffer. Searching his conscience, Job knows that he is not wicked and that he could not have committed any sin that deserved his calamity. All his life, he had believed that God was just. All his life, he believed that God rewarded the virtuous and punished the wicked. For the first time Job experiences a crisis of faith. Why did God afflict him? Job shudders at the thought: Is God unjust?

Job's inner turmoil and disappointment with God reflect the sentiment of countless sufferers. Job is the archetypal figure of innocent suffering. In the modern era, the young narrator of Holocaust survivor Elie Wiesel's memoir, *Night*, expresses the spiritual agony of an innocent sufferer. Experiencing with his father their first night in a Nazi concentration camp, the narrator laments: "Never shall I forget that night, the first night which has turned my life into one long night. Never shall I forget those flames which consumed my faith forever. Never shall I forget that nocturnal silence which deprived me, for all eternity, of the desire to live. Never shall I forget those moments which murdered my God and my soul and turned my dreams to dust. Never shall I forget these things, even if I am condemned to live as long as God Himself. Never."[20] Only a person of the deepest faith like Job could suffer such a loss of meaning, fearing that God has abandoned him.

Job eventually realizes the magnitude of the horrors that happened to him. He buried his ten children; he surveyed his great material losses; he left his home to mourn, sitting in ashes. In the Jewish tradition, when friends come to commiserate, the mourner is the first to speak. The poet takes full advantage of the mournful silence to enhance the drama. Having realized the full significance of his suffering, the patient Job of the prose Prologue is suddenly transformed. Having lost the will to live, Job breaks the silence, voicing his anguish from the ash-heap.

# JOB'S LAMENT

## Chapter 3   Job Curses His Birth

THE PROSE PROLOGUE COMPLETED, the tone of the story shifts radically. The omniscient narrator announces that after sitting with his friends in mourning for seven days and seven nights, "Job opened his mouth and cursed the day of his birth." Job could no longer contain his rage and despair. The poetic dialogue begins with an explosive outcry from Job, shattering the silence. We are plunged into the midst of Job's suffering. He faces the prospect of imminent death.

In an impassioned lament, the first of several, Job curses the day of his birth and the night of his conception. This monologue gives us a deeper insight into Job. He vents his grief of mind and heart. His words are not directly addressed to anyone but are overheard by his friends. While Job does not curse God explicitly, as the Satan predicted and his wife urged, Job does curse his own existence. He hates his life and longs for the peace of death. But because God gives life, for Job to curse his existence is blasphemy. A curse is a summoning of a supernatural power to harm a person or thing. In ancient times, a curse was more than a spoken wish. People believed that a curse puts forces in motion that inevitably bring about the intended evil. For the Israelites, as well as other ancient peoples, spoken words had dynamic power, especially when uttered as a curse. A curse was considered self-fulfilling, and once spoken becomes reality. A curse cannot be recalled, any more than an arrow once shot from a bow and rushing headlong to its target can return to the shooter. The words of Job throughout most of the book, while they could never actually harm God, revile him with blasphemy.

Job begins his blasphemies by pleading with God to wipe his birthday from the calendar. His life no longer has purpose. His world had been predictable under God's benevolent providence. But knowing that God alone could have caused his suffering, Job is despondent. For him, the cosmos has become a moral chaos, devoid of justice. Job experiences a dark night of the soul, his life bereft of the light of meaning. He feels deserted in a hostile universe. The poet William Butler Yeats famously lamented: "Things fall apart; the centre cannot hold. Mere anarchy is loosed upon the world."[1] For the first time, Job directly confronts the fragility of life and the prospect of his own death. Believing himself abandoned by God, everything seems absurd. If the day of his birth and the night of his conception had not existed, he would not exist. He would never have been born into the world of suffering.

In the first nine verses of his monologue, Job utters a series of maledictions, unified by contrasting images of day and night, light and darkness, life and death, order and chaos. In words almost identical to the lament of the prophet Jeremiah,[2] Job cries: "Let the day perish in which I was born, the night which said, 'There is a boy conceived.' Let that day be darkness. Do not let God from above seek for it, neither let the light shine on it." Job then parodies Genesis, reversing the divine words of creative action.[3] God began by creating the day out of chaotic darkness with the words, "Let there be light," and deemed his creation "good." But Job would have God undo the day of his birth as something evil that allowed him to exist: "Let darkness and the shadow of death claim it. Let a cloud dwell on it. Let all that makes black the day terrify it." Job would have the day of his birth returned to the primeval dark chaos. After creating the day, God separated the light from the darkness, originating the night. As for the night of his conception, Job curses: "Let thick darkness seize on it. Let it not rejoice among the days of the year. Let it not come into the number of the months." Instead of bringing the joys of conception and birth, "let that night be barren. Let no joyful voice come therein."

If God will not fulfill his anguished wish, Job would summon the ancient sorcerers of pagan religion to curse the day of his birth. He calls upon them to use their incantations to "rouse up Leviathan," a

Canaanite mythological sea monster. A symbol of the primeval chaos God overcame in creating the world, ancient people believed that Leviathan was capable of leaping from the sea and devouring the sun and the moon, causing an eclipse. Job wishes that Leviathan, representing his own inner chaos, would swallow the morning stars that gave light to his day: "Let the stars of its twilight be dark. Let it look for light, but have none, neither let it see the eyelids of the morning." Job concludes with the reason for cursing his day: "It did not shut up the doors of my mother's womb, nor did it hide trouble from my eyes." But, having been born, Job is doomed to suffer. His lament is more poignant because wishing to annihilate the day of his birth is futile. The past cannot be undone. His birth cannot be reversed.

Job devotes the second half of his monologue to a solemn lamentation, the most despairing in the Hebrew Bible. His anguish is expressed in rhetorical questions, each beginning with a desperate "Why?" Whereas the patient Job of the Prologue never asked why, the suffering Job now questions the value of human life. Believing that his life belongs to God, throughout his ordeal Job never contemplates suicide. Nevertheless, unable to reverse his conception, Job wishes that he had died immediately at birth: "Why did I not die from the womb? Why did I not give up the spirit when my mother bore me?" Job projects his bitterness at his mother, asking why she welcomed and nursed him. Had he died as a newborn, he would now be free from torment. It would have been even better to be a stillborn child, "who never saw light." But he was fated to be born: "Why did the knees receive me? Why the breast that I should nurse? For now should I have lain down and been quiet." A newborn child was customarily first placed on the father's knees before being fed by the mother. But being born and having lived to maturity, the despairing Job longs to die. He would then pass to Sheol, the Hebrew underworld. Although not mentioned explicitly in the Book of Job, references to Sheol are clear. It harbored the spirits of the dead, righteous and wicked alike. It is not the afterlife later developed by

Christians, a place of reward for the virtuous and punishment for the wicked. The ancient Israelites dreaded Sheol as a gloomy, dark, shadowy place, from which the dead never return. They are separated completely from God and those still living. They have no knowledge of what happens on earth, no happiness, no memory, and no hope of resurrection. But Job reverses the traditional conception of the Hebrew underworld, viewing it positively as a place of peace and a refuge from his suffering.

Had Job died at birth, he declares, "I would have been at rest, with kings and counselors of the earth, who built up waste places for themselves; or with princes who had gold, who filled their houses with silver." Having been a man of great riches and honor and suddenly lost everything, Job realizes that wealth and power are transitory. The Preacher in Ecclesiastes cries: "Vanity of vanities. All is vanity."[4] The magnificent palaces of kings are destined to ruin. The poet Shelley's "Ozymandias" declares: "Look on my works, ye Mighty, and despair!' Nothing beside remains: Round the decay of that colossal wreck, boundless and bare, the lone and level sands stretch far away." Job sees death as the great equalizer, striking all indiscriminately. All humans, kings and subjects, masters and slaves, rich and poor, powerful and weak, suffer the same fate. In death, Job would be their equal. Death erases the inequities of earthly life. Kings are stripped of their earthly power and wealth. The wicked can no longer harm the weak. Prisoners and servants are free from their masters. If death brings such peace, Job sees it as preferable to life.

Turning from himself, Job expands his lament to speak for all of suffering humanity. Having lost his children and material livelihood, and undergoing great physical and mental anguish, Job understands why many who suffer long for death. With interrogatives, he laments: "Why is light given to him who is in misery, life to the bitter in soul who long for death, but it does not come; and dig for it more than for hidden treasures, who rejoice exceedingly, and are glad when they can find the grave?" Multitudes of humans who suffer look forward to death. Not having died at birth or shortly after,

Job yearns for God to let him die now. For the first time, he singles out God as the source of his suffering: "Why is light given to a man whose way is hidden, whom God has hedged in? My sighing comes before I eat. My groans are poured out like water." Job's questions are addressed to God who gives humans life and causes their suffering. For a reason unknown to Job, God has become his adversary, darkening his path, depriving him of meaning. God "hedges" him in an intolerable life. God's "hedge" provides an ironic contrast to the Prologue, where the Satan says that Job is righteous only because God placed a "hedge" of protection about him.[5] But now God has placed an imprisoning "hedge" of suffering around him. Betrayed by God, Job feels trapped in a miserable life from which he longs to escape. He grieves because his adversity signifies that he is alienated from God. Where is the God of retributive justice in whom Job believes? Job has not yet explicitly accused God of injustice, but he has made an opening salvo.

What kind of a God permits the innocent to suffer? The question is central to the Book of Job. As an innocent sufferer, Job concludes his monologue with the reason for his dirge: "For the thing which I fear comes on me, that which I am afraid of comes to me. I am not at ease, neither am I quiet, neither have I rest; but trouble comes." This surprising admission suggests that Job has had an uneasy relationship with God, based largely on fear. Job has always known that God can act in dreadful ways. He had a horrible premonition that the God he worshipped would destroy him. The Hebrew God is a God of wrath as well as benevolence. He is a God of power, giver as well as destroyer of life. The same God who liberated the Israelites from the Egyptians later permitted the destruction of Jerusalem and its great Temple. While his conscience tells him he is righteous, Job had apparently always feared that he might inadvertently offend God, inciting his wrath. We see this fear as early as the Prologue, as the poet invites readers to read between the lines. Job was scrupulous in his religious observances, offering sacrifices on behalf of his sons on the mere possibility that they might have sinned and cursed God in their hearts. Job believes that God monitors the thoughts as well the actions of humans. The God of the Book of Job is woefully insecure. Doubtful of the allegiance of humans, he assigned the Satan to spy on them. The Prologue and the Epilogue reveal a God who demands that humans make animal sacrifices. Worst of all, the Satan manipulated God to unjustly afflict Job, his most righteous servant. The biblical notion of the "fear of God" ordinarily refers to the attitude of awe and reverence humans ought to have towards the Creator. But Job's reputed "fear of God" is not merely a sign of reverence, but also of unadulterated terror.

Is fear the reason for Job's blameless and upright life? Fear is the basis of religion. Indeed, religion has elevated the fear of God into a virtue. Throughout the Hebrew Bible, people live in dread of God, a wrathful punisher. In Exodus the capricious "Yahweh met Moses and wanted to kill him," apparently because he had not circumcised his son.[6] This dark side of God is depicted throughout the Hebrew Bible, with humankind victimized by the contradiction in the divine nature. But most biblical commentators fail to provide an honest assessment of the immoral aspects of God's character. Biblical scholar Norman Whybray observed: "The dark side of God is a subject that has received astonishingly little attention from Old Testament scholars....It is almost as though there is a scholarly consensus that any criticism of God's character in the Old Testament is inconceivable." [7] God has a demonic as well as a divine side.

Fearful of God's dark side, Job reflects an anxious piety in the Prologue. He believes that God demands sacrifices and total subservience, and that humans are held accountable for the slightest sin. Job worried that his good fortune was always under threat of suddenly being taken away by God. This fear of God pervades the Book of Job, enveloping all of the human characters. Job will be terrified of confronting the hostile deity to defend his integrity. He will view God as his ruthless enemy, a threat to his life, an abuser of humankind. He will also speak of a God whose face remains "hidden," a *Deus absconditus,* a God who conceals himself.

Throughout the Hebrew Bible, God hides his face to punish or to show disapproval. In the Book of Job, he does not reveal himself until the dramatic climax. Nevertheless, God is an ominous invisible presence throughout the dialogue between Job and his friends.

Listening to Job's curse and lamentation, his friends are shocked and angered. To them, Job's iconoclastic speech suited a sinner rather than a righteous man. Nourished on the theology of divine retribution, they assume that Job's suffering is penal, the result of some serious sin. Instead of examining his conscience to find sins for which to repent, Job calls upon God to annihilate the day of his birth. To make matters worse, he invokes pagan sorcerers also to curse his birthday by awakening the chaos represented by Leviathan. The friends had come to comfort Job, expecting him to welcome their counsel and do anything to regain God's favor. They thought Job would break the silence by uttering a traditional lament, including confession of guilt, praise of God and a plea for forgiveness. Instead they hear Job parody a lamentation psalm, calling upon God not to save him but to grant him a swift death. The friends regard this as blasphemy. Several times, the poet places parody in the mouth of Job to underscore the inadequacy of traditional religious language to deal with great suffering.[8] Job's parodies, especially of the Psalms, reflect his anguish over his radically altered relationship with God. Job's entire world has been turned upside down. His reversals and subversions of traditional religious forms reflect the reversals and subversions in his mind.

Job's curse upon the day of his birth leads his friends to question his innocence. Could a man who speaks so vehemently against God be completely innocent of sin? Surely, the just God would not afflict Job without reason. His friends had come to console him; not to participate in denouncing God. God's justice must be defended. Job must be shown the error of his ways and be persuaded to repent and plead with God to be forgiven.

"Job Rebuked by His Friends" (1825)
By William Blake

# FIRST CYCLE OF SPEECHES
## CHAPTERS 4-14

## Chapter 4   Eliphaz: Job is a Sinner

THE JOB POET PROVIDES NO STAGE DIRECTIONS for the drama. Nevertheless, we can imagine the shock upon the faces of Job's friends when he burst into his curse-lament. Indeed, after Job's initial stoic response to the dreadful events of the Prologue, no one anticipated his sudden outcry. The first to respond to Job is Eliphaz the Temanite, opening the fierce debate. Because he speaks first in each of the three cycles of dialogue, we assume that he is the oldest and perhaps regarded as the wisest. In Hebrew, the name Eliphaz means "my God is pure gold." Of the three friends, he speaks the longest, his words totaling more than the other two over the course of the entire dialogue. In the hands of the poet, the friends speak as adept rhetoricians, using the art of persuasion in their attempt to convince Job that his adversity is consistent with God's justice. The poet's sympathy is obviously with Job, who speaks much longer than any of his friends. Yet the poet allows the friends to argue their position with passion, eloquence and absolute conviction.

Eliphaz commences with a tactful exordium intended to make the bereaved Job receptive to his message. He presents himself with the utmost courtesy and prudence. Wishing to address Job's plight, he asks permission to speak: "If someone ventures to talk with you, will you be grieved?" Without waiting for Job's reply, Eliphaz insists on speaking: "But who can withhold himself from speaking?" He believes that Job's abusive cursing of his day of birth demands a response. God's character and justice must be defended. Attempting to console, Eliphaz praises Job for the comfort he has often given to righteous sufferers in the past, how he "instructed many," "strengthened the weak hands," "supported him who was falling" and "made firm the feeble knees." Eliphaz then expresses surprise that Job does not apply to his own suffering the conventional wisdom that he had offered to others. He chides Job: "But now it has come to you, and you faint. It touches you, and you are troubled." To Eliphaz, Job is like a physician who cannot heal himself. Job has apparently been spared great adversity in his life. It is easier to counsel others who suffer, but it is much different when the counselor himself suffers.

Job is not comforted by Eliphaz's opening words, a rebuke in the guise of conciliation. The reference to Job's "trouble," is an insensitive understatement, for Job is utterly devastated. Eliphaz is also reminding Job that he too, following tradition, had frequently counseled mourners that their sins caused their suffering, advising them to repent and seek forgiveness. Job now realizes how feckless and cruel such platitudes could be to the innocent sufferer. Eliphaz goes on to commend Job's exemplary life, unwittingly affirming the words of God in praise of Job in the Prologue. Eliphaz asks rhetorically: "Is not your piety your confidence? Is not the integrity of your ways your hope?" If Job is really pious, why has he no confidence that God will assist him? If Job has integrity, why has he lost hope? Ironically, Job's piety and integrity led to his being singled out by God for cruel suffering to test his faith. While ostensibly acknowledging Job's piety and integrity, Eliphaz implies that he might have neither.

Having delivered his exordium, Eliphaz proceeds with the rest of his rhetorical strategy. He sounds the principle theme of the friends: Job's suffering is consistent with the iron law of retribution. He reminds Job of their shared belief in the doctrine: the righteous prosper and sinners suffer. Eliphaz alludes to the doctrine by means of further rhetorical questions, calling for negative replies. Throughout their speeches, Job and his friends frequently ask rhetorical questions— common in wisdom literature— as a persuasive device. The purpose is not to gain information, but to imply an answer or judgment, to accuse or reprimand, or to influence a response. Eliphaz bids Job to consult his own experience: "Remember now, whoever perished, being innocent? Or where were the upright cut off?" God does not allow the innocent to perish prematurely. Eliphaz seeks to "console" Job by claiming that because he still lives, he must not be wicked. Only the wicked are destroyed. This would mean that Job's children perished because they were wicked. Eliphaz ignores the countless innocent people who die prematurely. Adherence to tradition blinded Eliphaz to reality. Did he never see people afflicted undeservedly? Did he never see virtuous people suffer premature death? But Eliphaz cannot allow exceptions to the retribution doctrine. He refuses to question God's justice

Divine retribution operates by an infallible relationship between cause and effect infused by God into the moral order. Humans are free to determine their own fate by their conduct. Eliphaz supports his argument with personal knowledge, using a traditional agricultural metaphor: "According to what I have seen, those who plow iniquity, and sow trouble, reap the same. By the breath of God they perish. By the blast of his anger they are consumed." Eliphaz has dropped his initial conciliatory tone. He insinuates that Job reaps the suffering he deserves. With great skill, Eliphaz has delivered a blow to Job's integrity. Job might be essentially righteous, but he would not suffer unless he has sinned.

Job is stunned. He wants desperately to believe that his suffering is a terrible mistake. For some inexplicable reason, God has withdrawn his favor from him. But does a perfect and absolutely just God make such dreadful mistakes? Once Eliphaz introduces the retribution doctrine, that those who sow wickedness reap disaster, Job realizes that despite his innocence, he is regarded as a sinner. Given their belief in God's justice, the friends cannot presume Job's innocence. For them, suffering is not so much a test of faith, as the Prologue instructs, but punishment for sin. Whenever a sinner is punished, the moral order of the world is vindicated. A just God would never afflict a person without reason. Eliphaz also implies that unless Job repents, he will join the ranks of the wicked. The wicked do not long survive. If they seem to prosper, it is but temporary, for God's ultimate judgment cannot be avoided. The wicked may be like lions, dangerous and powerful, but they are defenseless before God: "The roaring of the lion, and the voice of the fierce lion, the teeth of the young lions, are broken. The old lion perishes for lack of prey. The cubs of the lioness are scattered abroad." For Eliphaz, the lion is Job and the scattered cubs might be a callous allusion to his ten dead children. Like the proud and defiant lion, Job roars blasphemously, cursing his life and turning from God.

To further convince Job, Eliphaz tries another approach. In an effort to have Job admit that he has sinned, Eliphaz addresses the issue of innocent suffering. He holds that because no one is completely sinless, all people should expect some trials and adversity. Hence Job ought to accept his suffering without complaint. To lend authority to his argument, Eliphaz claims to have had a privileged supernatural experience. The Job poet enables Eliphaz to speak the language of a mystic: "Now a thing was secretly brought to me. My ear received a whisper of it." Eliphaz relates that in the midst of "visions of the night, when deep sleep falls on men, fear came on me, and trembling, which made all my bones shake." He continues: "Then a spirit passed before my face. The hair of my flesh stood up. It stood still, but I could not discern its appearance. A form was before my eyes. Silence, then I heard a voice." The apparition revealed its message in two rhetorical questions, demanding negative replies: "Shall mortal man be more just than God? Shall a man be more pure than his Maker?" This implies that for Job to protest his suffering is tantamount to claiming that his justice exceeds that of God. God always treats humans justly, whether he afflicts a righteous person or a wicked person.

Yet there is hope for Job. Eliphaz apparently distinguishes between righteous and wicked sinners. At this point, he does not place Job among the wicked, but clearly insinuates that because Job suffers, he must have sinned. Sinners who are essentially righteous have hope of restoration by God, while incorrigible wicked sinners do not. For the ancient Israelites, righteousness was not inconsistent with sin.[1] No person was deemed to be absolutely sinless. The Hebrew Bible records that Noah, Abraham and Moses sinned. Although imperfect, righteous persons strive to live according to God's laws. Wicked people live in serious sin, an expression of utter disdain for God and his moral laws. In contrast, the sins of the righteous are less serious and are followed by repentance and acceptance of God's punishment. Job never claims to be absolutely sinless, but he will insist that his suffering is incommensurate with any transgressions he might have committed.

Eliphaz wishes Job to understand that unless he is wicked, he will survive his ordeal. A merciful God has granted him time to repent if he is a righteous sinner. But for Job, Eliphaz's implied distinction between a righteous and a wicked sinner is not relevant. His intense suffering is unjust and could only be reserved for the wicked. According to Eliphaz's vision, God's justice cannot be challenged. No creature can presume to equal God's purity and justice. Since God does not even trust his serving angels, much less does he trust humans, "who dwell in houses of clay," their corporeal bodies, "whose foundation," as Genesis affirms, is "in the dust." Humans are easily crushed, like short-lived moths: "Between morning and evening they are destroyed," their death too insignificant to attract notice.

What was this "spirit," this "form" that revealed itself to Eliphaz? Was it God himself or an angel? Does Eliphaz imagine himself to be a prophet? He does not say that the revelation came from God. According to Hebrew scripture, God spoke to prophets in dreams.[2] Eliphaz's experience echoes other pericopes in Hebrew scripture. Abraham experienced fear and trembling when God commanded him to sacrifice his son Isaac.[3] The prophet Elijah experienced a theophany, a perceptible manifestation of God, at Mount Horeb. This came not in the conventional form, accompanied by crashing thunder and flashing lightning, but as a barely perceptible "gentle whisper."[4]

Eliphaz's supernatural experience is not credible. Although his dream has the trappings of a theophany, why did it reveal to him a mere commonplace? Job as well as Eliphaz already knew that no mortal is more righteous than God. Samuel Terrien characterizes Eliphaz's vision as a "pseudo-oracle." Terrien concludes: "While the typically Hebraic stories of visual or auditory experiences with revelatory purposes almost always bring man into direct rapport with the deity, Eliphaz claims only the vision of 'a ghost.'"[5] Eliphaz might have fabricated the dream to lend credence to the doctrine of retribution. Who would challenge a voice from God himself? In fact, Job would later accuse Eliphaz, along with the other two friends, of lying to defend God, a claim supported by the Epilogue. Hebrew scripture condemns false prophets who lie in God's name, claiming to be inspired by a dream.[6]

But Eliphaz did not deliberately lie about receiving a personal divine oracle. He feared God too much to implicate him in falsehood. A more plausible explanation is that Eliphaz's dream was not supernatural, but simply a nightmare. Like Job, overly scrupulous not only in his behavior but also in his thoughts lest he offend God, Eliphaz's nightmare was merely an objectification of his fears and guilt-ridden conscience. The two questions posed by the "spirit" actually apply to Eliphaz: "Shall mortal man be more just than God? Shall a man be more pure than his Maker?" The questions were self-referential. In depicting his mysterious nighttime visitor, the Job poet again subverts traditional religious conventions. Having parodied God's act of creation and the traditional lamentation in Job's opening monologue, the poet now parodies the biblical theophany. The still small voice, the "gentle whisper" heard by Elijah, is replicated by the mysterious "voice" of Eliphaz's nightmare, stimulated by his profound insecurity, terrified of the judgment of God.

# Chapter 5   Eliphaz: Job Should Repent

ELIPHAZ WISHES TO IMPRESS UPON JOB that God is his sole refuge. As an imperfect sinful human being, he must accept his suffering as just. No heavenly angel will take the side of a sinner against God: "Call now; is there anyone who will answer you? To which of the holy ones will you turn?" Eliphaz anticipates Job's forthcoming appeals for a third party from heaven— an "umpire," "witness," or "vindicator"— to defend him against God. Significantly, Eliphaz introduces the language of the law court that plays a fundamental role in Job's subsequent speeches. If Job hopes to "call" as a plaintiff against God, Eliphaz alleges, there would be no respondent. God would never grant Job a legal hearing. Presumed guilty, Job must repent and beg God for forgiveness: "Resentment kills the foolish man," Eliphaz proclaims. If Job continues to blaspheme God, he will suffer the untimely death of the wicked. Eliphaz then recounts how God deals with wicked fools. They might flourish, but only temporarily: "I have seen the foolish taking root, but suddenly," his house is cursed. Eliphaz cruelly insinuates that Job's children suffered because of his sin: "His children are far from safety. They are crushed in the gate. Neither is there any to deliver them, whose harvest the hungry eats up, and take it even out of the thorns. The snare gapes for their substance." The children of the wicked suffer for the sins of their deceased father. Powerless, they are oppressed at the gate, the location of the city's court, with no one to defend them. The bitter irony is not lost on Job. His own dead children were certainly "far from safety."

Eliphaz has alluded to Job's suffering to illustrate God's justice. After Job's prosperity had been established, it was taken from him suddenly according to the inexorable law of retribution. His material wealth was seized by wicked marauders. But Job's adversity, Eliphaz alleges, proves that he has sinned: "For affliction does not come out of the dust; neither does trouble spring out of the ground; but man is born to trouble as the sparks fly upward." Because of their sinful nature, humans suffer deservedly. In the eyes of Eliphaz and the friends, innocent suffering does not exist. This view is similar to the Christian doctrine of original sin, which teaches that because of the fall of man through Adam and Eve, humans have an innate tendency to violate God's law. Indeed, God himself declares, after destroying the world with the Great Flood, that "every inclination of the human heart is evil from childhood."[7]

To induce Job to repent, Eliphaz appeals to personal experience. He has "observed" that those who plow evil, reap evil; he has "heard" a hushed voice tell him that no mortal can be more righteous than God; and he has "seen" the foolish wicked prosper for a time, only to be destroyed by God's judgment. Confident that Job will understand his suffering as justified, Eliphaz tenders his personal advice. Trust God: "As for me," Eliphaz exhorts, "I would seek God. I would commit my cause to God." Job should follow the conventional wisdom teaching. Instead of cursing his life, Job should appeal to God. If Job is not a wicked but a righteous sinner, he should repent. A penitent Job, Eliphaz assures, will be restored, for God's providence works wonders. Eliphaz celebrates the miraculous saving power of God, "who does great things that cannot be fathomed, marvelous things without number." God nourishes his creation. He "gives rain on the earth, and sends waters on the fields." God is compassionate: "He sets up on high those who are low; those who mourn are exalted to safety." God punishes the wicked: "He frustrates the devices of the crafty, so that their hands cannot perform their enterprise. He takes the wise in their own craftiness; the counsel of the cunning is carried headlong. They meet with darkness in the daytime, and grope at noonday as in the night." God protects the poor and the needy: "He saves from the sword of their mouth, even the needy from the hand of the mighty. So the poor have hope, and injustice shuts her mouth." Hearing a celebration of the glories of God is bitterly ironic. Eliphaz's claim that under God's providence "injustice shuts her mouth," must have cut Job to the quick.

Eliphaz hopes that his final argument will break Job's resistance. Having presented the proverbial stick, Eliphaz now offers the carrot. He argues that suffering can be beneficial. The righteous, he alleges, should regard suffering as a blessing sent by God, a chastening call to repentance. In biblical wisdom literature suffering is often seen as God's way to provide loving warning and corrective discipline for the righteous but imperfect sinner. The Book of Proverbs counsels: "My son, do not despise Yahweh's discipline, neither be weary of his reproof; for whom Yahweh loves he reproves, even as a father reproves the son in whom he delights. Happy is the man who finds wisdom, the man who gets understanding."[8] According to Eliphaz, Job should be happy. God in his benevolence afflicted Job not to kill him, but to improve and correct him. God afflicts the sinner with suffering, but he also forgives and restores those who repent. There is hope for the righteous sinner like Job who trusts in God and mends his errant ways: "Behold, happy is the man whom God corrects. Therefore do not despise the chastening of the Almighty. He wounds, and binds up. He injures, and his hands make whole." This is Eliphaz's version of "what does not kill you makes you stronger," or "something good will come out of this." Such bromides are no comfort to the dying.

Eliphaz assures Job that if he humbly repents, the God who wounded him will restore him: "You shall know that your tent is in peace. You shall visit your fold, and shall miss nothing. You shall know also that your offspring shall be great, your offspring as the grass of the earth." Job will also live a long life, regarded as a great blessing in the Hebrew Bible: "You shall come to your grave in a full age, like a shock of grain come in its season." With the promise of such an idyllic restoration, Eliphaz expects Job to comply with his pious advice. But the cruel irony of Eliphaz's words could not assuage Job's pain. Even though he is righteous, his home had not been secure, his property had been stolen, and his children had been killed when their house fell upon them in a supernatural storm. Job is not interested in the material restoration Eliphaz promises. His dead children cannot be replaced. Job only wants his integrity affirmed.

Unbeknownst to Eliphaz, God and the Satan have wagered over whether Job's piety is pure. Were Job to repent merely to regain God's favor, he would demonstrate a selfish piety. Having striven to convince Job to repent and appeal to God's mercy, Eliphaz closes his speech with a succinct peroration. Speaking for each of the friends as the voice of hallowed tradition, he declares: "We have searched it, so it is. Hear it, and know it for your good."

Eliphaz awaits Job's response.

## Chapter 6   Job: My Protest is Justified

INSTEAD OF COMFORTING JOB, Eliphaz has infuriated him. According to Eliphaz, Job is a righteous man who has committed sins that merit suffering. Eliphaz has also hurt Job by implying that his sins caused the deaths of his children. He has exhorted Job to accept his tribulation as a merciful corrective from God and repent. If Job fails to repent, Eliphaz insists, he will be a wicked sinner and lose all hope of restoration. But Job cannot repent for sins he did not commit. To do so would violate his integrity as a "blameless and upright" person. Although Job shares his friends' belief in divine retribution, he knows in his conscience that God has afflicted him unjustly. Would God wish Job to violate his divinely-instilled conscience? Job refuses to plead for forgiveness. The Job poet raises a fundamental question: How does a person of integrity respond to injustice, especially when the perpetrator of injustice is God himself? Job's response will be powerful and incisive. Instead of accepting his suffering as deserved, Job will boldly assert his human dignity, demand his rights and mount a trenchant attack upon God's justice.

Job does not respond directly to Eliphaz. As if to illustrate the fecklessness of his friend's advice, Job begins by defending his blasphemous curse-lament. He has gone beyond the denial stage of grieving. Kübler-Ross explains: "When the first stage of denial cannot be maintained any longer, it is replaced by feelings of anger, rage, envy, and resentment. The logical next question becomes: "'Why me?'"[9] Job projects his anger at his friends. Are they blind to his plight? According to the doctrine of divine retribution, Job is not an innocent sufferer. Eliphaz counsels him to be patient, for "resentment kills the foolish man."[10] But Job cannot remain silent. He alludes to the metaphoric scales of justice, pointing out that his suffering is not proportionate to any possible transgression: "Oh that my anguish were weighed, and all my calamity laid in the balances! For now it would be heavier than the sand of the seas." In the scale of cosmic divine justice, only great sinners should suffer as he does. How dare Eliphaz ask Job to view his suffering as merciful correction? Does a loving God treat the righteous so cruelly? Job's friends fail to understand that the weight of his suffering accounts for his "rash" words. His rage is justified.

The angry Job of the dialogue contrasts starkly with the patient Job of the Prologue. Probably the most popular reference to Job occurs in the New Testament: "You have heard of the patience of Job, and have seen the end of the Lord; that the Lord is very pitiful, and of tender mercy."[11] But the word translated "patience" in the King James Bible actually means "endurance," bearing up under great suffering or hardship. Job is no longer patient. He is now a defiant rebel struggling to endure unjust treatment by God. Nor does the text, from beginning to end, support the existence of a merciful and compassionate deity.

Job's speech becomes even more strident. His religious faith rests on two pillars: belief in God's absolute justice and belief in his own integrity. As Job defends his integrity, his conception of God is gradually transformed. His innocent suffering drives him to the horrifying thought that God is not just. Eliphaz had earnestly exhorted Job to "seek God" for relief.[12] Yet Job points to God as the cause of his suffering. Throughout his speeches, Job will address God as a living, personal deity, not a philosophical abstraction. Job speaks to God, while his friends merely speak about God. The God of Job is the God of Israel who has a personal relationship with his human creations and is responsive to their needs. As the seventeeth-century French philosopher Blaise Pascal later exclaimed: "Fire. God of Abraham, God of Isaac, God of Jacob; [not the God of] philosophers and scholars."[13] This personal God, Job believes, has unjustly severed their relationship. The poet has Job depict the first of many graphic images of divine abuse: "The arrows of the Almighty are within me. My spirit drinks up their poison." God is the divine archer who shoots poison arrows at Job, sending an army of terror to afflict and kill him. In the Hebrew Bible, arrows represent God's wrath or judgment.[14]

Eliphaz has just told Job that he should be happy, that God "wounds and binds up, he injures, and his hands make whole."[15] But Job has lost too much to be happy. He believes that God has inflicted upon him a fatal wound. Having lost everything he cherished, except his integrity, Job cannot again become whole. He is gripped by fear: "The terrors of God set themselves in array against me." Job's calamities fell upon him like arrows, sudden, sharp, swift, and deadly, cutting him deeply with overwhelming force. Job accuses God of being a vicious predator who afflicts him for no reason. The Prologue proves Job to be right. Many commentators believe that Job is mistaken about God, driven by his suffering to impugn God unjustly. They hold that Job does not attack the real God, but the God of an imagination impaired by grief. They allege that Job attacks a caricature of God, not the God of compassion and absolute justice. Nevertheless, the text shows that Job assails the real God, the God who afflicts him undeservedly. This is the God of the Hebrew Bible, the God who wiped out the world and then repented for his rashness.

Job defends his acrimonious words as the natural response to his agonizing pain. He asks rhetorically: "Does the wild donkey bray when he has grass? Or does the ox bellow over his fodder?" Job will continue to "bray" and "bellow" as long as he suffers innocently. Extreme suffering justifies extreme words. The rabbinical tradition, though shocked at Job's language, suggested this mitigation: "No man is taken to account for what he speaks in distress; Job spoke as he did because of his dire afflictions."[16] Job's blasphemous speech is his only means to voice anger at God. Job would never surrender his integrity. Eliphaz's pious platitudes revolt him. He again asks rhetorically: "Can that which has no flavor be eaten without salt? Or is there any taste in the white of an egg? My soul refuses to touch them. They are as loathsome food to me." Instead of consoling, Eliphaz augments Job's suffering. Eliphaz alleged that God often wounds out of love to spur a sinner to a healing repentance. But Job sees no benevolence, only poison, in God's arrows. In deep anguish, Job struggles to comprehend why God, with whom he had fellowship in the past, has turned against him. As the dialogue progresses, Job will view God as his enemy.

Job will have nothing of Eliphaz's illusory promises of restoration. Distraught, Job utters a passionate second lament. He again subverts accepted religious forms. The traditional lament concludes with a plea that God save one's life. Job instead pleads with God to let him die: "Oh that I might have my request, that God would grant the thing that I long for, even that it would please God to crush me; that he would let loose his hand, and cut me off!" Rather than violate his integrity by confessing to some heinous sin he did not commit, Job's only wish is that his suffering end by a quick death. "Be it still my consolation," my only joy amidst my pain, "that I have not denied the words of the Holy One." The "Holy One" is Yahweh, the Hebrew God, speaking through his prophet, the second Isaiah: "I am Yahweh, the Holy One of Israel, your Savior."[17] Having lived by God's law and spoken the truth according to his conscience, Job could go to the grave peacefully. But while Job does not deny God, he fears that God has denied him.

Exhausted physically and emotionally, Job believes that he can no longer endure. Why should he endure when he has no ground for hope? He unburdens his soul in a series of rhetorical questions: "What is my strength that I should wait? What is my end, that I should be patient? Is my strength the strength of stones? Or is my flesh of brass?" Job feels forsaken by God: "I have no help in me," and "wisdom is driven quite from me." Deprived of everything he values, he has no reason to live. The thought of suicide is alien to him, but death is more attractive than life.

Job is gripped by a terrible dilemma. If he agrees to repent, he will violate his integrity, founded on adherence to God. But if Job refuses to accept guilt, he must conclude that God is unjust. Despondent, Job does not wish to postpone his death. If God were to grant his wish and promptly kill him, Job would at least die with his integrity unsullied. But killing Job would certainly undermine God's integrity. Not only has he afflicted Job unjustly, but if Job dies, the Satan's challenge could not be met. God will be disgraced. The Satan predicted that if God removes his hedge of protection, Job will curse him directly to his face. For God to win the wager with the Satan, Job must be allowed to live. God must grant him a hearing. Only in this way can it be determined whether Job will remain faithful or deny God by cursing him in a direct encounter.

Job now turns his attention to his friends as a group. Even though only Eliphaz has spoken thus far, Job knows that his friends, adhering to the wisdom tradition of divine retribution, believe he is a sinner. Eliphaz has set the tone by denying Job's innocence. Job is not comforted by the presence of his friends. He does not feel compassion from them. They watched him suffer for seven days and nights. True friendship is tested in time of adversity. Job expects his friends to side with him even if he has spoken impiously: "To him who is ready to faint, kindness should be shown from his friend; even to him who forsakes the fear of the Almighty." Job is learning an unpalatable truth about human nature. He compares his friends to deceptive brooks that overflow with water from melting ice and snow in the winter, but become dry from the summer heat when most needed. The Job poet speaks from knowledge attained from desert sojourners. Arabian caravans from Tema and traveling merchants from Sheba depart from their routes in search of water.

They enter the desert wasteland and perish from lack of water because the brooks have dried up. With bitter sarcasm, Job grieves: "My brothers have dealt deceitfully as a brook, as the channel of brooks that pass away; which are black by reason of the ice, in which the snow hides itself. In the dry season, they vanish." Referring sarcastically to his friends as "brothers," Job implies that that they have broken a fundamental bond with him. What happened to the love they had for each other? Friendship was especially important in the ancient world. Like unreliable brooks, Job's friends deceived him, leaving him to languish in his time of need.

Instead of comforting Job, his friends recoil at his disfigurement, the sign of a sinner. "Now you are nothing," Job exclaims, "You see a terror, and are afraid." The friends cannot admit that God, whom they regard as just, has afflicted an innocent man. They fear that if they side with Job, God will punish them for supporting a sinner. They fear God's vengeance. To admit Job's innocence, moreover, would overturn their belief in a moral universe. In desperation, Job reminds his friends that he never imposed on their friendship. He never asked them for money; he never asked them to risk their lives on his behalf. All he wants now is compassionate understanding and honesty, but they betray him. Knowing their friend, why do they deny that he is innocent? Why do they not join him in questioning God? They are obviously more concerned with defending God's justice and divine retribution than empathizing with Job's pain. Job is alone in his sorrow.

Eliphaz, and by implication Bildad and Zophar, must present Job with proof that he has sinned: "Teach me, and I will hold my peace. Cause me to understand wherein I have erred. How forcible are words of uprightness!" Job concedes the possibility of having sinned unintentionally, but his conscience is clear of any serious sins, especially those that might justify his calamity. If the friends would speak directly and show him his guilt, instead of falsely insinuating like Eliphaz, Job would listen. Yet Job knows that his friends cannot present any evidence that he had sinned. For them, Job's suffering is sufficient evidence. Job lashes out at them: "Your reproof, what does it reprove? Do you intend to reprove words, since the speeches of one who is desperate are as wind?" Indeed, Job's friends will assume that his angry words railing against God reflect the mind of a blaspheming sinner. Job assails his friends for their craven betrayal. Unable to control his anger, he compares them to treacherous men who would cast lots for helpless orphans or sell their friends into slavery.

An anguished Job pleads with his friends to look directly at him: "Be pleased to look at me." Doing so, they could not fail to see his innocence and honesty: "Surely I shall not lie to your face." Job is no hypocrite. His friends must treat him justly, he declares, for his "cause is righteous" and his integrity is at stake. Job knows that he has not committed any serious sins. He closes by affirming his devotion to the truth. His words might have been rash, as he admitted, but they are truthful: "Is there injustice on my tongue? Cannot my taste discern mischievous things?" Job expects the truth from his friends, as he speaks the truth to them. He pleads with his friends to believe what they see, an innocent man suffering.

Job's words reflect his profound sense of isolation. He alone can experience his pain. Speaking from their traditional religious beliefs, Job's friends do not really see or hear him. Job expected that their knowledge of his entire life should have been sufficient for them to affirm his righteousness. He fears that even God does not know him. His plight makes his friends extremely uncomfortable. Until his affliction, their world was completely predictable. They were certain that the God of absolute justice rewarded the virtuous and punished the wicked unerringly. But now Job, renowned for his righteousness, suffers. If Job suffers undeservedly, what security do the friends have that God will not likewise afflict them? Rather than comfort and understand, Bildad and Zophar will follow Eliphaz in maligning Job's character.

## Chapter 7  Job: My Suffering Overwhelms Me

DISILLUSIONED WITH HIS FRIENDS, a despairing Job turns to God. For the first of several times, Job addresses God directly. He vents his emotions in a moving monologue. From the vantage point of his personal suffering, Job sees God as imposing an intolerable burden on humanity: "Is not a man forced to labor on earth? Are not his days like the days of a hired hand?" Human life seems meaningless. With an ironic reversal of Genesis, Job compares God to a ruthless overseer who has condemned humans, supposedly created "in his own image," to lives of dismal servitude. The universe is supposed to be governed by a benevolent and just God. But Job bemoans that God has given him a terrible lot: "As a servant who earnestly desires the shadow, as the hireling who looks for his wages, so am I to possess months of misery, wearisome nights are appointed to me." Servants and workers can look forward to rest and wages for their labor, but Job can only expect sleepless nights on the ash-heap, suffering unbearable pain and overcome by grief: "When I lie down I say, 'When shall I arise, and the night be gone?' I toss and turn until the dawning of the day." He then gives a lurid picture of his excruciating skin affliction, with its suppurating sores: "My flesh is clothed with worms and clods of dust. My skin closes up, and breaks out afresh." To Job, the "hope" offered by Eliphaz is a cruel illusion. How long could Job survive in agony? He is in psychological conflict. Whenever he focuses on his pain and suffering, he prays that God grant him a swift death. But when he reflects on the prospect of dying without vindication, he laments the shortness of his life: "My days are swifter than a weaver's shuttle," Job wails, "and are spent without hope." The thread of his life is rapidly slipping away.

Job's mood shifts again as he addresses God, pleading for compassion: "Remember that my life is a breath." Job echoes Genesis, when God breathed life into man. In the traditional psalm of lament, God is often called upon to remember and bring relief to the sufferer. Job desperately seeks to bargain with God before he dies. If he dies, he reminds God, he will lose any chance of happiness: "My eye shall no more see good." No longer will mortal eyes perceive him: "The eye of him who sees me shall see me no more." But at least God's hostile eye will no longer torment him: "Your eyes shall be on me, but I shall not be." Human life is transitory and death is final: "As the cloud is consumed and vanishes away, so he who goes down to Sheol shall come up no more. He shall return no more to his house. Neither shall his place know him anymore." As noted, the ancient Israelites had no conception of an afterlife with rewards and punishments. Death was regarded as virtual extinction. Job therefore has no hope that God will act justly toward him after he dies. Once in the grave, a mortal's relationship with God ceases. Instead of being known to posterity as a person of integrity, honest with himself, Job would be condemned as a great sinner, an enemy of God.

Returning to the subject of his integrity, Job's anger reaches a crescendo. The belligerent stand he takes, wrestling with God, dominates the remainder of the poetic dialogue. Job will frequently digress from a speech directed at the friends in order to address God. Believing death to be near, Job refuses to be restrained. He will throw caution to the wind and speak the truth to divine power: "I will not keep silent. I will speak in the anguish of my spirit. I will complain in the bitterness of my soul." Kierkegaard highlights Job's bold protest. In the eyes of the young man in *Repetition*, Job "became the voice of the suffering, the cry of the grief-stricken, the shriek of the terrified, ... a faithful witness to all the affliction and laceration there can be in a heart, an unfailing spokesman who dared to lament 'in bitterness of soul' and to strive with God."[18] There should be more dissenting voices like that of Job.

As he promises, Job speaks out in anguish, firing a mocking rhetorical question at God: "Am I a sea, or a sea monster that you put a guard over me?" Job is obviously not the sea monster, the primeval force of chaos quelled by God in creating the cosmos. Nor is Job the mighty sea, which God separated from the land at the creation. Job then reminds God of the suffering he has caused him: "When I say, 'My bed shall comfort me. My couch shall ease my complaint;' then you scare me with dreams, and terrify me through visions: So that my soul chooses strangling, death rather than my bones." God is Job's sadistic torturer. Sitting on the ash-heap, without the comforts of bed or couch, Job's sarcasm is transparent. Plagued by horrible dreams and visions, he would prefer death by strangling rather than continuing to live. Reversing the petition of the traditional lament, Job calls upon God not for protection, but for death. He hates his existence. He implores God to cease his oppressive vigilance: "I loathe my life. I do not want to live forever. Leave me alone, for my days are but a breath." Without purpose, his integrity assaulted, Job wants God to stop harassing him and let him die in peace.

Job has not completed his furious diatribe. With a masterful parody, the poet has Job turn the great Eighth Psalm ironically on its head, expressing the opposite of the traditional meaning. The Psalmist expresses wonder that humans, insignificant compared to the immensity of creation, were given dominion over the earth by God. The Psalmist inquires, "What is mankind that you are mindful of them, human beings that you care for them? You have made them a little lower than the angels and crowned them with glory and honor."[19] The Psalmist depicts the exalted place of humans in the universe, having been created in the image of God. To this, Job retorts: "What is man that you should magnify him, that you should set your mind on him, that you should visit him every morning and test him every moment?" Job confronts God with the bitter truth. Instead of exalting humans, God abuses them, destroying their dignity. Why, Job cries, has God given him so much brutal attention? While Hebrew scripture refers to God as the watcher who protects his people,[20] Job subverts the metaphor to signify divine oppression. God's vigilance is not that of loving solicitude, but of suffocating espionage. No loving "hound of heaven" in the spirit of the poet Francis Thompson, the God of Job is a vicious stalker. Job transmutes the metaphor of God's eye from the eye of compassion to that of a sadist who takes pleasure in torturing humans with malicious surveillance. Divine providence has been supplanted by divine torment.

From the beginning, humans have struggled to find language adequate to speak about God. They have employed metaphors to highlight some human qualities they associate with the deity. Hence, God as Father, God as King, and God as Mother. The Job poet brings to the fore God's dark side— God as a demonic predator. As the psychologist Carl Jung argued, Job exposes the contradiction in God. God is not only compassionate and merciful; God is also cruel, savage, and ruthless. Experiencing undeserved suffering, Job dares to become the judge of God. According to Jung, "Job stands morally higher than Yahweh. In this respect the creature has surpassed the creator."[21] A perfect God does not do contradictory things. Nevertheless, the God of the Hebrew Bible is evil as well as good, destroying and preserving.

God is like an unstable parent who, for the most part cares for his children, but is also capable of turning on them, inflicting cruel punishment for the slightest infraction. Job's world is nightmarish, ruled by an omniscient deity who knows his every action and thought. Job wants to escape from the terrorizing deity: "Will you not look away from me nor leave me alone until I swallow down my spittle?" God has usurped the role of the Satan in the Prologue, going to and fro on earth spying on humans. Like the Satan, God's eyes are constantly upon Job. God needs no agents to do his bidding. Job asks God: "What do I do to you, you watcher of men?" Job demands to know why God has turned against him: "Why have you set me as a mark for you so that I am a burden to myself?" Job concludes his harangue with a simple request of God, using the legal language that pervades his forthcoming speeches: "Why do you not pardon my disobedience, and take away my iniquity?" If Job has sinned, would not a merciful God forgive? Job concedes the possibility that he might have inadvertently committed some minor sin. But no such sin would justify his tribulation. Job concludes that his death is imminent: "For now I shall lie down in the dust. You will seek me diligently, but I shall not be." God will seek Job for more torment, but it will be too late. At least in death, Job will escape God's relentless scrutiny.

## Chapter 8    Bildad: God is Just

UNTIL NOW IN THE DIALOGUE, Eliphaz, speaking for the friends, presumes Job's guilt without accusing him directly of sin. Although Job has not explicitly assailed God's justice, he has done so implicitly. Having heard Job's portrayal of God as a sadistic tormenter of humanity, Bildad the Shuhite must affirm the justice of God. Job and his friends believe in God's moral government of the universe. They believe that God is the transcendent source of purpose and justice. In order for the world to make sense to the friends, Job's suffering must be the consequence of sin. On the other hand, for the world to make sense to Job, his innocence must be confirmed.

Infuriated by Job's rhetoric, Bildad commences his speech with a caustic exordium. In the face of a challenge to God's justice, Bildad will not repeat Eliphaz's courteous opening. Bildad begins by rebuking Job with rhetorical questions. "How long," he asks sarcastically, "will you speak these things? Shall the words of your mouth be a mighty wind?" Bildad thus initiates the frequent exchange of insults between Job and his friends. Bildad mockingly affirms Job's complaint that his friends regard his words as mere "wind." Ignoring Job's attack upon the loyalty of his friends, Bildad circles back to Eliphaz's defense of God. Bildad confronts Job with two additional rhetorical questions, assuming negative replies: "Does God pervert justice? Does the Almighty pervert righteousness?" Thus Bildad explicitly introduces the idea of God's justice. He uses legal terms, "justice" and "righteousness," that Job will appropriate in order to demand a trial with God, a theme that dominates the remainder of the dialogue. If Job is innocent, God has indeed perverted justice and righteousness. God must be just, or the retribution theology is false. A God of justice is fundamental to monotheism. It is inconceivable to Bildad that God would act unjustly. Thus Job suffers because he is a sinner.

A just God, according to Bildad, rewards good and punishes evil. Thus suffering is the necessary consequence of sin. Bildad presents Job with a cruel demonstration of the working of God's justice: "If your children have sinned against him, he has delivered them into the hands of their disobedience." Job's ten children died as a result of God's punitive justice. Unlike his children, who must have been guilty of serious sin, Job still lives, indicating that his transgressions are less serious. If Job has sinned but repents, his ordeal will be temporary. Bildad offers Job the same hope as did Eliphaz: "If you want to seek God diligently, make your supplication to the Almighty. If you are pure and upright, surely now he would awaken for you." Bildad believes that instead of dying like his sinful children, Job can be restored as long as he is essentially "pure and upright." Bildad ironically echoes the words of the Prologue. He is not aware of God's affirmation of Job's character in the Prologue as "pure" and "upright." Job is righteous.

Yet Bildad, imprisoned by the wisdom tradition's retributive creed, reasons from the effect to the cause. Instead of arguing that the sinner suffers, the friends assume that the sufferer has sinned. Job's children died, so they must have sinned. Job suffers, so he must have also sinned. If Job makes proper supplication to God, Bildad promises, his present impoverished condition will be reversed beyond his expectations. Indeed, God would grant him more prosperity than he had originally: "Though your beginning was small, your latter end would greatly increase." Like Eliphaz, Bildad does not understand that Job is not interested in material restoration. Job refuses to see his affliction as evidence of God's justice. He wishes to have his integrity vindicated. Unbeknownst to Job, confessing sin in order to be rewarded would prove that his piety is self-interested.

Bildad then attempts to reinforce the retribution theology. While Eliphaz relied upon the authority of alleged divine revelation, Bildad falls back on hallowed tradition. Of the three friends, Bildad holds most rigidly to the ancient teaching. The retribution creed has been passed down over centuries. "Inquire of past generations," Bildad remonstrates, "find out about the learning of their fathers. For we are but of yesterday, and know nothing, because our days on earth are a shadow." A single life is not long enough to accumulate the wisdom of the ancestors. Bildad concludes: "Shall they not teach you, tell you, and utter words out of their heart?" Job must submit to the teaching of the hoary past found in the Hebrew Wisdom books. According to Bildad's perception, based on the wisdom of generations, Job cannot claim his suffering to be innocent. But established authority often relies on tradition to support erroneous beliefs.

Continuing his effort to persuade, Bildad next illustrates the traditional doctrine by analogies from nature drawn from wisdom literature. He insinuates that Job, unless he repents now, will join the godless wicked. Bildad compares the godless to plants, papyrus and reeds that require water to survive. He makes assertions in the form of two rhetorical questions, anticipating negative replies: "Can the papyrus grow up without mire? Can the rushes grow without water? While it is yet in its greenness, not cut down, it withers before any other reed." Like plants growing on the banks of the Nile River, the dying Job needs God for sustenance. Without God, the plants die: "So are the paths of all who forget God. The hope of the godless man shall perish." The godless are under the illusion that they are secure, but their "confidence shall break apart" like a frail "spider's web. He shall lean on his house, but it shall not stand. He shall cling to it, but it shall not endure." When the wicked prosper, the orthodox try to explain it as only temporary. Bildad concurs. The prosperous wicked are like well-watered plants in the sunshine, but when God uproots them their lives wither away. Such is the inevitable fate of the wicked.

Having chastised Job for his vehement language, Bildad appeals to ancestral faith to support the retribution creed, and advises Job to beseech God for forgiveness. Bildad's peroration illustrates that he remains unaware of Job's state of mind. Having shown Job the threat, the ruin of unrepentant sinners, Bildad softens his tone by concluding with hope. Like Eliphaz, Bildad holds out to Job the prospect of a glorious restoration. Job should trust in God's infallible retributive justice: "God will not cast away a blameless man, neither will he uphold the evildoers. He will still fill your mouth with laughter, your lips with shouting." At the same, time, "those who hate you shall be clothed with shame. The tent of the wicked shall be no more." Job could not fail to grasp the cruel irony in Bildad's conclusion. How could Job's mouth be filled with laughter after God has killed his ten children? Job's integrity, his "blameless" righteous life, did not shield him or his family from terrible misfortune at the hands of God.

## Chapter 9   Job: God is Unjust

THE DEFENSE OF GOD'S JUSTICE by Eliphaz and Bildad stirs Job to reflect further on his own situation. Following a pattern repeated throughout the dialogue, Job reverts to their earlier arguments. Eliphaz had asked, "Shall mortal man be more just than God?"[22] In turn, Bildad asked: "Does God pervert justice? Or does the Almighty pervert righteousness?"[23] Job could not disagree with the implied negative answers to these questions. All his life Job had believed in God's justice and that no mortal is more just than God. Bildad also affirmed that God will not "cast away a blameless man." Hence, Job begins his response by agreeing with his friends: "Truly, I know that it is so." But Job is now deeply troubled, for his conscience reveals that God afflicts him undeservedly. Job's experience leads him to the horrifying conclusion that, for some inexplicable reason, God has cast him away.

Job is the victim of an appalling injustice. Recalling Bildad's advice that he "make supplication to the Almighty," Job contemplates a way to do so. He will appeal to God, but not for mercy, as Eliphaz and Bildad advised. Begging for mercy would be to admit sin, violating his integrity. Instead, Job will appeal to God for justice. But Job hesitates as he poses a fundamental question: "But how can a man be just with God?" His question is a legal one. If God, as Bildad insists, does not cast away a blameless man, how can a mortal like Job, unjustly afflicted, challenge God in court? In principle, the God of absolute justice ought to reward the virtuous and punish the wicked. But what recourse is open to a righteous person who suffers unjustly? Can God be compelled to rectify his own injustice? Eliphaz had advised Job to admit guilt and commit his cause *to* God.[24] Instead, the righteous Job wants to make his case *against* God.

With a move tantamount to a revolution in the Hebrew Bible, Job wishes to hold God accountable to the same moral standard as humans. Job dares to regard God as his equal in the eyes of the law. He is not the patient Job of the Prologue who refused to "charge God with wrongdoing,"[25] Job now seeks to litigate against God. The metaphor of a trial involving God occurs elsewhere in the Hebrew Bible. While God is said by the prophets to place Israel on trial for her sins, Job reverses the procedure, taking the radical step of indicting God for injustice. The prophet Jeremiah also reverses the legal procedure when he speaks of instituting a suit against God for allowing the wicked to prosper.[26] Unlike Job, Jeremiah fails to pursue the litigation.

Henceforth, Job's speeches abound in legal language, reflecting an established system of legal procedure in the ancient Near East.[27] Certain that he has committed no grievous sin to justify his suffering, Job will strive to defend his integrity against God in court. The Book of Job is unique in the Hebrew Bible in that the metaphor of a trial with God dominates the plot. Indeed, the legal aspect of the book is complex. God plays three roles. Depending upon the context, God is the plaintiff who accuses Job, the defendant who must answer Job's charges, and the judge of Job's integrity. At the same time, Job acts alternately as defendant, accused of sin, and as plaintiff, charging God with injustice. Whether as defendant or accuser, Job believes that the truth will bring him public vindication from God.

Referring to God in legal terms implies that God is subject to a standard of justice. Job's lawsuit must be viewed against the background of ancient Israel's conception of its relationship with its personal God. According to Erich Fromm, humankind first envisioned God as an absolute monarch who destroyed the world with the Great Flood, alleging that humans were wicked, and regretting their creation.[28] After drowning countless men, women, children, and animals, God repents and makes a covenant with Noah. The idea of a covenant, argues Fromm, was "one of the most decisive steps in the religious development of Judaism." The covenant between God and Noah was succeeded by the Mosaic covenant between God and the ancient Israelites. With this covenant, God and the Israelites became partners in a treaty. God was transformed from an "absolute" to a "constitutional" monarch. Obligated to abide by the rules of the covenant, God could no longer act arbitrarily, but must fulfill the requirements of retributive justice. Humans could now insist on their rights under the covenant and challenge God to abide by his promises.[29] The covenant is not explicitly mentioned in the Book of Job. But since the Israelites believed that Yahweh was not only the God of Israel, but also of humanity as a whole, even people outside the covenant could expect justice from God. The doctrine of retribution, prevalent throughout the ancient Near East, depended upon an ethical relationship between God and humanity. While the people were morally obligated to obey divine law, God was obligated to act justly. Both God and humans were expected to uphold their moral obligations.

Job's conscience and sense of justice moved him to take legal action against God. He rebels against his innocent suffering. He wishes to confront God face-to-face. This quest to see the face of the deity was considered perilous. The Hebrew Bible taught that God is too awesome for any mortal to behold. As God warned Moses, "You cannot see my face, for no man may see me and live."[30] Seeing God, Job would experience what the Christian theologian Rudolf Otto later called the *mysterium tremendum*, the mystery of the majestic divine before which one trembles in terror.[31] But Job demonstrates the utmost courage. Courage is not the absence of fear, but the ability to confront and manage fear. Despite the odds, Job is willing to risk his life by confronting God to achieve justice.

While Job might welcome death, he does not wish to die until he can defend himself before God. Job manifests the bargaining phase of grief. According to Kübler-Ross, those who are dying often seek to bargain with God. Job vacillates. In the early part of his dialogue with the friends, he pleads with God to end his torment by allowing him to die as soon as possible. But he soon realizes that dying without vindication is worse than death itself. Like many people dealing with a terminal illness, therefore, Job sought to postpone his death. If God would permit him to survive until he can vindicate his integrity, he could die in peace. Job must find a means to challenge the deity. He wishes to "dispute" or contend with God and "prove" his innocence, as in a court of law. Job imagines himself as the defendant, charged with sin, with God as his accuser.

Yet Job finds the prospect of confronting God in a law court overwhelming. The idea that God would permit himself to be challenged legally is patently absurd. There is no greater adversary than God. As if answering his own question, Job fears that humans could not be just before God because God is invincible. Even though innocent, a human could not withstand God's cross-examination. If God "is pleased to contend with him, he cannot answer him one time in a thousand." God's unbridled power leads Job to despair of a successful lawsuit. Eliphaz had tried to convince Job that only God's power could relieve his suffering. But Job does not see benevolence in God's power.[32] Job parodies the conventional doxology, focusing not upon God's benevolence and absolute justice, but his awesome destructiveness: "God who is wise in heart, and mighty in strength: who has hardened himself against him, and prospered?" In the eyes of Job, God cannot be trusted to exercise his power justly. Hence, no human could successfully challenge God in court. God's arbitrary power is unstoppable. He could easily undo his creation: "He removes mountains, and they do not know it, when he overturns them in his anger. He shakes the earth out of its place. Its pillars tremble. He commands the sun, and it does not rise, and seals up the stars. He alone stretches out the heavens and treads on the waves of the sea. He makes the Bear and Orion, and the Pleiades," constellations of the south. Job praises God not to call attention to his glory, but to show the futility of legally confronting an omnipotent and destructive adversary. The fact that God causes earthquakes and eclipses, created the heavens and the stellar constellations, makes Job mindful of the immense disparity between the deity and himself.

For Job, God is hidden. Job quotes a line almost verbatim from Eliphaz's doxology: God "does great things past finding out; yes, marvelous things without number." Reversing Eliphaz, who used the words to praise God's saving grace toward penitent sinners, Job stresses divine destructive power and inaccessibility. With God hidden, Job fears that his quest for justice is hopeless. Not having a material form, God cannot be seen: "Behold, he goes by me, and I do not see him. He passes on also, but I do not perceive him." God is Job's invisible enemy. As sovereign of the universe, God is not morally accountable to humans. The God of Job is not one of absolute justice, but of absolute power: "Behold, he snatches away. Who can hinder him? Who can ask him, 'What are you doing?'" Indeed, God does what he wants, including killing Job's children and servants as well depriving him of his livelihood and physical health. God cannot be restrained. Even the armies of the sea monster Rahab, symbol of primordial chaos, shrink before his feet: "How much less shall I answer him and choose my words to argue with him?" With such a God—elusive, unaccountable, invisible, and terrifying— Job despairs of vindicating his integrity.

Returning to legal language, Job visualizes a terrifying scene of a trial with God. The obstacles that he would face as a defendant would be insurmountable. As ruler of the world, God is not subject to a higher standard of justice. Even though Job is "righteous," God would not "answer" him. Job would be compelled to "make supplication" to God, his "judge." Job feels his mortal impotence before God who, whether he is the accuser or defendant, will be the ultimate judge. Overwhelmed, Job fears that he would be compelled to plead with God for mercy instead of justice. He would succumb to God's power. If Job succeeds in summoning God to court, he does not believe that God would respond: "If I had called, and he had answered me, yet I would not believe that he listened to my voice." Faced with God's awesome presence, Job fears that he would be rendered helpless and speechless. Anticipating God's later speeches from the whirlwind at the conclusion of the book, Job imagines a frightening scene in the heavenly court as he is blown over by a divine storm of accusatory words. God "breaks me with a storm, and multiplies my wounds without cause. He will not allow me to catch my breath, but fills me with bitterness." Once again, Job ironically echoes the Prologue, when God admitted to afflicting him "without cause," killing his children in a storm.[33]

For God's might is right: "If it is a matter of strength, behold, he is mighty! If it is a matter of justice, 'Who,' says he, 'will summon me?'" Like a tyrant, God is a law unto himself, subject to no one, especially a human creature. Job alleges that, like a clever prosecuting attorney, God would pervert his innocence into guilt, compelling him to become a witness against himself: "Though I am righteous, my own mouth shall condemn me. Though I am blameless, it shall prove me perverse." Terrified, Job might admit guilt without defending himself. His friends had warned that contesting God would bring about his death. Pitted against an omnipotent deity, Job momentarily forsakes his vindication in favor of a quick death: "I am blameless, I do not respect myself. I despise my life."

His despair mounting, Job issues his most scathing attack upon God. Until now he had accused God of "hedging" or oppressing him, or of shooting poisonous arrows into him; but now Job accuses God of being immoral. God is indifferent to Job's integrity. Job fires his broadside. Innocent suffering demonstrates that God does not care whether a person is blameless or wicked. Reversing the claims of Eliphaz that the innocent never perish prematurely and Bildad that God does not reject the blameless and strengthen the wicked,[34] Job unleashes his fury, accusing God of perverting justice. It makes no difference to God whether Job is righteous or wicked: "It is all the same. Therefore I say he destroys the blameless and the wicked." These blasphemous words are a stinging indictment of God. Job accuses God of gross immorality by ignoring ethical distinctions. When disaster strikes a nation, God permits the good as well as the evil to perish.

In the Prologue, when God afflicted Job unjustly, the narrator affirms that he "did not sin with his lips."[35] But Job has grown from an abject servant to a defiant rebel who blasphemes God. Job no longer sees a moral order in the world. He raises an incisive question. If God indiscriminately destroys people without regard to their conduct, what is the incentive for a moral life? Why should anyone be righteous? Why should anyone fear being wicked? God kills the innocent and the wicked without discrimination. There could be no more devastating indictment of the deity. With one blow, Job repudiates the moral basis of the ancient Hebrew religion. But if God does not have moral standards, Job despairs of achieving vindication.

An unjust God is prevalent in the Hebrew Bible. When God intended to destroy the good as well as the evil people of Sodom, Abraham interceded, arguing like an attorney for the defense: "Far be it from you to do things like that, to kill the righteous with the wicked, so that the righteous should be like the wicked. May that be far from you. Should not the Judge of all the earth do right?"[36] But Job goes much further than Abraham in challenging God. Job accuses God of perverting justice. Rebutting the assertions of his friends, Job holds that God actually favors the wicked and laughs at the suffering of the innocent. Indeed, God ensures the triumph of wickedness by clouding the reason of judges, preventing them from seeing the truth and adjudicating fairly: "If the scourge kills suddenly, he will mock at the trial of the innocent. The earth is given into the hand of the wicked. He covers the faces of its judges." As we have seen, the ancient Israelites had no understanding of secondary causes. Whenever the wicked triumph, God is the cause. Suffering and injustice were not attributed to blind fate or accident. As Job laments, God is directly responsible for the world's injustices: "If not he, then who is it?"

Having reviled God's injustice, Job becomes sorrowful. Returning to his individual plight, he bemoans, as he did in his previous speech, the transitory nature of his life. Time is running out for him to vindicate himself, for he is certain that he will soon die. His language is brilliantly figurative: "Now my days are swifter than a runner. They flee away, they see no good, they have passed away as the swift ships, as the eagle that swoops on the prey." Eliphaz and Bildad promised Job that if he repented for his sins, his future would be bright. But Job will not violate his integrity. His life apparently racing to its end, he considers his remaining alternatives. He might drop his demand for a legal hearing: "If I say, 'I will forget my complaint. I will put off my sad face, and cheer up.'" But he could not forget that God caused his suffering. How could Job not protest the deaths of his innocent children and servants, the destruction of his property, and the divine assault upon his body? If Job were to disregard his complaint, he would forsake his integrity and die in disgrace. While he does not fear dying, he fears that death will come before his innocence is vindicated. In despair, Job addresses God directly, accusing him of already convicting him: "I know that you will not hold me innocent." Job is convinced that God intends to destroy him. He laments: "I shall be condemned. Why then do I labor in vain" to win vindication? Even if he were to purify himself of whatever made him unacceptable to God, the effort would be futile: "If I wash myself with snow, and clean myself with lye, yet you will plunge me into the ditch." Job would become so repugnant, that "my own clothes shall abhor me." Job believes that God is determined to condemn him without a fair trial. He is not granted the presumption of innocence. No matter what he does, Job believes that he will be found guilty.

With the path to vindication seemingly blocked, the heroic Job refuses to relinquish all hope. He reiterates the enormous obstacle before him. Job is a human, while God is omnipotent, a transcendent being. Job seems to recognize that the anthropomorphic God of scripture is mere metaphor: "For he is not a man, as I am, that I should answer him, that we should come together in judgment" before the heavenly court. How could Job ever convince God of his innocence? The idea of Job acting as a plaintiff, accusing God of punishing him unjustly seems impossible. The ontological gulf between God and humans cannot be bridged. A small David faced the largest Goliath. Having God condescend to appear with Job in the heavenly court, having divine justice challenged, and responding to interrogation by a human, was beneath the dignity of a deity. Hence from the outset Job knew that, despite his innocence, his chances of winning a lawsuit were slim. For God would be both prosecutor and judge.

Spurred by his desperate predicament, Job searches for another way out. Perhaps God could be compelled to act justly. From Job's fertile imagination springs the startling idea of an umpire who might mediate his dispute with God. Such a mediator might lift God's threatening rod from Job, enabling him to defend himself without fear. The juridical notion of a mediator who places his hand upon two disputing human parties, judging impartially between them, is found elsewhere in the Hebrew Bible. But Job's wish for a mediator who could impose a restraint upon God himself is blasphemy. Eliphaz had warned Job not to expect any angelic intervention on his behalf.[37] Nevertheless, Job fantasizes that if an unbiased mediator were to stand between God and himself, a just resolution might be reached. Under the supervision of an umpire, Job might receive a fair trial. No longer fearing the rod of God's punishment, Job could conduct his defense.

But who might this umpire be? Perhaps a member of God's heavenly court, some angel, might intervene to mediate between Job and God. This wish for a mediator reflects the bargaining phase of coping with death. Job is desperately grasping at some means to save his integrity before he dies. But he quickly realizes his mere wishful thinking and drops the notion: "There is no umpire between us that might lay his hand on us both." An omnipotent God would never submit to the authority of a mediator. In the *Babylonian Talmud*, a pious rabbi considered Job's notion blasphemous. Rab reprimanded: "Dust should be placed in the mouth of Job. Is there a servant who argues with his master?"[38] God is subject to no one. He cannot be held to a higher standard. Job and God are not equal before the law.

## Is God Above the Law?

In raising the possibility of an umpire to mediate between himself and God, Job unwittingly introduces a philosophical question that Plato posed in his dialogue, the *Euthyphro*. Now known as the "Euthyphro dilemma," Socrates states it succinctly: "Is the pious loved by the gods because it is pious, or is it pious because it is loved by the gods?"[39] Are compassion, honesty, and justice intrinsic virtues, or are they virtues simply because God commands? If God commands an action *because* it is good, this implies that morality is independent and antecedent to God. If so, God himself would be subject to a higher moral standard. But Job and his friends held what is today known as the divine command theory of ethics. Morality is whatever God commands. Nevertheless, This view can be used to justify atrocities. If God wills that suffering be inflicted on an innocent person, it would be justified. Such reasoning makes God's command that the Israelites annihilate the Canaanites morally right.

Biblical religion, exemplified by the Hebrew prophets, reflected the divine command theory. Justice and goodness were regarded as inseparable from God. According to Yehezkel Kaufman, author of *The Religion of Israel*, the principal distinction between Jewish monotheism and pagan polytheism is that Jewish monotheism rejected the pagan notion of a transcendent "metadivine" realm, prior to and independent of the gods, whose decrees they must obey.[40] Along similar lines, Abraham Heschel explains the essential difference between an ethics derived from philosophy and one derived from religion: "There are no ultimate laws, no eternal ideas. The Lord alone is ultimate and eternal. The laws are His creation, and the moral ideas are not entities apart from Him.... God is not the mere guardian of the moral order. He is not an intermediary between a transcendental idea of the good and man....If the moral law were something absolute and final, it would represent a destiny to which God Himself would be subject. Far from being sovereign, God would then fall into dependence on rigid, objective norms."[41] When Job introduces the possibility that God might be sued in court, subject to an impartial umpire, he raises the question whether the deity himself is subject to moral standards. Can God choose to make an evil action good? If God is subject to a higher moral standard, he is not God, for he would then not be sovereign. The Hebrew religion recognized no power or law higher than God. If Job loses his proposed litigation against God, there is no Supreme Tribunal to which he can appeal.

## Why Does God Permit the Innocent to Suffer?

With his sweeping indictment of God, Job unwittingly raises the perennial theodicy problem. If God is perfectly just and good, why do innocent people suffer? Is there a moral order in the world? Entrenched in the retribution dogma, Job's friends are blind to the theodicy problem. God is just and suffering is the consequence of sin. But if God is the cause of all things, as Job's contemporaries believed, he must be the cause of evil. Indeed, the Prologue makes it clear that God caused Job's innocent suffering. Despite the friends, the theodicy problem cannot be ignored. The existence of evil is the fundamental challenge to monotheism. The problem of innocent suffering was especially difficult for the Israelites because, as strict monotheists, they could not attribute evil to a cause independent of God. There was no devil to blame for evil.

The theodicy problem has often been articulated by means of three propositions. First, God is omnipotent; second, God is perfectly good and just; and third, evil exists, including innocent suffering. The traditional monotheist cannot logically hold all three propositions together. Job and his friends are left with the following options. To accept Job's calamity as undeserved, would mean to deny either God's power to prevent it, or his goodness to will its prevention. Rather than deny God's power or goodness, the friends, upholding the retribution creed, deny Job's innocence. Job's suffering is punishment for sin. If Job is innocent, God is guilty. A just God would not afflict Job undeservedly. The friends cannot conceive of an unjust God.

Given their monotheistic theology, it is no surprise that the friends accuse Job of sin. On the other hand, Job concludes the opposite of the friends. His personal experience of innocent suffering contradicts the retribution doctrine. Knowing that his suffering is undeserved, he must deny either God's omnipotence or his goodness and justice. Throughout the dialogue, Job will affirm God's omnipotence, but challenge his goodness and justice. The question of God's morality is raised on almost every page of the Book of Job. The only way to avoid this question is to deny the theodicy problem, which many believers do, or to deny God's existence. Atheists are not constrained to ask questions about the goodness and justice of

God. But it is a problem for theists. Grappling with innocent suffering in a world purportedly under divine providence, the Job poet is among the first theodicists.

Modern apologists for God often attribute evil to human free will and the inflexible laws of nature. Evil exists because humans are created with the freedom to choose between good and evil. God could not intervene to prevent moral evil without abrogating human freedom. At the same time, God created a world ruled by natural laws. God does not intervene to prevent natural disasters. But in the world of Job, God is not distant from his creation, allowing it to operate independently. Indeed, the Hebrew Bible is replete with examples of God's direct intervention in human affairs and nature. A prominent example occurs in the Book of Exodus, where God interfered with the freedom of the Egyptians, preventing them from continuing to enslave the Israelites. God's liberating mission also included his intervening in nature by sending plagues upon the Egyptians and parting the Red Sea.

The unsatisfactory resolution of the theodicy problem would eventually contribute to belief in life after death. Only in this way could God's goodness and justice be vindicated in the face of evil. If God could not fulfill absolute justice in this life, the hope is that it will be fulfilled in the next. John Milton's *Paradise Lost* is a theodicy, its express purpose being to "assert Eternal Providence and justify the ways of God to men."[42] Christians like Milton could attribute much of the world's evil to original sin, the corruption of human nature, and the virtuous could look forward to receiving their rewards in the afterlife. Saint Paul declared: "All that we suffer in this life is nothing in comparison with the glory which is destined to be disclosed for us."[43] But we have noted that belief in an afterlife is foreign to Job's culture. Not until the Book of Daniel, probably the oldest book in the Hebrew Bible, do we find an explicit belief in life after death.[44] Nevertheless, for many, belief in immortality does little to resolve the problem of reconciling God's existence with innocent suffering. A benevolent God ought to have created a world devoid of horrific evil.

In the late nineteenth century, Fyodor Dostoevsky, who struggled to maintain his Christian faith, highlighted the theodicy problem in his novel, *The Brothers Karamazov*. The character Ivan Karamazov rejects God's world because of the prevalence of innocent suffering. Ivan finds morally repulsive the notion that suffering will be justified at the end of the world when God will reveal that it fits into some higher providential harmony: "Imagine that you are creating a fabric of human destiny with the object of making men happy in the end, giving them peace and rest at last, but that is was essential and inevitable to torture to death only one tiny creature— that baby beating its breast with its fist, for instance—and to found that edifice on its un-avenged tears, would you consent to be the architect on those conditions? Tell me, and tell me the truth." Ivan soundly rejects such a world: "I renounce the higher harmony altogether. It's not worth the tears of that one tortured child who beat itself on the breast with its little finger and prayed with its unexpected tears to 'dear, kind God.'"[45] For many people today, the concentration camps of Auschwitz and countless other examples of horrendous evil call into question the God of traditional theology. As Richard L. Rubenstein, leader in the "death of God" movement during the 1960s, averred in his book, *After Auschwitz*: "Our images of God, man, and the moral order have been permanently impaired. No Jewish theology will possess even a remote degree of relevance to contemporary Jewish life if it ignores the question of God and the death camps. How can Jews believe in an omnipotent, beneficent God after Auschwitz?"[46]

## Chapter 10   Job: I Will Continue to Protest

DESPITE THE FORMIDABLE ODDS AGAINST HIM, Job continues to wrestle with God. He is determined to compel God to abide by his own higher standard of justice. Job will pursue his case, even at the risk of his life, which matters nothing to him compared to his integrity: "My soul is weary of my life," he cries. Putting aside his hope for a third party to intervene between himself and God, Job imagines what he would say were he to confront God alone as a plaintiff in a courtroom, even if his words would be futile: "I will give free course to my complaint," Job declares. "I will speak in the bitterness of my soul." Addressing God, he would demand a fair trial: "Do not condemn me. Show me why you contend with me." Anticipating Anglo-American jurisprudence, Job insists on the right to due process. In Job's mind, he has already been tried, convicted, and punished without ever knowing his crimes.

Job has a right to confront the charges against him. If granted an audience with God, he would courageously pose a series of questions to determine why he suffers. Perhaps God takes pleasure in afflicting him. With bitter sarcasm, Job inquires: "Is it good to you that you should oppress, that you should despise the work of your hands, and smile on the counsel [plans] of the wicked?" Such behavior is not expected from a God of justice. Perhaps God, Job mocks, has the limited eyesight of humans, making it difficult for him to distinguish between right and wrong? "Do you have eyes of flesh? Do you see as man sees?" An omniscient God should be able to see into the minds of humans. Perhaps God's life is so short that he must rush to uncover some sin in Job: "Are your days as the days of mortals, or your years as man's years that you inquire after my iniquity, and search after my sin?" While Job might appear guilty in the mortal eyes of the world, God is aware of his innocence: "You know that I am not wicked. There is no one who can deliver out of your hand." Only God can remedy the injustice he has done to Job. But God ignores Job's desperate plea to know the reason for his suffering.

Nevertheless, Job appeals to God's compassion: "Your hands framed me and fashioned me altogether, yet you destroy me." With the traditional invocation of a lament, Job prays to God to remember him: "Remember that you have fashioned me as clay. Will you bring me to dust again?" The metaphor of God the potter, lovingly creating man, appears elsewhere in the Hebrew Bible. According to Genesis, God created everything with his word; only man was created by God's hands from the dust of earth, signifying a special relationship.[47] The prophet known as the third Isaiah declares: "Yahweh, you are our father. We are the clay, you our potter. We all are the work of your hand."[48] Job wonders why God, after lovingly creating him, now wishes to destroy him. He reminds God that he had been the beneficiary of divine solicitude from the moment of his conception: "Have not you poured me out like milk, and curdled me like cheese? You have clothed me with skin and flesh, and knit me together with bones and sinews. You have granted me life and loving kindness. Your visitation has preserved my spirit." But something went wrong in Job's relationship with God. Job is the victim of terrible divine injustice. The benevolent God has become the destroyer God, the evil "watcher of humanity."

Job suddenly drops his pathetic appeal to God and launches into a vehement accusatory outburst. He has a horrifying thought: God secretly planned to destroy him from the beginning, subjecting him to the closest surveillance, waiting to crush him. God lavished prosperity upon Job merely to make his ruin more agonizing. God's apparent benevolence disguised a sinister design: "You hid these things in your heart. I know that this is with you: If I sin then you mark me. You will not acquit me from my iniquity." Job laments that God pursues him for the slightest transgression: "If I am wicked, woe to me!" But if Job is righteous, as he affirms, he still suffers: "If I am righteous, I shall still not lift up my head, being filled with disgrace, and conscious of my affliction." Whether Job is righteous or wicked makes no difference to God, who is arbitrary. Although Job is innocent, God has brought shame upon him. His affliction marks him as a sinner.

Honor and shame are integral to ancient cultures. Shame is different from guilt.[49] In a shame culture, such as Job's, the worth of individuals is determined by how society views them, whether they are praised or condemned. Praise brings honor; condemnation brings shame. The experience of guilt is associated with conscience, whether or not one adheres to their fundamental values. Shame and honor are public, imposed by society, while guilt is private, imposed by individuals upon themselves, based upon self worth. Condemned by society as a sinner, an enemy of God, Job suffers shame. He has lost his good reputation as a blameless and upright person. But as long as his conscience affirms his innocence, he never suffers guilt. Indeed, if Job were to experience guilt, it would prove the friends correct that he is a sinner. Throughout his ordeal, wrestling with God, Job upholds his integrity, regardless of the shame he suffers from his community. But God is also subject to shame. When the Satan challenges the authenticity of Job's faith, God's reputation is threatened. God's concern that humans might worship him for selfish reasons insulted his pride, leading him to betray Job, his loyal servant. For this treachery, it is God who should experience guilt, violating the standard of justice he allegedly upholds as sovereign of the universe.

We have seen Job's isolation, separated from society and berated by his friends. Deprived of dignity and his standing as the greatest man in the East, Job's agony is augmented because society viewed suffering as evidence of sin. Indeed, he is regarded as a living proof of divine retribution. Falsely accused, Job can only bow his head in shame. Unwittingly, Job disproved the Satan's claim in the Prologue that "skin for skin, all that a man has he will give for his life." Winning public vindication is more important to Job than life itself. Yet as long as Job lives, God assaults his honor by his vicious hunting, as the powerful lion stalks prey: "If my head is held high, you hunt me like a lion. Again you show yourself powerful to me." Job alleges that if he persists in his protest, God will augment his misery to show that he is a wicked sinner: "You renew your witnesses against me, and increase your indignation on me. Changes and warfare are with me." Job is overwhelmed by the juggernaut of divine injustice.

Gripped by despair, Job sees his entire life as meaningless. He bewails an incomprehensible contradiction in God. Why did God create Job if he meant to destroy him? "Why, then, have you brought me out of the womb?" Renewing the plea for death of his early speeches, Job cries: "I wish I had given up the spirit, and no eye had seen me. I should have been as though I had not been. I should have been carried from the womb to the grave." He begs God for some peace before he dies. "Are not my days few?" He renews his request that God take pity and look away from him: "Cease then. Leave me alone, that I may find a little comfort, before I go where I shall not return from." The poet might have been familiar with the Babylonian myth of the goddess Ishtar, in which the underworld is called the "land of no-return." Death would end Job's torment. Gone is the depiction of death in his first speech, where Sheol is a place of peace, free from life's tribulations. Images of darkness reflect Job's deep depression. He would pass to Sheol, "the land of darkness and of the shadow of death; the land dark as midnight, of the shadow of death, without any order, where the light is as midnight." With no thought of resurrection, Job now seems resigned to dying without being vindicated.

## Chapter 11  Zophar: Job Deserves Greater Suffering

A T THE END OF JOB'S LONG OUTBURST, Zophar, the third friend and presumably the youngest, is aghast. He sat with Job in mourning for seven days and nights. He listened patiently as Eliphaz and Bildad struggled to reason with Job, promising him restoration if he confesses sin and asks God for forgiveness. Zophar heard Eliphaz appeal to personal religious experience. He heard Bildad invoke the authority of tradition. And he heard Job reject every appeal and accuse his friends of treachery. Zophar was shocked by Job's defiance, angered by his perversion of sacred prayers, and dumbfounded by what he regarded as Job's hypocrisy, concealing some serious sin. Zophar was most angered by Job's claim that God subverts justice by rewarding the wicked and punishing the innocent. Zophar heard Job's blasphemy, characterizing God as a savage predator who enjoys hunting human victims, afflicting them for the slightest transgression. And Job now has the audacity to imagine that he can summon God to court and indict him. Job's sinful pride must be quelled; God must be defended.

Zophar begins his tirade with two accusatory rhetorical questions: "Should not the multitude of words be answered? Should a man full of talk be justified?" Addressing Job directly, he asks: "Should your boastings make men hold their peace? When you mock, shall no man make you ashamed?" Zophar believes himself better equipped to answer Job than the two other friends. Bildad had rejected Job's speech as a "mighty wind."[50] In turn, Zophar calls Job's speech "idle" or meaningless rhetoric, without substance. The friends could have sought support in proverbial Hebrew wisdom: "Sin is not ended by multiplying words, but the prudent hold their tongues."[51] Job has mocked the temporal retribution creed, denying God's justice. He has mocked traditional prayers, subjecting them to bitter parody. Moreover, he has the effrontery to demand that God appear and point out his supposed sins. According to Zophar, Job says to God, "My doctrine is pure. I am clean in your eyes." But Zophar misrepresents Job. While Job did argue his innocence, we have noted that he never claimed to be "pure" in the sense of perfectly sinless. Job did say he was "blameless,"[52] and he did insist that God knew he was "not wicked,"[53] but he was referring to his "integrity." While Job concedes that he might be guilty of sinning from ignorance, his conscience testifies that he has not committed any sin to justify great suffering.

Zophar sarcastically suggests that God should fulfill Job's wish for a judicial hearing. If Job were to confront God, he would be correctly humiliated: "Oh that God would speak, and open his lips against you, that he would show you the secrets of wisdom!" God would reveal to Job his sins, making his guilt clear. Of course,

Zophar cannot provide any evidence of Job's sins. But wisdom, Zophar maintains, has "two sides," one practical, accessible to humans, the other transcendent, belonging to God alone. Ironically, Zophar implies that only God knows why Job suffers. Having heard Job's indignant replies to Eliphaz and Bildad, including his blasphemies, Zophar throws off all restraint. Rebutting Job's claim that God recognizes his innocence, Zophar declares: "Know therefore that God exacts of you less than your iniquity deserves." Presuming to speak for the Almighty, Zophar insists that if God would condescend to respond to his impious challenger, he would make Job realize that his sins are even greater than he is willing to acknowledge. Zophar is the first friend to accuse Job explicitly of sin. No more insinuations. Apparently, Job is an even greater sinner than Eliphaz or Bildad imagine. Job's sins have activated the inexorable principle of retribution. How dare Job assail God, accusing him of injustice? Only God's mercy has preserved Job from even greater agony. Instead of contemplating a lawsuit, Job should praise God for his benevolence and repent immediately before it is too late.

Having defended God's justice, Zophar confronts Job with God's transcendence. Foreshadowing Yahweh's speeches at the book's climax, Zophar presents a hymn to God's infinite wisdom. According to Zophar, Job presumes to know about God what he could not know, and that he could do what no other human can do. Zophar rebuffs Job's impious presumption with rhetorical questions, predictably calling for negative replies: "Can you fathom the mystery of God? Can you probe the limits of the Almighty?" God's wisdom, Zophar proclaims, is inscrutable, extending throughout every dimension of the created world. The limits of God's wisdom "are high as heaven. What can you do? They are deeper than Sheol. What can you know?" The extent of God's wisdom "is longer than the earth and broader than the sea." Confronted by such a God, who sees and knows all, what can Job do on his own behalf? Zophar is alleging that even if Job cannot comprehend the reason, he must accept his suffering as justified by God's providence. While Zophar does not claim more than human wisdom for himself, he believes he is wise enough to know that God is just and that Job is a sinner. But Job never denies that God's wisdom surpasses human understanding. Neither can he deny the testimony of his conscience that God is unjustly afflicting him.

Zophar argues that no person can escape divine justice. God knows all the sins of humankind. If God imprisons Job or "convenes a court" to judge him, "who can oppose him?" Job himself had regrettably conceded as much. Zophar accuses Job of trying to conceal his sin. Job had insisted to his friends that he told the truth: "I shall not lie to your face"[54] But Zophar charges Job with hypocrisy, a sinner who refuses to admit guilt. Reversing Job's lament about God the malicious watcher, Zophar praises God's surveillance of humans. Job must acknowledge that the omniscient God "knows false men. He sees iniquity also, even though" he does not always subject it to immediate punishment. According to Zophar, God knows Job's iniquity and is punishing him justly. Concluding his insults, Zophar evokes a proverb to imply that the incorrigible Job lacks the intelligence to see that he cannot escape God's judgment: "The empty-headed man becomes wise when a man is born as a wild donkey's colt."

Having extolled God's infinite wisdom and omniscience, Zophar comes to the final part of his speech. Following the cyclical pattern of the friends' rhetoric, Zophar offers Job, like Eliphaz and Bildad, a viable escape from God's wrath. Unable to question the simplistic doctrine of retribution, the friends, we have noted, believe that the innocent do not suffer. If Job is suffering innocently, their belief in divine justice will be undermined. But if Job admits sin and repents, there is hope for him. God will forgive and restore him. Zophar assures: "If you set your heart aright, stretch out your hands toward him." Implying that Job has been corrupt, Zophar enjoins: "If iniquity is in your hand, put it far away. Do not let unrighteousness dwell in your tents." Zophar has no doubt that Job is a sinner.

Zophar insinuates that Job has contaminated his "tent" or household with evil. Zophar then paints an idyllic picture of a repentant Job's restoration: "Surely then you shall lift up your face without spot. You shall be steadfast, and shall not fear: For you shall forget your misery. You shall remember it like waters that have passed away." His conscience clear, Job would be able to lift his head again in honor, having overcome the shame his tribulation brought. His agony will be merely a past memory, virtually insignificant.

Zophar speaks as if it would be easy for Job to forget the loss of his children. Zophar reverses the dark images that Job used to express his death wish at the conclusion of his previous speech. Job has spoken of his passing down to Sheol, "the land of darkness...dark as midnight...where the light is as midnight."[55] Zophar presents a radically different picture of Job's restoration: "Life will be clearer than the noonday. Though there is darkness, it shall be as the morning. You shall be secure, because there is hope. Yes, you shall search, and shall take your rest in safety. You shall lie down, and no one shall make you afraid, and many shall court your favor." Job will be blessed with peace and security, and, his reputation restored, many will again seek his help. Like Eliphaz and Bildad, Zophar does not know that if Job were to repent to be restored by God, he would unwittingly demonstrate the Satan's allegation that his virtue was conditional, dependent upon divine favor.

Switching from the first to the third person, Zophar ends by giving Job a solemn warning. While there is hope for the repentant sinner, there is none for the wicked, whose eyes look in vain for deliverance: "The eyes of the wicked shall fail. They shall have no way to flee. Their hope shall be the giving up of the spirit." The fate of the unrepentant sinner is an untimely death. But Job will reject Zophar's counsel, just as he had rejected the exhortations of Eliphaz and Bildad. Job will not compromise his integrity. He is willing to die defending his righteousness.

## Chapters 12   Job: God is a Destroyer

BY THIS TIME, JOB KNOWS that he will not be able to convince his friends of his innocence. Blind adherents of the traditional teaching, they cannot believe that his suffering is undeserved. Defending orthodoxy, they present a united front, assailing Job as a hypocritical sinner. Eliphaz began the assault by alleging that while Job may be essentially righteous, he is nevertheless a sinner. How else could Job's great suffering be explained? Bildad dealt a cruel blow by suggesting that Job's children died because they sinned. And Zophar tried to convince Job that his sins are much greater then he realizes. The friends have also demeaned Job's attempts to argue his innocence. Eliphaz warned that the resentful words of a foolish sinner can only lead to his destruction. Bildad ridiculed Job's words as "blustering wind," and Zophar as "idle talk." Each of the friends exhorted Job to relinquish his quest for vindication. He should repent and be reconciled to God before it is too late. Each promised Job that if he repents God will restore his previous prosperity.

As Job listened to each of his friends, he grew increasingly frustrated. The authority of tradition is in their favor. Nevertheless, Job's personal experience of innocence contradicts the retribution creed. As a righteous person, he does not deserve his torment. Job must be true to himself. He cannot confess sins he did not commit. To make a false confession would destroy his integrity. According to his conscience, he is not an enemy of God. No one can compel Job to violate his conscience. Job had been under the illusion that he could count on his friends' comfort and understanding in his time of greatest need. Instead of supporting their friend, they subject him to ridicule and malicious insinuations. Refusing to submit to their exhortations, Job is emboldened to pursue his lawsuit with God. Rather than respond directly to Zophar, Job speaks to the friends as a group as they sit before him.

Barely able to restrain his anger, Job begins with irony and sarcasm. In their self-righteousness, the friends assumed an air of superiority over Job. Addressing the friends, he declares that they "are the people" who are wise, "and wisdom will die with you." But Job too has wisdom: "I have understanding as well as you; I am not inferior to you." So far, the friends have uttered commonplaces. Like his friends, Job knows that God is omnipotent and majestic. Like his friends, Job knows that humans are completely dependent upon God. Like his friends, Job knows the doctrine of retribution, that God rewards the righteous and punishes the wicked. Job also knows that no mortal can withstand God's wrath: "Yes, who does not know such things as these?" Nevertheless, Job's innocent suffering compels him to conclude that God is not absolutely just. Before his calamity, God had always responded to Job's prayers. Because of Job's righteousness, he had been rewarded by God with prosperity, health, and a large family. But having lost all, Job struggles to comprehend why God's love has been replaced by wrath. Stigmatized as a sinner, Job is ridiculed by his friends and community, an object of scorn instead of respect: "I am like one who is a joke to his neighbor. The just, the blameless man is a joke," mocked as a hypocrite. Job's misery has brought him shame. He is bitter at his friends who, convinced they are favored by God, show "contempt for misfortune" because they see it as evidence that Job has sinned. The friends ignore how often God violates retributive justice, harming the innocent and supporting the wicked. Job will attempt to show the friends what they refuse to see. Injustice pervades the world. "The tents of robbers prosper," Job laments, "and those who provoke God are secure, who carry their God in their hands." Here Job may be alluding to the marauding Sabeans and Chaldeans who stole his flocks and murdered his servants. Such violence could not have happened without God's approval. As Job charged in his previous speech, God actually favors the wicked. Indeed, here Job alleges that the wicked are extensions of God's hands, the direct cause of evil.

Job contends that the injustice of God should be obvious to all. Using a theme from wisdom literature that humans can learn from nature, Job avers that even the animals of the earth are wiser than Job's friends. If animals could communicate with humans, they would tell the friends that violence, brutality, and injustice rule the world. "Ask the animals," Job insists, "and they shall teach you; the birds in the sky, and they shall tell you; or speak to the earth, and it shall teach you. The fish in the sea shall declare to you." The earth and animals would affirm that God is the cause of everything, including the suffering of the innocent and the prosperity of the wicked. Animals, Job alleges, instinctively know that the wicked prosper. Animals are victims of a ruthless struggle for existence, devoid of morality or justice. The poet Tennyson wrote of "Nature, red in tooth and claw." Smaller, slower animals are devoured by vicious, faster, more powerful animals. Destruction and survival have nothing to do with moral character. Job inquires: "Who does not know that in all these, Yahweh's hand has done this, in whose hand is the life of every living thing, and the breath of mankind?" God is directly responsible for both good and evil. Significantly, Job uses the holy name of the Hebrew covenantal God, Yahweh, revealed in the third chapter of Exodus, rather than a generic divine name. The poet might be emphasizing that Job's adversary is the Hebrew God who plotted with the Satan in the Prologue, the God who destroyed the world in the Great Flood, and who subjected Abraham to a cruel test, ordering him to sacrifice his son Isaac.[56]

Despite their reputed wisdom, Job's friends fail to see that God is complicit with evil and wickedness. In the face of experiential knowledge, the trite moralizing of Job's friends rings false. Job cannot accept their advice because it fails the test of reason and common sense. Job asks his friends: "Does not the ear try words, even as the palate tastes its food?" Instead of offering advice of true wisdom, the friends intensify Job's agony by pressing him to relinquish his claim to innocence.

Job recalls the rebuking questions Zophar put to him: "Can you fathom the mysteries of God? Can you probe the limits of the Almighty?"[57] Zophar and the other friends sang doxologies in praise of God's infinite wisdom and power. Job begins with a sentiment typical of doxologies: "With God is wisdom and might. He has counsel and understanding." Like the friends, Job has seen the effects of God's wisdom and power. But for Job, God is far from benevolent. Victimized by God, Job's view of the deity has undergone a fundamental change. Once again, Job uses parody to vent his anger. He subverts the traditional psalm of praise, imitating the language of an orthodox doxology to emphasize God's destructive rather than his creative power. Nature, politics, society, religion and international affairs fall victim to God's indiscriminate, arbitrary power: "Behold, he breaks down, and it cannot be built again. He imprisons a man, and there can be no release. He withholds the waters, and they dry up. Again he sends them out, and they overturn the earth. With him is strength and wisdom. The deceived and the deceiver are his. He leads counselors away stripped. He makes judges fools. He loosens the bond of kings. He binds their waist with a belt. He leads priests away stripped, and overthrows the mighty. He removes the speech of those who are trusted, and takes away the understanding of the elders. He pours contempt on princes, and loosens the belt of the strong. He uncovers deep things out of darkness, and brings out to light the shadow of death. He increases the nations, and he destroys them. He enlarges the nations, and he leads them captive. He takes away understanding from the chiefs of the people of the earth, and causes them to wander in a wilderness where there is no way. They grope in the dark without light. He makes them stagger like a drunken man." Job's depiction of God's subversive power could not fail to offend his friends as sheer blasphemy. Instead of a force for unadulterated goodness in the world, Job sees an arbitrary and capricious God who destroys as much as he creates.

While God ought to support goodness and destroy evil, justice is conspicuously absent from Job's doxology. Destroying, overthrowing, disarming, and humiliating, God rules human society without justice. Job's doxology gives no indication that nations, rulers, judges, priests, and advisors rise and fall according to their virtue or wickedness. This conforms to Job's earlier lament that God "destroys the blameless and the wicked."[58] While according to the Hebrew wisdom tradition, a just government originates from God, Job laments that God causes such chaos in the world that a just government is impossible. Human reason, wisdom, counsel and judgment are subject to God's fickle dominion. Instead of protecting the deceived and oppressed and punishing the deceiver and oppressor, God is indifferent. The distinction between good and evil, the virtuous and the wicked, is completely obliterated. Where is the just God of the prophets who is concerned with human suffering? For Job, the world is ruled by a deity who is indifferent to morality. If a human ruler committed the crimes God committed, much of the world would rise up in moral outrage. Instead of a God of perfect justice, Job sees God as an arbitrary force of destruction. Disorder rules the world. Nothing is secure.

## Chapter 13   Job: I Would Argue My Case With God

LIKE HIS FRIENDS, JOB has always upheld the doctrine of divine retribution. A just God ought to reward the righteous and punish the wicked: "My eye has seen all this. My ear has heard and understood it. What you know, I know also. I am not inferior to you." Yet while Job can understand the friends' perspective, they fail to understand his. Job sees the dark side of God that his friends refuse to see. The reputed God of justice has afflicted Job, a righteous man. Rejecting the friends' counsel that he confess his sins and beg God for mercy, Job renews his determination to confront God directly with his injustice: "I would speak to the Almighty." Job visualizes appearing in God's courtroom to initiate his lawsuit. His friends, who should know him and vouch for his integrity, should be witnesses in his defense. But Job is convinced that they would betray him. Unable to contain his rage, he accuses the friends of being "physicians of no value," "forgers of lies," who misdiagnose the cause of his suffering.

While the friends could not allay Job's physical and psychological torment, they could at least comfort him in his grief. Instead of wisdom, they offer pious platitudes. Job urges them to cease speaking: "Oh that you would be completely silent! Then you would be wise. If only you would be altogether silent! For you, that would be wisdom." Although the friends are not sympathetic to his cause, Job proceeds to rehearse for them the argument he would make before God. Using forensic language, he implores: "Hear now my reasoning. Listen to the pleadings of my lips." Job does not trust his friends to be impartial witnesses if called upon by God to testify. Job accuses them of speaking falsely against him to gain favor with God. The eighteenth-century philosopher Immanuel Kant comes to Job's defense: "Job spoke as he thought, as he felt, and as every man in his position would feel. His friends, however, spoke as if they were overheard by the Almighty whose behavior they were judging, and as if they cared more for winning his favors by passing the right judgment than for saying the truth."[59]

Job presses the friends with a series of accusatory rhetorical questions: "Will you speak unrighteously for God, and talk deceitfully for him? Will you show partiality to him? Will you contend for God?" Will the friends, in order to defend God, testify untruthfully that Job has sinned? Hebrew scripture forbids perjury: "You shall not give false testimony against your neighbor."[60] Will the friends blame Job rather than God for his affliction? Will they sacrifice Job to support the flawed dogma of retribution? Will they continue to insist that God never afflicts the innocent or permits the wicked to prosper? If the friends deny the truth in order to gain God's favor, they, not Job, would be guilty of self-interested piety.

Continuing his legal language, Job warns the friends that their perjury would not withstand God's cross-examination: "Is it good that he should search you out? Or as one deceives a man, will you deceive him?" If they lie, they will incur the wrath of God, who can see into their hearts. Ironically anticipating the prose Epilogue, Job predicts that God will take his side: "He will surely reprove you if you secretly show partiality. Shall not his majesty make you afraid, and his dread fall on you." Their hackneyed religious formulas, Job affirms, are worthless "proverbs of ashes," their arguments supporting God are feckless "defenses of clay." With such untrustworthy friends as witnesses, Job knew that the chance of securing a legal success against God was slim.

Job's warning that his friends ought to fear lying before God reveals a paradox in his thinking, evidence of a deep conflict in his conception of God. How could Job expect God to treat him justly in court? Job cannot relinquish his memory of God's just and benevolent treatment of him in the past. Job's God is ambivalent. Despite his trenchant attack upon divine justice, Job retains the belief that God will grant him a fair trial, that God values truth, and that God can be persuaded to judge rightly. A strict monotheist, Job has no power higher than God to hear his appeal. Recoiling from God's demonic side, Job seeks refuge in God's divine side. He pleads to God, his judge, against God, his adversary. As the eleventh-century Spanish poet Ibn Gabirol appealed to God: "I will flee from thee to thyself."[61]

Even though Job refuses to believe that God has treated him justly, as the Jewish philosopher Martin Buber observes, "Job's faith in justice is not broken down. But he is no longer able to have a *single faith* in God and justice….He believes now in justice in spite of believing in God, and he believes in God in spite of believing in justice. But he cannot forego his claim that they will again be united somewhere, sometime, although he has no idea in his mind how this will be achieved."[62] Job's ambivalence towards God mirrors his oscillating emotions as he confronts the prospect of dying without vindication. Job's reason and heart are in conflict. Reason tells him that God is unjust. Despite his integrity, God afflicts him. But in his heart Job hopes that God will ultimately act justly towards him. When angered by his suffering, Job characterizes God as a malicious terrorist who torments humans and hides his face. But when Job confronts the prospect of death without vindication, his hope transforms God into a deity who will ultimately reveal a face of justice. This God will realize that Job's suffering is a cosmic anomaly and affirm Job's integrity. Throughout the dialogue with the friends, Job's vision of God shifts as rapidly as his emotional states.

Job's innocent suffering reflects a contradiction in God himself. Like human beings, who create God in their own image, God is plagued by an antinomy. As the nineteenth-century German philosopher Ludwig Feuerbach observed, a people's conception of God is a projection not only of their highest aspirations, but also of their destructive and cruel attributes. A century before, the French philosopher Voltaire quipped: "In the beginning, God created man in his own image. Man, being a gentleman, returned the compliment." Scripture is regarded as God's self-revelation. The Hebrew Bible depicts a contradictory God. Like humans, God is benevolent and cruel, pacific and violent. Job's conception of God stems from his personal experience of a contradictory God. Why did the God who rewarded his righteousness suddenly turn against him, treating him as a contemptible sinner? In his attempt to sue God in court for injustice, Job is in effect appealing to the good side of God to undo what the dark side has done.

Despite Job's innocent suffering, he never denies God's existence. Atheism was antithetical to the ancient Semitic mentality. Scripture does not seek to prove God's existence. Throughout the Hebrew Bible, God is a living reality. A world without God would be a world without meaning. When the Psalmist proclaims: "The fool says in his heart, 'There is no God,'"[63] he is not speaking of the philosophical atheist who literally denies God's ontological existence, but of the practical atheist, the wicked person who acts as if God does not exist. Philosophical atheism did not appear prominently in the West until the eighteenth century. In modern times, Elie Wiesel, like Job, retains his belief in God while vehemently protesting God's absence during great innocent suffering. Recalling his experience as a young boy in the Nazi German concentration camps at Auschwitz and Buchenwald, Wiesel affirms: "How I sympathized with Job! I did not deny God's existence, but I doubted God's absolute justice."[64] Wiesel explains in his *Memoirs* that, like Job, he protests God's injustice, his silence and his absence: "My anger rises up within faith and not outside it."[65] Martin Buber expressed similar sentiments: "How is a life with God still possible in a time in which there is an Auschwitz? The estrangement has become too cruel, the hiddenness too deep. One can still 'believe' in the God who allowed these things to happen, but can one still speak to Him? Can one still hear his word? .... Can one still call to Him?"[66] Like Wiesel and Buber, Job is a disillusioned believer. What pains Job most is his realization that God is no longer the absolutely good and just God who sustained him in his happy days.

Having been forewarned to testify truthfully, the friends might have wished to defend their veracity, but Job cuts them short: "Be silent, leave me alone, that I may speak," he commands. "Let come on me what will." Job acknowledges that to challenge God is to risk his life: "Why should I take my flesh in my teeth and put my life in my hand?" Having lost hope in assistance from his friends, Job now chooses to confront God alone, without a mediating umpire. What can a person do when his conscience impels him to challenge divine rectitude? Job's only hope is for a face-to-face dialogue in which God will recognize his mistake and acquit him. In his previous speech, Job admitted that no human could win a lawsuit against God. The price of such presumption might be death. But Job is determined to defend his innocence directly before God's face, whatever the consequence: "Behold, he will kill me. I have no hope. Nevertheless,

I will maintain my ways before him." His mood shifting, Job is confident that his integrity will enable him to prevail: "This shall be my salvation; that a godless man shall not come before him." Job will stand before God with a blameless conscience.

Job's boldness should not be underestimated. Calling for a hearing before God's court is a call for a theophany, from the ancient Greek, meaning a revelation of God. Theophanies occur throughout the Hebrew Bible, such as when God manifests himself to Moses in the burning bush.[67] People do not actually see God in his essence. The Israelites believed that no mortal could see God and live, especially a sinner.[68]   But people do see a palpable physical manifestation of his presence. In these instances, God always takes the initiative. But in this case, Job wishes to seize the initiative by in effect ordering God to appear and defend himself.

For a third time, Job enjoins his friends to remain silent as he presents his defense: "Hear diligently my speech. Let my declaration be in your ears." Confident of his innocence, Job explicitly declares that his integrity will be affirmed: "I have set my cause in order. I know that I am righteous." Would God treat him unjustly? Job's plea recalls that of the patriarch Abraham: "Should not the Judge of all the earth do right?"[69] Despite opposition from his friends and God's silence, Job has become stronger, summoning inner resources that he was only dimly aware of before. Within his mind, Job has assembled his arguments and steeled himself for a dialogue with God. Confident of success, Job challenges anyone, mortal or God, to bring credible charges against him, disproving his righteousness: "Who is he who will contend with me?" If evidence of his guilt can be produced, Job declares, "then would I hold my peace" and accept death.

Job now turns from his friends to address God directly.  Job asks God to grant him two concessions that he believes necessary to guarantee a fair trial. Job is now in the bargaining stage of mourning, striving to find a way to vindicate his integrity before he dies. As his friends listen, Job reveals what he wishes to say to God: "Only do not do two things to me. Then I will not hide myself from your face." First, God must remove Job's physical suffering so that he can argue calmly and persuasively. While he has been able to meet his friends' arguments in the midst of his torment, arguing with God will tax him to the limit. Second, God must lift the terror that Job, indeed all humans, have of him. With these pre-trial conditions satisfied, Job might be able to confront God in the heavenly court. Addressing God not as a judge but as a legal adversary, Job offers him the choice of acting as either plaintiff or defendant: "Call, and I will answer; or let me speak, and you answer me." Because he suffers unjustly, Job believes that he has a right to know the nature of his alleged crimes against God. Because God has not revealed them, Job devises an astute legal move. If God takes the initiative, attempting to justify Job's penalty, God will be the plaintiff or accuser, summoning Job, the responding defendant. If God refuses to act, Job will take the offensive, becoming the plaintiff, and sue God for injustice. He will seek to enjoin God to present evidence of his sins. In either instance, as plaintiff or defendant, God must face Job in court.

Having prepared his case, Job is confident that either as plaintiff or defendant he will prevail in court. God's sense of justice will compel him to affirm publicly Job's integrity. Justice dictates that a defendant must know the nature of his crime. With an ancient sense of *habeas corpus*, Job assumes the role of defendant and demands that God present the charges formally against him: "How many are my iniquities and sins? Make me know my disobedience and my sin." In a trial, the burden of proof lies with the accuser. Job concedes that he might have sinned inadvertently, but he is not admitting to serious sin. He merely challenges God to present proof of his transgressions, deliberate or unconscious. Job is like Josef K in Franz Kafka's *The Trial*. Without having done anything wrong, Josef is arrested. Like Job, falsely accused and assumed to be guilty, Josef spends the entire novel trying to learn the charges against him as he awaits a promised trial. After a year of desperate attempts to vindicate himself Josef is taken away and executed without a trial. According to literary critic, Northrup Frye, *The Trial* "reads like a kind of midrash on the Book of Job."[70] Both Josef and Job remain ignorant of their alleged crimes. Like Josef, Job's placid world is transformed into a surrealistic nightmare as he struggles to comprehend what has happened to him. In order to defend himself, Job demands that the charges be specified in an indictment. Whatever sins he might have committed, they do not justify the magnitude of his suffering.

Job then boldly interrogates God: "Why do you hide your face, and hold me as your enemy?" Job appears to pun on his own name. As we have noted, the Hebrew word for Job (Iyyob) is similar to the word for enemy or foe (Oyeb). Job is asking whether God has mistaken him for an enemy. Capitalizing on the similarity between the two words, the Jewish *Talmud* embellishes Job's encounter with God: "Said Job to God: Master of the Universe! Have you confused Iyyob (Job) with Oyeb (enemy)?"[71] God protests that he is not confused. He would never confuse Job with an enemy. But the Book of Job demonstrates that God does treat Job as an enemy. The God who destroyed Job's family and reputation was not his friend. Job wonders why almighty God would plague a fragile human with severe suffering: "Will you harass a driven leaf? Will you pursue the dry stubble?" Indeed, Job feels that God is tossing him helplessly in the wind. Job's feeling of utter helplessness before God's immorality is captured by Shakespeare in *King Lear*: "As flies to wanton boys, are we to the gods. They kill us for their sport."[72]

Using the language of criminal procedure, Job accuses God of trumping up charges, writing down "bitter things against me." God, declares Job, might indict him for "iniquities of my youth," but these could not have been serious enough to merit his torment. Had Job been a serious sinner as a youth, he would not have prospered as he did. Job imagines himself already convicted and imprisoned like a dangerous criminal and branded like a slave: "You put my feet in the stocks, and mark all my paths. You set a bound to the soles of my feet." God does this to a dying man, "decaying like a rotten thing, like a garment that is moth-eaten." One cannot escape such a sinister deity. Martin Luther understood how Job could speak so harshly of God even though, according to Luther, he was wrong in doing so. Facing death and believing that God has abandoned him, Job's "words show what kind of ideas a man, however holy he may be, has against God, when he gets the notion that God is not God, but only a judge and wrathful tyrant, who applies force and cares nothing about a good life." Luther adds: "This is the finest part of this book."[73]

## Chapter 14   Job: I Would Bargain with God

JOB'S MOOD AGAIN DEGENERATES to despair, as he reflects upon the human condition: "Man, who is born of a woman," Job cries, "is of few days, and full of trouble. He grows up like a flower, and is cut down. He also flees like a shadow, and does not continue." Shakespeare's Macbeth echoes the same sentiment: "Out, out, brief candle! Life's but a walking shadow, a poor player that struts and frets his hour upon the stage and then is heard no more. It is a tale told by an idiot, full of sound and fury, signifying nothing."[74] God is obsessed with Job who poses no threat to him. Recalling his description of God as the predatory watcher of humanity, Job taunts his divine adversary: "Do you open your eyes on such a one, and bring me into judgment with you? Who can bring a clean thing out of an unclean? Not one." If no human, as Eliphaz claims, is pure before God, why has Job been unfairly singled out for excessive punishment? Unlike the Psalmist who pleads with God to look upon him with succor, Job beseeches God to leave humans like himself alone: "Seeing his days are determined, the number of his months is with you, and you have appointed his bounds that he cannot pass, look away from him and let him alone, till he has put in his time like a hired laborer." Left alone, Job could die in peace.

The prospect of death depresses Job. He will die without vindication. There will be no resurrection: "There is hope for a tree, if it is cut down, that it will sprout again, that the tender branch of it will not cease. Though its root grows old in the earth, and its stock dies in the ground, yet through the scent of water it will bud, and sprout boughs like a plant." No such hope exists for Job: "A man dies and is laid low; he gives up the spirit and where is he?" When dead, Job will cease to exist: "As the waters fail from the sea and the river wastes and dries up, so a man lies down and does not rise. Until the heavens are no more, they shall not awake, nor be roused from their sleep." For Job, death means extinction. Once dead, his hope to vindicate himself in a trial with God would be lost forever.

Once again, Job's hope revives. The kaleidoscope of his emotions shifts from profound pessimism to faint optimism. Pursuing his effort to bargain with God, Job conjures up a fantastic notion. He again petitions God: "Oh that you would hide me in Sheol, that you would keep me secret, until your wrath is past." Even though blameless, Job must interpret his suffering as a sign of God's anger. Hebrew scripture records instances in which God's wrath was temporary. God declares through the second Isaiah: "In a surge of anger, I hid my face from you for a moment, but with everlasting kindness I will have compassion on you, says the Lord your Redeemer."[75] Job fantasizes that God might seclude him temporarily in Sheol. The capricious God who now treats Job as an enemy might again treat him as a beloved son. His wrath spent, God will recall Job from temporary death and restore their relationship. With great pathos, Job wishes that God would "appoint me a set time, and remember me!" Genesis records that Noah thought himself abandoned by God at the time of the Great Flood, but God remembered him and the waters receded.[76] Is it possible that God would remember Job in Sheol? Job asks: "If a man dies, shall he live again?" If God would grant his wish, Job will endure his service in Sheol, waiting for deliverance: "All the days of my warfare would I wait, until my release should come." In due time, God would summon Job to court and Job would respond: "You would call, and I would answer you." Hearing Job's case, God would exonerate him.

But Job admits that his wish to be hidden in Sheol, waiting for vindication from God, is impossible. Instead, God pursues him with a vengeance: "Now you number my steps. Do you not watch over my sin?" God continues to afflict Job while refusing to reveal the charges against him. Indeed, God hides the charges like a priceless treasure: "My disobedience is sealed up in a bag. You fasten up my iniquity." Job realizes that, once dead, he could never return from Sheol. His wish was only a momentary fantasy. Job despairs that he cannot prevail against God: "The mountain falling comes to nothing. The rock is removed out of its place; the waters wear the stones. The torrents of it wash away the dust of the earth. So you destroy the hope of man." Whereas the Psalms look to God as a refuge, Job sees God as a malicious destroyer. The famous twenty-third Psalm speaks of a God absent from the Book of Job: "Yahweh is my shepherd: I shall lack nothing....He restores my soul. He guides me in the paths of righteousness for his name's sake. Even though I walk through the valley of the shadow of death, I will fear no evil, for you are with me."[77] Job experiences a different God. From his individual despair, Job speaks on behalf of the forsaken innocent sufferer: "You forever prevail against him, and he departs. You change his face, and send him away." Once dead, a person knows nothing of what happens on earth: "His sons come to honor, and he does not know it. They are brought low, but he does not perceive it of them." But as long as Job lives, he must endure physical pain and spiritual anguish: "His flesh on him has pain, and his soul within him mourns." Job expects to die without vindication, his integrity maligned by all.

By this point, each character has spoken. The first cycle establishes the pattern of the remainder of the dialogue. The friends argue that Job is a sinner who must repent. Job indignantly rebuffs their accusations, insists on his innocence, and begins to focus on gaining a legal hearing before God. A principal issue of the first cycle is God's character, the friends defending him, while Job accusing him of injustice. The most prominent attribute of God in the speeches of both Job and the friends is power. While the friends celebrate God's power as an instrument of retributive justice, Job views God's power as arbitrary and destructive, often directed to immoral ends. Job's protest against God provoked the friends to launch a three-pronged attack upon his integrity. They have been conditioned to believe that the doctrine of retribution reflects God's moral order. They presume to represent the voice of reason and tradition. Eliphaz focused on God's absolute purity. Fancying himself a mystic with a special communication from God, Eliphaz proclaimed that all humans are sinners. Hence, Job should accept his suffering. Bildad focused on God's absolute justice. Fancying himself a scholar arguing from tradition, Bildad insists that according to ancient teaching, innocent suffering does not exist. Job's tribulation must be the consequence of sin. Bildad also cruelly alleges that Job's children perished because they were sinners. Finally, Zophar focused on God's absolute inscrutability. Presuming to speak for God, he rattles Job by insisting that his suffering is less than he deserves.

The friends adhere to the retribution creed as if it were a scientific law. God supposedly rewards the virtuous and punishes the wicked with perfect justice. Accordingly, the friends argue deductively from this invalid syllogism: All suffering is the result of sin; Job suffers, therefore Job has sinned. If suffering is the result of sin, as the friends argue, the fault is with Job, not God. Yet the friends insist that Job should not lose hope. Instead of proudly insisting on his integrity, Job should humbly repent and throw himself upon God's mercy. The Job of the Prologue who patiently accepted his calamity would be more pleasing to God. Each friend concludes his speech in the first cycle with a glowing depiction of the restoration a repentant Job would receive. At the same time, each of Job's speeches concludes in dark pessimism as he wishes for death, lamenting that God hides his face from his suffering. The conventional wisdom of the friends did not apply to Job. He adamantly resists their counsel, refusing to compromise his integrity. Job's knowledge of his innocence enables him to confront the traditional theology critically.

# SECOND CYCLE OF SPEECHES
## CHAPTERS 15-21

## Chapter 15   Eliphaz: Job Undermines Devotion to God

THE SPEECH OF ELIPHAZ OPENS the second round of the
dialogue, in which the relationship between Job and the friends
further deteriorates. Job's attack upon God enrages Eliphaz. He is
determined to overcome Job's resistance. While Eliphaz tried to be
gentle in his first speech, he will not tolerate Job's shocking
blasphemies against God. He commences by attacking Job for
speaking impious nonsense in the guise of wisdom. He begins with
two insulting rhetorical questions: "Should a wise man answer with
vain knowledge, and fill himself with the east wind?" The east wind
was the scorching sirocco that blew from the desert. Eliphaz is
reproving Job's speeches as mere rhetorical wind. Such speeches,
Eliphaz alleges, do not benefit Job: "Should he reason with
unprofitable talk, or with speeches with which he can do no good?"
Job's undeserved suffering, as we have seen, led him to challenge
the retribution doctrine, the basis of morality. But if Job is correct in
arguing that God is unjust, why should any human act righteously?
Job's speeches, Eliphaz charges, "do away with fear, and hinder
devotion to God." While the friends strive to convince Job to repent,
they have not been able to point to a single sinful act he committed.
But Eliphaz is convinced that Job's blasphemy proves that he is a
sinner. There is no need for a trial with God, for Job's own words
incriminate him: "Your iniquity teaches your mouth, and you choose
the language of the crafty. Your own mouth condemns you, and not
I. Your own lips testify against you." As the Jewish high priest
Caiaphas declared when Jesus was brought before him: "He has
spoken blasphemy. Why do we need any more witnesses?"[1] Job
would have no chance in God's court; the verdict would be a
foregone conclusion.

Job had disparaged the wisdom of his friends, arguing that even animals know that God does not act according to retributive justice. With a series of rhetorical questions, requiring negative replies, Eliphaz advances an *ad hominem* argument denouncing Job's claim to superior wisdom as a sinful pride. Anticipating the speeches of God from the whirlwind, Eliphaz rebukes Job by asking him sarcastically whether he is the epitome of wisdom: "Are you the first man who was ever born? Were you brought out before the hills? Have you heard the secret counsel [plans] of God?" Perhaps Job fancies himself Adam, the first man, on intimate terms with God. Perhaps Job is Wisdom personified, who declared: "Before the mountains were settled in place, before the hills, I was born."[2] Or perhaps Job is a prophet, privy to God's plans for humanity.[3] How can Job compare his meager wisdom, Eliphaz inquires, with the wisdom of the ages? How dare Job presume to know God's plans for the universe? Throwing Job's earlier words back upon him,[4] Eliphaz persists: "Do you limit wisdom to yourself? What do you know that we do not know? What do you understand, which is not in us?" The conflict between Job and his friends is centered on the question of wisdom. The friends represent the traditional wisdom of divine retribution, crumbling in the face of reality, while Job represents an emerging wisdom, struggling to come to a more accurate conception of God and the moral order of the universe. Ironically, had Job heard God's secret counsel, he would know the cause of his suffering.

According to Eliphaz, the friends represent the hallowed wisdom of the ages, gleaned from observation and experience, passed from generation to generation: "With us are the gray-headed and the very aged, much elder than your father." The doctrine of retribution reflects this wisdom. Convinced that sinners reap what they sow, the friends have pleaded with Job to repent, promising him restoration to God's favor. But to no avail. The frustrated Eliphaz presses Job: "Are the consolations of God too small for you, even the word that is gentle toward you?" Speaking for the friends collectively, Eliphaz presumes that their consolations represent God's will. Job should be grateful that he still has hope. If he confesses sin and accepts his calamity as punishment, God will forgive and restore him. By rejecting these consolations, Eliphaz implies, Job is guilty of sinful pride. But Job will not compromise his integrity. His friends have failed to console him. Indeed, they side with God and presume to sit in judgment against Job. Ascribing to them the title of "friend" becomes increasingly ironic as the dialogue progresses. Eliphaz finds Job's blasphemy inexplicable: "Why does your heart carry you away? Why do your eyes flash, that you turn your spirit against God and let such words go out of your mouth?" The ancient Israelites regarded the heart as the center of the reason and will. Eliphaz is chastising Job for having turned his reason and will away from God, as only a sinner would.

Having denigrated Job's speech, Eliphaz proceeds to share his own self-professed wisdom. Without referring to divine revelation as he did in his first speech, Eliphaz reiterates his view that humanity is depraved. He asks rhetorically: "What is man, that he should be clean? What is he who is born of a woman, that he should be righteous? Behold, he puts no trust in his holy ones. The heavens are not clean in his sight; how much less one who is abominable and corrupt, a man who drinks iniquity like water!" If God does not even trust his angels, how could he trust corrupt humans whose thirst for evil is insatiable? By definition, all humans are sinners. According to Eliphaz, because Job is a sinful human, he cannot claim to be innocent. Since even the angels or "holy ones" are impure in the sight of God, Job dare not challenge divine justice. Indeed, Eliphaz implies that Job's blasphemies make him akin to one who feeds on evil. But Eliphaz's overstates his argument. He is unable to exalt God without demeaning humanity. His view of humankind as corrupt, wicked, and hopelessly sinful, anticipates that of John Calvin, whose sermons on the Book of Job reflect a God before whom humans tremble. Did Eliphaz consider himself among the "abominable and corrupt" human race? If human beings are so corrupt, God must regret having created them.

Eliphaz closes with a lengthy verbal barrage, aiming to impress upon Job the traditional wisdom on the fate of the wicked. While the first cycle featured the doctrine of retribution in its full form, with God rewarding the righteous and punishing the wicked, throughout the second and third cycles, the friends focus only on the dismal consequences for the wicked. Job's angry rebellion against God and his refusal to repent convince the friends that he is teetering on the brink. Instead of being a righteous sinner, with hope for redemption, Job risks being destroyed by God as a wicked sinner. Sensing a lost battle, the friends cease exhorting Job to repent, shifting their tactic to outright condemnation. They want Job to see himself in their lurid depictions of the punishment of the wicked.

Following the lead of Bildad's first speech, Eliphaz appeals to the authority of tradition: "I will show you, listen to me," Eliphaz urges pompously. "That which I have seen I will declare; what wise men have been told by their fathers," and passed on over many generations. Eliphaz claims to have personally witnessed the truth of the ancient wisdom that God punishes the wicked. How could Job challenge the wisdom of the ages? How could he dare claim that God favors the wicked? The success of the wicked is merely apparent and temporary, alleges Eliphaz, for they live in constant fear of God's vengeance. Eliphaz concentrates on the horrendous consequences in store for Job if he fails to repent. With several transparent allusions to Job's tribulation, Eliphaz seeks to demonstrate the infallible working of divine retribution. He concentrates on the psychological suffering of the wicked. The wicked man is plagued by guilt. Even when he appears to prosper, he is already subject to extreme mental agony: "The wicked man writhes in pain all his days, even the number of years that are laid up for the oppressor. A sound of terrors is in his ears." The wicked man is overwhelmed by fear of sudden violent death: "In prosperity the destroyer shall come on him. He does not believe that he shall return out of darkness." The "sword" of God awaits him. The wicked person is also reduced to being a vagabond, searching desperately for food in times of famine. Aware "that the day of darkness is ready at his hand," "distress and anguish" besiege him like a "king ready to the battle."

Eliphaz portrays for Job the fate of the wicked person—his terror, his insecurity, his impoverishment, and his untimely death. And why is the wicked person visited by such horror? With an obvious reference to Job, Eliphaz punctuates his tale: "Because he has stretched out his hand against God, and behaves proudly against the Almighty." Reversing Job's image of God directing a military assault against him, Eliphaz argues that the wicked person defiantly attacks God with a "thick shield." For Eliphaz, Job is an unjust aggressor against God reaping the bitter fruit of his sin. But Job is akin to the mythical Prometheus, who rebelled against Zeus, stealing fire as an indispensible gift to humankind. In defending his integrity, Job is a hero to those who would resist the abuse of power, even heavenly power.

Resuming his insinuations against Job, Eliphaz uses vivid images to show that the wicked who appear to prosper suffer a sudden change of fortune. The wicked person "has covered his face with fatness, and gathered fat on his thighs," but he is fated to live "in desolate cities, in houses which no one inhabited, which are ready to become heaps." Eliphaz continues to direct his words at Job: "He shall not be rich, neither shall his substance continue, neither shall their possessions be extended on the earth." Moreover, the children of the wicked man will not flourish and he will suffer a premature death: "The flame shall dry up his branches. By the breath of God's mouth" he shall be destroyed. Further describing the demise of the wicked, Eliphaz declares, "let him not trust in emptiness, deceiving himself; for emptiness shall be his reward." The destruction of the wicked person "shall be accomplished before his time." Like an "unripe grape" on the vine, or an "olive tree" that drops its flower, his life will be barren. Eliphaz concludes his diatribe by insinuating that Job is wicked and that his impiety has brought upon him the wrath of God. Eliphaz intimates that Job's former material prosperity had been rooted in deceit and corruption: "For the company of the godless shall be barren, and fire shall consume the tents of bribery. They conceive mischief, and produce iniquity. Their heart prepares deceit." Relegated to the godless by Eliphaz, Job seems to have no hope of vindication.

## Chapters 16   Job: God Wants to Murder Me

JOB HAS GROWN INTOLERANT of his friends' insipid platitudes: "I have heard many such things." The friends relish their lurid descriptions of the wretched fate of the wicked, but Job's experience tells him otherwise. The friends' original mission had been to comfort and support Job in his grief. But they have been abject failures. Job accuses them of being "miserable comforters." Never having greatly suffered themselves, they cannot comprehend the gravity of Job's anguish. C. S. Lewis captures the frustration aroused by insensitive comforters. While grieving for his wife, Lewis was willing to listen to the truth of religion, "but don't come talk to me about the consolations of religion or I shall suspect that you don't understand."[5] Presuming to be theologians, Job's friends respond to his affliction with "vain words," praising God's justice and accusing Job of sin. As if stepping from the Book of Proverbs, they view Job's suffering through the lens of the retribution theology that did not apply to Job's case. Deceitful as a dried-up brook, they merely compound his torment. They are unwitting allies of the Satan, provoking Job to increasingly blasphemous speech. Owing to the friends, "Job's comforters" has become a proverbial phrase of disparagement. They are not true friends. Instead of commiserating, allowing Job to lament and voice his rage, they are self-righteous accusers, rebuking and seeking to silence him.

In fairness to the friends, they too, like Job, are victims of God's injustice. They are undoubtedly pious, sincere men who initially demonstrate compassion for Job by journeying from afar to sit and mourn with him. But they too bear the consequences of God's cruel contest with the Satan over Job's righteousness. Their rash and increasingly vituperative words against Job stem from their sincere effort to defend God. They have no idea that they are participating in a sinister plan to test Job's faith. By accepting the Satan's challenge, God causes the estrangement between Job and his friends. Looking upon Job from the vantage point of their secure and comfortable lives, it is easy for the friends to pontificate.

Kierkegaard, haunted by the Book of Job, provides insight on how people often react to the suffering of others. He wrote in his *Journal:* "The significance of this book really lies in showing the cruelty we men commit when we look upon unhappiness as a guilt, a crime....In order to protect oneself against it one explains suffering as guilt; it is his own fault. Oh cruelty of man." The friends needed to believe that Job's misery was his own fault and therefore preventable. They could not see Job's suffering as the act of a tyrannical God. Their greatest failing was not having the courage to put themselves in Job's place. Kierkegaard expresses a truth that Job's friends refuse to acknowledge: "Perhaps you believe that such a thing cannot happen to you? Who taught you this wisdom, or on what do you base your assurance? Are you wise and understanding, and is this your confidence? Job was the teacher of many. Are you young, and your youth your assurance? Job had also been young. Are you old, on the verge of the grave? Job was an old man when sorrow overtook him. Are you powerful? Is this your assurance of immunity? Job was reverenced by the people. Are riches your security? Job possessed the blessing of lands. Are your friends your guarantors? Job was loved by everyone. Do you put your confidence in God? Job was the Lord's confidant. Have you reflected on these thoughts, or have you not rather avoided them, so that they might not extort from you a confession, which you now perhaps call a melancholy mood? ... No man knows that hour when the messengers will come to him, each one more terrifying than the last."[6]

Job argues that if they could exchange roles, with the friends suffering instead of him, he would not speak like them. It is easy to sermonize when one is not suffering: "If your soul were in my soul's place, I could join words together against you, and shake my head at you." But Job alleges that he would be a true comforter: "I would strengthen you with my mouth. The solace of my lips would relieve you." Indeed, Eliphaz acknowledged that in the past Job had instructed and strengthened many who suffered.[7] But what counsel could we imagine Job, conditioned by the same retribution doctrine as his friends, provide to sufferers?  Would Job have been a sympathetic comforter had one of his friends been in his place?

Until Job suffered, he never questioned divine retribution. He should have anticipated that the friends would blame him rather than God for his calamity. Job's pain makes him forget that for him, as for the friends, the retribution creed had been axiomatic. The sufferer is not granted the benefit of the doubt. Hence if a friend suffered, Job too might have looked to sin as the cause. He too might have repeated the tired platitudes about the restoration of the repentant sinner. Would Job have remained patient if a friend, insisting on his innocence, rejected his counsel to confess and repent? Would Job have sided with a friend against God? Would the scrupulous Job, who offered sacrifices to the deity out of fear that his sons might have cursed God in their hearts, side with a friend who sought to challenge God's justice? Would Job have assumed that his afflicted friend must have committed a secret sin? While compassionate and just, Job would probably find it difficult to react significantly different than his friends if they suffered and sought his counsel.

Dropping further consideration of his friends, Job returns to his pain which, whether he speaks or remains silent, is unrelenting: "Though I speak, my grief is not subsided. Though I forbear, what am I eased?" If Job appeals to God, his cries are unanswered; if he protests, his friends attack him as a blasphemous sinner; if he accepts his ordeal and does not speak, his silence will be interpreted as an admission of guilt. With nothing to lose, Job continues his protest.

Receiving no solace from his friends, Job once again addresses God directly. In a poignant monologue, Job condemns God for causing his suffering. "God," he laments, "you have surely worn me out" and destroyed my family. Job's physical torment is viewed by everyone as evidence of serious sin: "You have shriveled me up. This is a witness against me. My leanness rises up against me. It testifies to my face."

Job presents a horrifying picture of divine violence. God is a vicious predatory animal who "has torn me in his wrath, and persecuted me. He has gnashed on me with his teeth. My adversary sharpens his eyes on me." Unwittingly, Job identifies God with the Satan, "the adversary" who plotted with God against him. Job voices his bitter anguish. He has been disgraced and ostracized, as the community, along with the three friends, joins God in the attack: "They have gaped on me with their mouth. They have struck me on the cheek reproachfully. They gather themselves together against me." As Job's enemy, "God delivers me to the ungodly, and casts me into the hands of the wicked." God is a brutal malevolent deity who batters him mercilessly and mortally wounds him with poison arrows: "I was at ease, and he broke me apart. He has taken me by the neck, and dashed me to pieces. He has set me up for his target. His archers surround me. He splits my kidneys apart, and does not spare. He pours out my gall on the ground." The righteous Job is treated like the mythical Titan Prometheus, bound to a rock, where each day the eagle of Zeus tore at his liver. Job is tortured like a victim of the later Spanish Inquisition. God's violent assault is relentless: "He breaks me with breach on breach. He runs on me like a giant." Job's hope for vindication seems bleak. Having undertaken to wrestle with God, he is being crushed by his adversary's overwhelming force. But even if God chooses to destroy him, Job is hopeful of at least a moral victory.

Commenting on Job's attack upon God, biblical scholar Gerhard von Rad wrote: "No one in Israel had ever depicted the action of God towards men in this way before....Here is a new tone which has never been sounded before: God as the direct enemy of men, delighting in torturing them, hovering over them like what we might call the caricature of the devil, gnashing his teeth...and splitting open Job's intestines."[8] The image of God the warrior is common in Hebrew scripture, which extols a God of battle who casts the Egyptians into the sea and subdues the Canaanites to assist the Israelites.[9] God was given the title "Yahweh of Hosts," signifying power in war.[10] The Psalmist sings: "Who is the King of glory? Yahweh strong and mighty, Yahweh mighty in battle."[11] Indeed, God commanded the Israelites to conquer their enemies, massacring men, women, and children, along with livestock.[12] God slew not only the enemies of Israel, but many Israelites as well, as punishment for disobedience.[13] He slaughtered the first-born of every Egyptian family.[14] He required the death penalty for violating the Sabbath,[15] for heresy[16] and for blasphemy.[17] If Job could have read Yahweh's history, he would never have expected justice from his adversary. When the American revolutionary Thomas Paine read the history of Yahweh and his people, he concluded: "Whenever we read the obscene stories, the voluptuous debaucheries, the cruel and torturous executions, the unrelenting vindictiveness, with which more than half the Bible is filled, it could be more consistent that we called it the word of a demon, than the word of God."[18]

As Job's friends behold him, a pathetic figure, he bemoans his fate. A bereaved father, he wears sackcloth, the coarse garment of mourners. By now the cloth adheres to his rotting skin as he lay on the dirty ash heap: "I have sewed sackcloth on my skin." His grief has become inseparable from his being. Suffering is stamped on his countenance: "My face is red with weeping. Deep darkness is on my eyelids." But once again, he parodies the traditional lamentation, the language of suffering. Job believes that God intends to murder him, just as he murdered his children. Hence Job cannot conclude by praising God and appealing for deliverance. Instead, he defiantly reaffirms his innocence. He has not sinned either in action or thought: "There is no violence in my hands, and my prayer is pure."

Unlike God, Job's hands are free of violence, and he maintains his integrity.

Significantly, Job no longer yearns for death. He is consumed by his quest for vindication. God's injustice and violence should not go undetected. Resuming his legal language, Job visualizes a witness to the crime. If he dies from his agony, God will be guilty of judicial murder. Job's death would be legal, for God is sovereign, but unjust. Job's anger and grief reaching a feverish pitch, he cries out in a passionate apostrophe to the earth that his unjust murder be avenged: "Earth, do not cover my blood. Let my cry have no place to rest." These words appear today, in various forms, on a number of Holocaust memorials in Europe. Job wishes his cry against God, his murderer, to resound throughout earth and heaven. With this verse, the poet parodies the story of Cain and Abel in Genesis. When Cain murdered Abel, God confronted Cain, asking: "What have you done? The voice of your brother's blood cries to me from the ground."[19] God then cursed Cain. Job turns God's own words against him. God is now Cain, the murderer, and Job is Abel, his victim. The subtext implies that God, if he murders the innocent Job, would deserve to be cursed like Cain.

In defiance, Job declares that his murder will not be hidden. Just as he had longed for a mediator to stand between God and himself, only to dismiss the fancy, Job is now confident that someone in heaven will witness the crime and defend his innocence against his friends and God: "Even now, behold, my witness is in heaven. He who vouches for me is on high." Although Job is ridiculed by his friends and ignored by God, his heavenly witness will be his advocate and "maintain the right of a man with God." In his first speech, Eliphaz sought to forewarn Job against attempting to turn to one of "the holy ones" of God to defend him.[20] But this is what Job now does. While a number of commentators have attempted to identify Job's "witness" as God himself, the text shows that the witness is not God, but some angel or heavenly being.[21] The Prologue indicates that the Satan was joined by other angels in

God's heavenly council. And Eliphaz had asked Job if he is privy to the secrets of God's council, indicating the presence of heavenly subordinates.[22] The Job poet might have been influenced by the ancient Near Eastern belief that each person has a patron god whom he can call upon to intervene on his behalf in the divine council.[23] Orthodox commentators distort the text by fabricating a God who plays the contradictory roles of both Job's accuser and his defense witness.[24] Why would God testify against himself? The words of Job demonstrate that God is his enemy, not his witness.

No doubt Job is conflicted about the nature of God, believing that the deity who treated him unjustly would ultimately vindicate him. But the belief of a desperate person does not justify tendentious interpretations arguing that God is not really Job's enemy, but his benevolent father, playing the various roles of witness, advocate, or vindicator. Convinced that God is determined to murder him, Job can hardly expect God to defend him as a witness against himself. A dying man, Job clings to the hope that he still has time to vindicate himself. Perhaps death is not imminent: "For when a few years have come, I shall go the way of no return." Nevertheless, the fear that he might die without vindication haunts Job throughout the remainder of the dialogue.

## Chapter 17   Job: I Have No Hope

THE EMOTIONAL PENDULUM SWINGS back to despair. Job thinks of his rapidly declining life and feels the shame cast upon him by the community: "My spirit is consumed," he wails, "my days are extinct, and the grave is ready for me. Surely there are mockers with me. My eye dwells on their provocation." Assailed by God, Job is a broken man psychologically, physically, and spiritually." The community has become God's accomplice, regarding Job as the proverbial sinner who suffers God's wrath: "He has made me a byword of the people. They spit in my face." In desperation, Job appeals to God who is, paradoxically, his adversary and judge. Only

God, who knows the truth and sees into the human heart, can vouch for Job's integrity: "Give a pledge, be collateral for me with yourself." Job cannot rely upon his friends for support: "Who is there who will strike hands with me?" God has "hidden their heart from understanding." Based on their rigid theology, the friends assume Job's guilt. Job asks God not to "exalt them" by condemning him. As the Psalmist implores God: "I have done what is just and righteous. Do not leave me to my oppressors. Ensure your servant's well-being."[25] Job warns the friends that falsely accusing him to gain God's favor will bring suffering upon their children: "He who denounces his friends for plunder, even the eyes of his children shall fail. Thus Job can only rely on the God who abuses him to guarantee him justice. Will the divine God emerge to save him from the demonic God? Should we demand perfect logic from a desperate dying man? As the French philosopher Pascal observed, "The heart has its reasons of which reason knows nothing."[26]

Job's heart is broken: "My eye also is dim by reason or sorrow." Meanwhile his body wastes away: "All my members are as a shadow." Seeing a righteous person suffer, he insists, "upright men shall be astonished," and "the innocent shall stir up himself against the godless." Yet the righteous person like Job is undeterred: "He who has clean hands shall grow stronger and stronger." Filled with righteous indignation, Job glares at the friends, daring them, and by extension the community, to refute his case against God: "As for you all, come on now again; I shall not find a wise man among you."

Job falters momentarily, relapsing again into despair. He concludes his speech by lamenting his coming death. Overcome by emotion, he forgets his valiant quest for vindication. Zophar had promised Job that if he repents, "though there is darkness, it shall be as the morning. You shall be secure, because there is hope."[27] Job reverses Zophar's imagery. His words are those of a dying man: "My spirit is consumed. My days are extinct, and the grave is ready for me." Job fears that for him there is only night and darkness: "My days are past, my plans are broken off, as are the thoughts of my heart. They change the night into day, saying 'the light is near' in the presence of darkness." Returning to the theme of death, he visualizes the grave as his new home and family, his decaying body consumed by worms: "I look for Sheol as my house. If I have spread my couch in the darkness, if I have said to corruption:'You are my father;' to the worm, My mother,' and 'my sister;' where then is my hope? As for my hope, who shall see it? Shall it go down with me to the gates of Sheol?" Shall Job and his hope "descend together into the dust?" Experiencing the darkest moment of his ordeal, Job fears that he will die without vindication, maligned as a great sinner and enemy of God. But Job has inner resources he has yet to tap.

## Chapter 18   Bildad: God Punishes the Wicked

UNMOVED BY JOB'S PASSIONATE LAMENT, Bildad responds by attacking his turbulent language. In his first speech Bildad ridiculed Job's words as a "mighty wind."[28] But Job continues to vilify God. Exasperated, Bildad impatiently inquires: "How long will you hunt for words? Consider, and afterwards we will speak." Bildad appears to believe that if only Job reflects, he will relent. But by this point no constructive intellectual exchange is possible. Attached to the divine retribution creed, the friends are convinced that Job's suffering is the result of sin. Job, for his part, is convinced of his innocence and more determined to defend his integrity. Neither side is willing to compromise.

Bildad is incensed because he believes Job looks upon his friends as unintelligent, incapable of reasoning. Indeed, Job alleged that animals are wiser than the friends, for even beasts know that the wicked prosper?[29] Job had lamented that God "tore me in his wrath, and persecuted me."[30] Bildad rebuts that Job's rage, not God, is responsible for his destruction: "You tear yourself in your anger." Bildad fears the theological revolution of Job's attack upon God's justice. To admit that Job suffers innocently would undermine the belief in a moral universe ruled by a just God. If Job is right, God is necessarily wrong. According to Bildad, Job is motivated by pride, expecting the moral universe to be overturned simply to satisfy him. The law of retribution teaches that the sinner must suffer. Bildad asks rhetorically: "Shall the earth be forsaken for you? Or shall the rock be removed out of its place?" God will not suspend the moral law of the universe so that Job can be vindicated, making him the exception to God's law of retribution. As a sinner, Job must suffer. But Job believes that God himself has already overturned the moral order. Job's lawsuit is intended to restore faith in God's justice. If Job, an innocent person, is pronounced guilty, there is no moral order.

Bildad devotes the remainder of his speech to the fate of the wicked. Job has maintained that divine justice is absent from the world. The wicked not only prosper, but even enjoy God's favor. According to Job, God has made a travesty of the doctrine of retribution. Nevertheless, as we have noted, the doctrine is essential to the friends' cause. Hence, the friends propound the creed again and again, hoping to pierce Job's defenses and lead him to repent. Through the genius of the Job poet, the friends describe the operation of divine retribution by means of a remarkable variety of images. At the same time, Job counters his friends, using equally vivid images to argue that experience demonstrates that the innocent do suffer and the wicked do prosper. Neither Job nor the friends change their minds. Henceforth, Job becomes even bolder in pursuing his lawsuit against God, while the friends become more forceful in threatening Job with the dire consequences of refusing to repent.

Regarding Job as an unrepentant sinner, Bildad sees no need to remind him that the righteous prosper. He focuses on the correlative point that the wicked suffer. Echoing the second speech of Eliphaz, Bildad paints a dire picture of the destiny of the wicked, using wisdom literature tropes to show darkness overcoming light, darkness representing suffering and death, light representing prosperity and life. Once again Bildad implies Job's association with the wicked. He intends to shock Job into repentance. Using a standard image from the wisdom tradition,[31] Bildad affirms: "The light of the wicked shall be put out," for they have lost God's favor. "The spark of his fire shall not shine. The light shall be dark in his tent. His lamp above him shall be put out. The steps of his strength shall be shortened. His own counsel shall cast him down." The wicked person is never secure; he lives under threat from numerous unavoidable traps. He is pursued with a vengeance rivaling that of the ancient Greek Furies. Suddenly he is caught: "He is cast into a net by his own feet, and he wanders into its mesh. A snare will take him by the heel. A trap will catch him. A noose is hidden for him in the ground, a trap for him on the path." The words "net," "snare" and "trap" indicate that the wicked cannot escape their fate. With implied allusions to Job, Bildad argues that fear plagues the wicked person: "Terrors shall make him afraid on every side, and shall chase him at his heels. His strength shall be famished. Calamity shall be ready at his side." His body is "devoured" by disease, leading to death, "the king of terrors." His home will be a place of desolation, destroyed by the fire of God: "There shall dwell in his tent that which is none of his. Sulfur shall be scattered on his habitation."

While Bildad's first speech concluded with an appeal to Job to seek God's forgiveness, his second speech is aggressive from start to finish, focusing only on the dreadful consequences for the unrepentant. In his laments, Job refused to include any gesture of penitence. Drawing obvious parallels between Job and the wicked person, Bildad delivers a foreboding message, rubbing salt into Job's emotional wounds. With no children or descendants and no survivors where he once lived, the godless man is completely forgotten. Having lost his home, his property, and his family, the wicked person completely loses his identity. In his first lament, Job longed for the peace of death.[32] Bildad insists that death is no comfort to the godless. The wicked person's entire family perishes with him: "His roots shall be dried up beneath. Above shall his branch be cut off." With no belief in an afterlife, the ancient Israelites hoped to receive a semblance of immortality by remaining in the thoughts of posterity. But Bildad insists that the wicked are deprived of this consolation. Bereft of honor and family, the wicked person is completely forgotten: "His memory shall perish from the earth. He shall have no name in the street. He shall be driven from light into darkness and chased out of the world." Aware that Job's children died, Bildad claims that the wicked man "shall have neither son nor grandson among his people, nor any remaining where he lived." Job had insisted that only the "godless" would be afraid to defend themselves before God. Bildad's insinuation is clear. If Job continues his impious effort to move the mountain of the moral order from its divinely fixed "place," he will die prematurely and disappear forever into the dark realm of death, "the place of him who does not know God." Yet Bildad fails to understand that Job would rather be completely forgotten than surrender his integrity.

## Chapter 19  Job: My Redeemer Lives

A DRAMATIC CLIMAX in the poetic dialogue, this is one of the most moving and controversial chapters in the Book of Job. Deserted by his friends, Job is desperate to win vindication while he still lives, but at least posthumously. He opens by lamenting the mental anguish his friends inflict upon him. They sought to undermine his defense, scoffing at his speech as mere wind directed against a just God. They reject his claim to innocence, associating him with the wicked; they mock his bold idea of litigating against God; they regard him as a hypocrite; and they exhort him to confess sins he did not commit. Bildad's cruel speech, branding Job as wicked, reflects the conviction of the friends. Bildad had asked Job "how long" would his blasphemous speeches continue.[33] Job flings the question back upon the friends collectively, crying: "How long will you torment me and crush me with words? You have reproached me; you are not ashamed that you attack me." Their words dampen his spirit as much as his physical affliction tears his body. Job insists that even if "it is true that I have erred, my error remains with myself," between himself and God alone. He has not harmed his friends. Why do they add to his agony? Rather than give Job the benefit of the doubt, tending to his broken heart, they humiliate him to "magnify themselves," pointing to his misery as evidence that he is a wicked sinner. But Job maintains that he suffers not from any sin but from God's violence. Bildad insisted that God does not "pervert justice,"[34] but Job believes that God indeed does pervert justice. He declares emphatically: "Know that God has subverted me, and has surrounded me with his net." Bildad warned that the wicked are trapped in nets of their own making.[35] Job retorts that he is innocent and that God unjustly tosses the net about him. God must be held accountable.

Once again, Job directly accuses God of injustice. He deplores God's vicious onslaught against him, an innocent man. God refuses to heed Job's anguished pleas and grant him a judicial hearing: "Behold, I cry out of wrong, but I am not heard. I cry for help, but there is no justice." Similarly, the prophet Habakkuk lamented: "How long, Lord, must I call for help, but you do not listen. Or cry to you 'Violence,' but you do not save."[36] Instead of relieving Job's plight, God seeks to annihilate him. Job paints a horrifying picture of the ruthless crimes that God has committed against him, both physically and psychologically. God has killed Job's family, reduced him to poverty, and afflicted him with a loathsome skin disease: "He has walled up my way so that I cannot pass, and has set darkness in my paths." God impedes Job's every effort to vindicate himself. Job had been honored like a prince among the people, wearing his righteousness like a crown. But God "has stripped me of my glory, and taken the crown from my head." Job is an object of shame in the community. Like a demonic predator, God hunts Job like he is a wild animal, destroying his hope: "He has broken me down on every side, and I am gone. My hope he has plucked up like a tree." Job's entire life has been uprooted. His words, "walled up," "darkness," "stripped," "broken," "gone," and "plucked up" convey his feeling of running from a divine juggernaut. God pursues him with personal vengeance: "He has kindled his wrath against me. He counts me among his adversaries." Echoing his earlier description of God as an aggressive warrior, Job imagines a divine army marching to attack and crush him: "His troops come on together, build a siege ramp against me, and encamp around my tent." Indeed, God's army has consisted of marauding Sabeans who stole his oxen and donkeys and killed his servants, a fire from heaven that destroyed his sheep and more servants, Chaldeans who stole his camels and killed still more of his servants, a whirlwind that destroyed his house and killed his children, and friends who have betrayed him.

God's violent aggression has isolated Job from his community. Kübler-Ross wrote of the painful loneliness experienced by many of the dying. Social relations constitute a large part of a person's identity. Confronted by a debilitating and possibly contagious terminal illness, Job is completely alone. His extended family, his relatives and friends, his servants, even his wife, avoid rather than comfort him in his grief. The suffering that God inflicted reduces Job to a social pariah, viewed by all as a terrible sinner. No one supports Job; no one pities Job: "He has put my brothers far from me. My acquaintances are wholly estranged from me. My relatives have gone away. My familiar friends have forgotten me. Those who dwell in my house, and my maids, count me for a stranger. I am an alien in their sight. I call to my servant, and he gives me no answer. I beg him with my mouth." Job is deprived of the affection of his wife, mother of his ten children: "My breath is offensive to my wife." So disgraced is Job, that "even young children despise me. If I arise, they speak against me. All my familiar friends abhor me. They whom I loved have turned against me." Job's existence is detested by all. His plaintive words, "estranged," "gone away," "forgotten," "stranger," "alien," "offensive," "loathsome," "despise," and "against me," reflect his sense of profound isolation. God has stripped Job of everything that made life meaningful to him— except his integrity.

With great pathos, Job laments how God maliciously afflicted his body, reducing him to an emaciated skeleton: "My bones stick to my skin and to my flesh," he grieves, having escaped death so far only "by the skin of my teeth." Abandoned by God and condemned by society, Job makes a final pathetic appeal to his friends to respond to his plight as they should: "Have pity on me, have pity on me, you my friends," he cries plaintively, "for the hand of God has touched me." The irony is poignant. God had done the Satan's bidding, twice stretching out his hand in the Prologue, bringing disaster upon Job.[37] Job's tribulation deserves compassion from his friends. He cannot comprehend their hostility. They judge and disparage him, inflicting him as deeply as God's arrows. Job cries: "Why do you persecute me as God does?" But they cannot pity and defend a man touched by God's punishing hand. Instead of strengthening him, the friends are frustrating obstacles during his stages of grief. His anger draws their anger. His hope to confront God elicits their ridicule. His attempt to articulate his grievance against God incites them to accuse him of pride. To the friends, as we have seen, Job's suffering testifies to his great sin. They regard him as a living demonstration of divine retribution. But to Job, the friends are like cannibals who wish to join God in devouring him. Job appeals to their consciences: "Are you not satisfied with my flesh?" Seeing no compassion in their faces, Job knows that any further appeal for their support would be in vain.

Dismissing his friends, Job's fortitude enables him to rise again from despair to hope as he reaches the climax of his speech. Despite the overwhelming odds, Job refuses to be crushed. Not even death can stop him. Uncertain of winning vindication before dying, Job turns to posterity. He wishes that a permanent public record of his case against God be preserved so that, if he should die shortly, a future advocate might defend him. Although dead, Job's innocence and honor would be established for posterity. With escalating emotion, he exclaims: "Oh, that my words were now written! Oh that they were inscribed in a book! That with an iron pen and lead they were engraved in the rock forever!" Job imagines something like the sixth century BCE inscription carved into a stone cliff at Mount Behistun, describing the military triumphs of the Persian King Darius. Job wishes to inscribe forever his "words" defending his innocence and protesting God's injustice. A book is liable to perish, but if engraved in stone, Job's words would be indelible testimony of his integrity for all posterity to see. The Ten Commandments were engraved on stone tablets to perpetuate God's moral law. Job's testimony, also engraved on stone, would confirm his innocence. On the basis of his permanent words, Job might be acquitted in the future. Perhaps he envisions a stone set prominently in the city square of Uz, near the seat from which he dispensed justice to his fellow citizens. The stone might bear words similar to these: "Here lies Job, a blameless and upright man who suffered innocently and died defending his integrity." Ironically, the poet preserved Job's words, giving voice to all innocent sufferers, past, present, and future. The reputation of Job, one who wrestled bravely with an unjust God, is imperishable.

But Job has a sudden thought. He could not witness his vindication beyond the grave. When a man dies, he had lamented, "his sons come to honor, and he does not know it."[38] Job does not want to die before God acknowledges his integrity. Out of the depths of his anguish Job rises to the supreme confidence that God will exonerate him while he still lives. With great emotion, Job cries: "I know that my redeemer lives. In the end, he will stand upon the earth." This is the most famous verse in the Book of Job. Over the centuries, the majority of Jewish and Christian commentators have erroneously indentified Job's redeemer as God himself. But this is to divide God in two, with a just God defending Job against an unjust God.[39] While it is true that God is viewed by scripture as a redeemer who delivers Israel from its enemies,[40] throughout his speeches Job insists that God is not his friend or defender, but his adversary.

Many readers, including the early Church fathers, have tried to read Job's cry of faith in his vindication through the lens of Christian theology, claiming that Job's redeemer prefigures Jesus Christ. The beautiful soprano aria from Handel's *Messiah* has encouraged this misreading. But for Christians, the role of Jesus is fundamentally different. While Jesus is regarded as the redeemer of humanity from the consequences of sin, Job's redeemer is really his avenger, bringing him justice against God. This redeemer would have the power to bring God to court, defend Job, and compel God to vindicate him.[41] Job's idea of a redeemer, a third party who takes Job's side to argue that God is unjust is sheer blasphemy. But we have seen that the poet has no fear of having Job defy religious sensibilities. Throughout much of the poetic dialogue, Job regards God as his implacable enemy. Those who insist that God is Job's redeemer need only read the Prologue to see that God, who inflicted the righteous Job, is his enemy, not his friend.

In speaking of his "redeemer," the poet has Job use the Hebrew word *go'el*, which also translates as "vindicator." *Go'el i*s a legal term originating in ancient Israelite family law. It refers to the nearest relative or close friend charged with the legal duty to restore the rights or avenge the wrongs of a family member. The custom is found in all ancient societies as a means of preserving the family or clan. The duties included redeeming a family member from slavery,[42] buying back property lost because of debt,[43] and marrying a widow to provide a male relative with progeny.[44] But the most important responsibility of a *go'el* was to act as the "blood avenger," avenging the blood of a relative unjustly murdered by someone outside the family.[45] Given that Job believes that God intends to murder him, his *go-el* or redeemer will be a blood avenger. Job knows, of course, that his redeemer cannot avenge his death by killing God, who is not made of flesh and blood. Nevertheless, if Job should suffer an untimely death from God's wounds, the redeemer will exact vengeance by exposing God's injustice and restore Job's integrity for posterity. The myth of a God of absolute justice would be dead.

Like Job's emotional cries for an "umpire," and a "witness," his appeal to a "redeemer" is a projection of a deep wish to be vindicated before he dies. Job seeks desperately to postpone death until his honor is restored. He would accept death as long as God confirms his integrity, affirming him as a righteous person. Racing against time, Job first fantasized that God would grant him temporary refuge in Sheol until his wrath abated. God would then restore him to life and renew their relationship. Dismissing this notion as impossible, Job imagines a series of celestial third-party figures standing between God and himself, enabling Job to vindicate his integrity before death. Job's idea of a redeemer is his boldest yet, for such a redeemer would be more than a mediator or witness on Job's behalf, but a "blood avenger." This implies the greatest blasphemy that the Job poet could have conceived.

Job's redeemer would not be a human, but most likely a celestial being or angel who will plead for him. Such a being, like the Satan, would have a legitimate function in God's heavenly entourage. Yet Job's notion of a third party— whether an umpire, a witness in heaven, or a redeemer— interceding for him against God once again raises the philosophical Euthyphro dilemma. Is God subject to a higher standard of justice? Are things just because God decrees them just, or does God decree them just because they are intrinsically just? Job's hope for some intercessor expresses his faith in a moral order that God himself must obey.

At this point, the Hebrew text is notoriously obscure, raising important questions and eliciting a variety of interpretations. Would Job's vindication occur before or after death? We hold that Job expects vindication just before death, his disease in its final stage: "In the end," "after my skin is destroyed," Job's avenger will "stand upon the earth"— a legal term to signify standing up in court— to defend Job on the basis of the written record.[46] Job had boldly declared that, even at the risk of death, "I will maintain my ways before him."[47] Job could not, of course, witness a post-mortem vindication. The spirits in Sheol, we have noted, have no knowledge of events on earth. Nor could Job expect to be brought back from the dead to be exonerated. He has denied the possibility of a resurrection from the dead.[48] Job had imagined arguing his case before God and being vindicated while still alive. God would no longer hide his face. Job's emotion reaching the highest pitch, he proclaims: "After my flesh is destroyed, then in my flesh I will see God, whom I, even I, shall see on my side. My eyes shall see, and not as a stranger." To see God was a privilege of the righteous.[49] Like Abraham, Moses, and Isaiah, Job would experience a direct physical manifestation of God. The New English Bible translation best captures the legal lens through which Job sees his case against God: "In my heart I know that my vindicator lives and that he will rise at last to speak in court; and I shall discern my witness standing at my side and see my defending counsel, even God himself, whom I shall see with my own eyes, I myself and no other."[50] In Job's imaginary courtroom are assembled all parties to his case. Job, the accused, sits in the dock. Standing at his right side is his witness, ready to testify on his behalf. The awaited vindicator rises to prove Job's righteousness. Seeing God with his own eyes, Job will be vindicated.

Overcome with emotion, Job cries: "My heart is consumed within me." One visualizes Job collapsing on the ash-heap, anticipating his vision of God, who will acknowledge him "not as a stranger," but as a righteous servant. Job is confident that his integrity will be confirmed and his relationship with God restored, preferably before, but at least after death on the basis of the written record. Descending from his ecstatic height, Job closes with yet another grim warning to his friends. If they continue to persecute him, alleging that he is a serious sinner, God will punish them severely. "Be afraid of the sword," Job admonishes, "for wrath brings punishments of the sword, and you may know there is a judgment." Job again fails to notice the contradiction in his thinking. Recalling the divine favor he experienced in the past, Job expects that the God who is his enemy will ultimately act justly, and punish the friends for maligning his character.

# Chapter 20   Zophar: God Punishes the Wicked

Z OPHAR HAS LISTENED WITH GROWING INDIGNATION while Job parodies sacred religious conventions and mocks divine retribution. He has heard Job's blasphemous invective against God. He has also heard Job express supreme confidence that his innocence will be vindicated with the assistance of a heavenly redeemer. Thus far, the friends have failed to convince Job to repent or suffer death from God's wrath. Zophar now delivers his second and final speech, as he will soon recede from the dialogue. Unlike Eliphaz and Bildad, he will not speak a third time. Ignoring Job's plaintive call for pity and understanding, the angry Zophar hopes to strike a fatal blow at the heart of Job's defense. His speech is a *tour de force,* replete with accusatory insinuations, demonstrating considerable skill in parodying Job's speeches.[51] If Job dared to twist conventional lamentations in his favor, Zophar parodies Job's words to associate him with the wicked.

Ignoring Job's emotional cry for pity, Zophar begins by focusing on himself. He is insulted by Job's threat that the friends will be punished by God for maligning his character. Having "heard the reproof which puts me to shame," Zophar declares that he will respond from the "spirit" of his "understanding." Addressing Job's allegation that God permits the wicked to prosper, Zophar devotes his entire speech to defending the traditional doctrine of divine retribution. Like Eliphaz and Bildad, Zophar argues from the effect to the cause. Job suffers greatly, therefore he must have sinned greatly. If Job is innocent, God is unjust and the traditional teaching is false. Zophar's first speech dwelt upon both aspects of retribution, the prosperity of the righteous as well as the destruction of the wicked. By this time in the dialogue, we have noted, the friends have decided to concentrate entirely on the fate of the wicked, implying that Job is most likely among them. Zophar resorts to the stock argument of defenders of divine retribution to explain the prosperity of the wicked. Their success is only temporary. Following the lead of Eliphaz and Bildad, Zophar subjects Job to a third depiction of the inescapable destruction of the wicked. With mock astonishment, Zophar asks Job: "Do you not know this from old time, since man was placed on earth, that the triumphing of the wicked is short, the joy of the godless but for a moment?" The doctrine of retribution is an infallible truth, stemming from time immemorial.

Challenged to explain Job's suffering, the friends insist on blaming the victim. Lacking concrete evidence, they infer that Job's blasphemous language must come from someone who had been a sinner prior to his catastrophe. Circling back to the friends' argument on the fate of the wicked, Zophar insinuates that Job is among them, guilty of the sin of pride for attacking God. When Job demanded a trial before a heavenly court, Eliphaz denounced the proud wicked man who "stretched out his hand against God."[52] Echoing the biblical story of humanity's attempt to construct the Tower of Babel to reach God, Zophar avers that although the wicked person's height may "mount up to the heavens, and his head reach to the clouds," he will "perish forever like his own dung. Those who have seen him shall say, 'Where is he?'" The wicked person disappears like a dream, no more to be found, "chased away like a vision of the night." Zophar insinuates that pride preceded Job's disgraceful fall. Job, hailed as the greatest man of the East, has been overthrown by God for his sins. Mocking Job's reference to God, "the watcher of men," unable to see him after he dies, Zophar repeats Job's words almost verbatim, affirming that when the wicked person dies, "he shall fly away as a dream, and shall not be found. He shall be chased away like a vision of the night. The eye which saw him shall see him no more, neither shall his place any more see him." With heartless reference to Job's personal loss, Zophar affirms that the wicked man's children will be compelled to make restitution for the wealth he stole. Finally, his doom having been sealed, the wicked man will die in the prime of life: "His bones are full of his youth, but youth shall lie down with him in the dust."

Zophar demonstrates insight on the psychology of the wicked. For the wicked man, evil exerts a fatal attraction, ultimately bringing about his destruction. With graphic language alluding to Job, Zophar argues that evil is most manifest in the wicked man's insatiable appetite for wealth: "Wickedness is sweet in his mouth, though he hides it under his tongue" to savor its morsels, until it inevitably turns to the poison. Whatever happiness the wicked person enjoys is impermanent: "He has swallowed down riches, and he shall vomit them up again," Zophar declares. "God will cast them out of his belly." The wicked man cannot escape divine judgment: "He shall suck cobra's venom. The viper's tongue shall kill him." The wicked man "has oppressed and forsaken the poor" and violently seized their homes. Throughout the ancient Near East, abusing the poor was considered a grave offense. The wicked person, insists Zophar, does not enjoy his ill-gotten riches: "He shall not look at the rivers, the flowing streams of honey and butter. That for which he labored he shall restore, and shall not swallow it down." Tormented in conscience, there is "no quietness within him. He shall not save anything of that in which he delights." Zophar thus insinuates that Job had sinfully acquired his wealth by exploiting the poor and seizing their houses, making him an impious hypocrite.

Continuing his diatribe, Zophar argues that the wicked man is consumed by insatiable greed: "There was nothing left that he did not devour. Therefore his prosperity shall not endure." But ultimately, divine retribution cannot be avoided. With another obvious allusion to Job, Zophar holds that when the wicked man is most prosperous, "God will cast the fierceness of his wrath on him." Rather than offer Job the hopeful message of his first speech, Zophar no longer exhorts him to repent. Job's stubborn refusal to bow to tradition, Zophar believes, has brought him to the brink of the final catastrophe. With gruesome imagery, he concludes by depicting God violently crushing the wicked. Once again, he parodies Job's earlier words. Job had lamented that God charged him like a warrior, making him the unjust target for divine arrows.[53] Zophar rebuts that

God relentlessly chases and destroys only the wicked. If Job suffers from God's arrows, he deserves it as a sinner. There is no escaping divine wrath. God violently assaults the wicked. Zophar rivals Homer's *Iliad* in his graphic depiction of violence: "He shall flee from the iron weapon. The bronze arrow shall strike him through. He draws it out, and it comes out of his body. The glittering point comes out of his liver. Terrors are on him." Zophar concludes: "All darkness is laid up for his treasures." The fire of God's wrath "shall devour him," consuming what is left of his possessions. Job could not fail to recall that it was the fire of God that destroyed his sheep and servants.[54]

Before closing, Zophar cannot resist a final parody of Job's words. Job had called upon heaven and earth, all creation, as witnesses in his defense: "Earth, do not cover my blood. Let my cry have no place to rest," he implored. "Even now my witness is in heaven."[55] In his following speech, Job proclaimed that a redeemer blood avenger, probably an angel from heaven, will defend his integrity before God: "I know that my redeemer lives."[56] Seeking to shatter Job's hope, Zophar submits a vindictive retort, alleging that heaven and earth together will testify to a wicked person's guilt. Zophar declares: "The heavens shall reveal his iniquity," afflicting him with suffering, and "the earth shall rise up against him," casting him from society. The wicked person's material possessions are swept away: "The increase of his house shall depart. They shall rush away in the day of his wrath." Zophar does not conclude by summoning Job to repent. The depiction of the horrible fate of the wicked should suffice. Like Eliphaz and Bildad, Zophar punctuates his speech by reminding Job of God's justice. The success of the wicked is but temporary. Their destruction is certain: "This is the portion of a wicked man from God, the heritage appointed to him by God."

# Chapter 21  Job: The Wicked Prosper

JOB'S RESPONSE TO ZOPHAR'S CUTTING DIATRIBE, linking him to the wicked, closes the second cycle of speeches. Once again, Job's exordium calls the three friends to attention: "Listen diligently to my speech. Let this be your consolation." Their silence is better consolation for Job than their words. Although their original intent had been to commiserate with his suffering, they fail to listen sympathetically. Whenever Job protests his innocence, they accuse him of being a sinner. Whenever he challenges God, they accuse him of blasphemy. Job remembers that Eliphaz presumed to equate the friends' "consolations" with those of God.[57] Job had responded by calling them "miserable comforters."[58] If they cannot comfort him with words, they could at least listen as he makes his case. Because he will attack God for misgoverning the world, allowing the wicked to prosper, Job expects them to resume their ridicule: "After I have spoken," he declares, "mock on." The longer Job suffers, the more he needs someone to listen. In pleading with the friends to remain silent while he vents his anguish, he might have wistfully recalled the seven days and nights they sat with him in utter silence. Rather than finding fault with him, they had let him try to cope with his grief. But his friends are now his accusers.

Job reminds the friends that his grievance is directed not at humans such as themselves, but at God, the cause of his catastrophe. He asks rhetorically: "As for me, is my complaint to man? Why should I not be impatient?" Were God a mortal, Job might expect imperfect justice. But the God of absolute justice must act justly. Until Job suffered innocently, he never imagined that he would someday be compelled to vindicate his integrity. According to the retribution teaching, God punishes the wicked unfailingly. Nevertheless, hearing Zophar elaborate on the wretched destiny of the wicked, Job could not disagree more. Too often, the virtuous suffer and the wicked prosper. Why does God allow this? The question torments Job. He is not alone in challenging God for allowing the wicked to prosper. The prophet Jeremiah queries: "You are always righteous, Lord, when I bring a case before you," he declares gingerly. "Yet I would speak with you about your justice: Why does the way of the wicked prosper? Why do all the faithless live at ease?"[59] The Wisdom Teacher in Ecclesiastes is also troubled: "There is something else meaningless that occurs on earth: The righteous who get what the wicked deserve, and the wicked who get what the righteous deserve. This too, I say is meaningless."[60] God's inequitable treatment of the innocent and the wicked, in direct conflict with the retribution dogma, causes Job great consternation. The continued success of the wicked contradicts the traditional view that God's upholds justice.

As the friends listen in silence, Job hopes to jolt them into questioning their simplistic retribution dogma. He asks them to look directly at him. The sight of an innocent man, reduced by God to skin and bones, wracked with pain, scraping his festering sores with a broken piece of pottery, ought to horrify them: "Look at me and be astonished. Lay your hand on your mouth." If they look directly at him, the suffering would shock them. They should see their own humanity in Job. He is living proof that the righteous suffer. God is abusing an innocent man. The friends should also be shocked by God's injustice. Reflecting on the overwhelming evidence of the prosperity of the wicked, Job is appalled: "When I remember, I am troubled. Horror takes hold of my flesh."

Attached to the retribution dogma, the friends relish their gruesome descriptions of the demise of the wicked at the hand of God.[61] But Job will fire a broadside at their creed confronting them with the truth that the wicked often prosper. In his diatribe, Zophar parodied Job's words, associating him with the wicked. But Job too is a master rhetorician. He uses the words of the friends to parody their creed. Job begins with three deft strokes, countering claims made by each of the friends that the wicked suffer God's wrath. Zophar maintained in his second speech that the wicked man suffers a premature death: "His bones are full of his youth, but youth shall lie down with him in the dust."[62] Job rejects this claim with a rhetorical question, asked by countless innocent sufferers over centuries: "Why do the wicked live, become old, and grow mighty in power?" Bildad claimed in his second speech that the wicked man has no offspring.[63] Job counters: "Their child is established with them in their sight, their offspring before their eyes." Finally, Eliphaz proclaimed in his second speech that the wicked man "writhes in pain all his days. A sound of terrors is in his ears" as he awaits the sword of God's judgment.[64] Job rebuts: "Their houses are safe from fear, neither is the rod of God upon them." Job's counterpoints underscore the immense gulf between him and the friends. They have diametrically opposed views of God's government of the world. While Job never denies that many wicked suffer, he believes that God is too often tardy in exacting his judgment.

Job continues to rebut the friends by calling attention to the happiness of the wicked: "Their bulls breed without fail. Their cows calve, and do not miscarry. They send out their little ones like a flock." The wicked person's children dance: "They sing to the tambourine and harp, and rejoice at the sound of the pipe. They spend their years in prosperity" and, unlike Job, "in an instant they go down to Sheol," without suffering. Job cannot contain his bitterness. Even though he devoted himself to a "blameless" life of integrity, God plagues him with suffering while the wicked prosper despite their rejection of God: "They tell God, 'Depart from us, for we do not want to know about your ways. What is the Almighty that we should serve him?'" Ironically, according to Job's depiction, the wicked display the self interest that Job was accused of by the Satan: "What profit should we have, if we pray to him?" The wicked are what are called practical atheists, believing in the existence of God, but ignoring God's moral law. They have no fear of divine retribution and commit their sins with impunity. They would serve God only to benefit themselves. But the wicked, Job alleges, fail to see that the God they ignore is responsible for their success: "Their prosperity is not in their hand." Despite their wickedness, God incomprehensibly rewards the godless, ignoring moral distinctions. Job made this point earlier when he charged: "The earth is given into the hand of the wicked." God is to blame: "If not he, then who is it?"[65] But Job would rather be a righteous sufferer than among the flourishing wicked. He emphatically denounces their beliefs and behavior: "The counsel [plans] of the wicked" are "far from me." Job is not among the wicked, and yet God allows him to suffer.

The wicked continue to thrive throughout long lives. Reversing Bildad's claim that "the light of the wicked shall be put out,"[66] Job counters with a stinging rhetorical question: "How often is the lamp of the wicked put out?" Zophar proclaimed that the wicked suffer the wrath of God.[67] Job rejects this contention with two more rhetorical questions: "How often is it that the lamp of the wicked is put out, that their calamity comes on them, that God distributes sorrows in his anger? How often is it that they are as stubble before the wind, as chaff that the storm carries away?" Indeed, the Psalmist assured that the wicked are "like chaff which the wind drives away."[68] While the wicked sometimes suffer, Job sees that too often they escape God's judgment. Job anticipates the objection that when the wicked prosper, their children are punished for their transgressions. This belief in deferred retribution was common among the ancient Israelites. According to the Book of Exodus, God does not leave the guilty unpunished, but "visits the iniquity of the fathers on the children, on the children's children, on the third and on the fourth generation."[69] According to Lamentations, "Our fathers sinned and are no more. We have borne their iniquities."[70] But Job finds it unjust that the children of the wicked person should suffer for his wickedness: "You say, 'God lays up his iniquity for his children.'"[71] This is no punishment, cries Job: "Let him recompense it to himself, that he may know it. Let his own eyes see his destruction. Let him drink of the wrath of the Almighty." Deferring punishment to their children will hardly deter the wicked sinner: "For what does he care for his house after him when the number of his months is cut off?" Once dead, the wicked know nothing of what happens on earth.

Can Job or any human presume to question God's justice? Job asks rhetorically: "Shall any teach God knowledge, since he judges those who are high?" Job's question is ironic, implying a rebuke. For God knows the difference between justice and injustice. But God does what he wishes, and is not accountable to a higher authority. Experience demonstrates that God acts not according to any rational moral principle, but arbitrarily. Job submits the example of two individuals: "One dies in his full strength, being wholly at ease and quiet. His pails are full of milk. The marrow of his bones is moistened. Another dies in bitterness of soul, and never tastes of good. They lie down alike in the dust. The worm covers them." Both are certain to die, but too many wicked people enjoy a healthy and prosperous life, while too many good people suffer a life of grief and misery. A person's fate has nothing to do with whether they are good or evil. God does not invariably reward the righteous and punish the wicked as he ought. And once they are dead, retribution is too late. But, as Job regrettably acknowledges, no one can tell God what to do.

Job's speech, concluding the second cycle of the dialogue, subverts the Wisdom teaching of the Psalms and Proverbs. The doctrine of divine retribution depended upon the unfailing operation of two correlatives: the righteous will prosper and the wicked will suffer. Enlightened by his personal experience, Job now questions the divine retribution principle. The thought horrifies him. If God does not reward and punish justly, there is no incentive to be righteous. If God does not enforce justice, the notion of a moral order is subverted. An arbitrary God rules the universe. If there is no transcendent justice, Job's integrity would be irrelevant. The medieval Christian theologian Thomas Aquinas was sensitive to the flaw in the retribution creed that caused Job such consternation. Aquinas concedes that the apparent arbitrary distribution of happiness and suffering in the world induced many to doubt divine providence, concluding that human affairs are governed by mere chance. Writing in his *Literal Exposition on Job*, Aquinas observes: "Good things do not always happen to good men or bad things to bad men. On the other hand, neither do bad things always happen to good men or good things to bad men. Rather, both good and bad things happen to good and bad men indifferently."[72] Aquinas seeks to demonstrate that, despite appearances, human affairs are ruled by divine providence. Unlike the Job poet, Aquinas believes that God's justice will prevail not in this life but in an afterlife.

For Job and his friends, divine retribution can only occur in this life. Job knew that the friends would reject his heretical contention that God fails to enforce retribution. For their lives to have meaning, the friends must believe that the wicked will suffer the wrath of God in this life, the only life. Aware of the futility of trying to convince the friends, Job looks directly at them, sensing hostility from their visages. He addresses them sharply: "I know your thoughts, the devices with which you would wrong me." Job is aware that that they intend their descriptions of the fate of the wicked to apply to him. They vilified his character, accusing him of great sin, first by insinuation and then blatantly. If Job, reputed to be righteous, has lost everything, they too are vulnerable to the same fate. They must defend their theology at all cost. Each friend has emphasized the utter destruction of the wicked.[73] Job highlights their erroneous belief: "You say, 'Where is the house of the prince? Where is the tent in which the wicked lived?'" Job refutes the friends' contention that the wicked always suffer. The house of the evil prince remains standing. The tent of the wicked is secure. Job hammers the friends with several rhetorical questions: "Have you not asked wayfaring men? Do you not know their evidences," that the wicked are spared God's judgment? The testimony of travelers, presumably including the Job poet, who have seen other parts of the world, belies the naïve retribution creed. The friends remain blind to innocent suffering and the flourishing of the wicked. Job inquires bitterly about the wicked person: "Who shall declare his way to his face? Who shall repay him what he has done?" Not God. Ironically, Job's anger at the wicked parallels his anger at God. God is like a wicked ruler who abuses his subjects. If granted a face-to-face encounter with God, Job intends to confront him with his unjust ways.

Bildad and Zophar spoke confidently of the terror that the wicked suffer as God sends them to a shameful death.[74] Looking towards his own death in disgrace, Job rebuts that many wicked wealthy and powerful persons die with honor. There is no day of reckoning, no final divine judgment and retribution. Bildad alleged that the memory of the wicked perishes from the earth.[75] Job demurs. With great pomp and ceremony, the coffins of the wicked are "borne to the grave." Countless admirers flock to join their funeral processions, and a vigil is kept at their tomb, preserving their memory for posterity. Even the soil of the earth where they lie buried is "sweet" to them, making them comfortable in death as they were in life. The grieving Job fears that, although a righteous man, unlike many of the wicked, he will die without mourners, scorned as a sinner by his community, forgotten in a lonely grave. Given these harsh realities, Job punctuates his speech with a sarcastic barb at his friends. Their retribution theology has blinded them to the truth. Job concludes the second cycle of speeches, bitterly dismissing the friends: "How can you comfort me with nonsense, because in your answers there remains only falsehood."

Failing to convince Job to repent, the friends augmented their attack in the second cycle of speeches. Reflecting the cyclical nature of the dialogue, the friends sought to intimidate Job, circling back repeatedly to the dismal fate suffered by the wicked. While their first cycle speeches defended the just nature of God, their second cycle speeches sought to impress on Job the retribution suffered by the wicked. Sinners in the hands of an angry God! The theme is reiterated with multiple variations. The friends do not temper their stern warnings with words to comfort Job in his ordeal. Nor do they resume their pleas for Job's repentance. But Job remains undaunted.

The more forcefully the friends argue that he is a sinner who deserves suffering, the more Job rails against God's injustice.

Unlike Job's speeches in the first cycle, the second cycle reveals a hero determined to win vindication. Opposition from the friends has driven Job inward, bringing him to deeper self-awareness, enabling him to discover the strength that lies in conscience. While there is no word for "conscience" in the Hebrew Bible, Job clearly has an innate sense of right and wrong. From this Archimedean point, he challenges God. Like Socrates, Job is a hero of integrity, a righteous person acting from an inviolable moral center. Conscience enables Job to examine his past life to confirm his righteousness. Compelled by his innocent suffering to choose between his righteous conscience and the conventional belief in a God of absolute justice, Job chooses his conscience. God himself affirms in the Prologue that Job is unique in his righteousness: "There is no one like him in the earth."[76] Adhering to the testimony of his conscience, Job continues to wrestle with God. In opposition to the retribution doctrine, he rejects the contention of the friends that God crushes the wicked. With angry words, blasphemous to the friends, Job accuses God of violent aggression and intending to murder him. Job envisioned a heavenly witness to his murder who will testify to his innocence. Finally, Job's spirit soared as he expressed confidence that a vindicator will take his side against God. Either before or after death, Job hopes to triumph, winning from God a public vindication of innocence.

# THIRD CYCLE OF SPEECHES
## CHAPTERS 22-31

### Chapter 22    Eliphaz: Job is a Wicked Sinner

L ISTENING TO JOB'S BLASPHEMOUS SPEECH, Eliphaz reaches his boiling point. How dare Job contend that God allows the wicked to prosper! How dare Job accuse God of acting arbitrarily, without regard for strict justice! In his speech of the first cycle, Eliphaz addressed Job with courtesy, encouraging him to have hope. Since all humans are sinful, all should expect some tribulation. If Job repents, God would restore him. But Job continues to reject any suggestion that he repent for sins not committed. In this, Eliphaz's third and final speech, he abandons all pretense of courtesy. Having heard Job adamantly affirm that he is innocent and that God has treated him unjustly, Eliphaz makes a final effort to convince Job that not repenting will lead to disaster. Unlike the other friends, Eliphaz no longer merely insinuates Job's guilt, but takes the outrageous step of blatantly accusing him of being a wicked sinner, teetering on the threshold of destruction.

From the beginning, Job traced his suffering to God's injustice. According to Eliphaz, Job believes wrongly that his supposed integrity matters to God, who would be obligated to reward him. God, argues Eliphaz, owes nothing to any human. He appeals to logic. God transcends benefit and loss: "Can a man be profitable to God? Is it any pleasure to the Almighty that you are righteous? Or does it benefit him that you make your ways perfect?" Eliphaz contends that God has no ulterior motive to subvert justice by rewarding the wicked and punishing the innocent. While God is pleased when humans are virtuous and angered when they are wicked, he is not dependent upon their behavior. Transcendent and perfectly self-sufficient, God does not profit or lose when humans are righteous or wicked. Humans, not God, suffer from sin; and humans, not God, benefit from virtue. God is supremely objective, meting out rewards to the innocent and punishment to the wicked not arbitrarily, but in a perfectly just manner. Because God has no motive to punish Job unjustly, Eliphaz concludes, Job has brought his affliction upon himself by sinning. But the Prologue indicates that God is deeply affected by human actions. Eliphaz might have thought that his description of God would bolster his argument. Yet his notion of a God, distant and unaffected by human affairs, is antithetical to the Hebrew Bible. The Hebrew God is a living covenantal God, intimately involved with humanity. Indeed, God is vulnerable to humanity, ironically dependent upon his creature Job. God's pride, insulted by the Satan, relies upon Job meeting the Satan's challenge.

Despite his attempt to be logical, Eliphaz's traditional theology leads him to an erroneous conclusion. Like Bildad and Zophar, he infers from Job's suffering that he has sinned. And because Job suffers greatly, his sins must be great. Proceeding from this feeble basis, Eliphaz launches a cruel assault upon Job's character, accusing him of having hid grievous transgressions. Earlier, Job accused his friends of preparing to bear false witness against him, testifying before God that he is a great sinner. Job's fears are now materialized by Eliphaz, who represents the conviction of the friends. Insisting on his legal right to know the charges against him, Job had demanded that God supply him with a formal indictment, specifying his sins. Desperate to corroborate divine retribution, Eliphaz fabricates the specific list Job requested. Having listened to Job's denials throughout several speeches, the frustrated Eliphaz is prepared to betray his friend. While Eliphaz initially appeared to be the kindest friend, he now reveals himself as the cruelest. He claims that Job is a serious sinner. Eliphaz proceeds with more rhetorical questions, again assuming negative replies: "Is it for your piety that God reproves you; that he enters with you into judgment?" Were Job innocent, he would not need to defend himself in God's court. The root of Job's suffering is obvious to Eliphaz: "Is not your wickedness great? Neither is there any end to your inequities." But Eliphaz is unwittingly ironic. God had singled out Job for innocent suffering precisely because of his superior piety.

With no evidence and no witnesses, the desperate Eliphaz charges Job with committing several grave social crimes against humanity violating the accepted moral values of the ancient Near East. Consistent with the dubious logic of the friends, Eliphaz argues from the effect, Job's great suffering, to the cause, Job's supposed great sins. Israelite law and moral standards decreed by the prophets provided for the protection of the poor from corrupt practices of the rich and powerful. Eliphaz portrays Job as one who acquired his wealth by abusing power and oppressing the helpless. According to Eliphaz, Job exploited his own relatives for financial gain and refused to aid the needy: "You have taken pledges from your brother for nothing, and stripped the naked of their clothing. You have not given water to the weary to drink, and you have withheld bread from the hungry. You have sent widows away empty, and the arms of the fatherless have been broken." As a perpetrator of severe injustice, Job brought upon himself the wrath of God. Echoing Bildad's speech depicting the wicked man as entangled in a "net," a "trap," a "snare," a "noose," and surrounded by startling "terrors,"[1] Eliphaz concludes: "Therefore snares are around you. Sudden fear troubles you" like the "darkness, so that you cannot see, and floods of waters cover you." In accord with the law of retribution, Job suffers justly, living in constant terror, like a drowning man engulfed by rising water. Eliphaz's portrayal of Job as a grievous sinner, an obvious lie, is ironic, given God's affirmation of Job's righteousness in the Prologue.

Having fabricated a catalogue of Job's sinful acts, Eliphaz also accuses him of sinful beliefs. He alleges that, like the wicked, Job assumes that his sins can be hidden from God. According to Eliphaz, Job says: "Is not God in the heights of heaven? See the height of the stars, how high they are!" When Job accuses God of failing to distinguish between the righteous and the wicked, he implies that

God lacks perfect knowledge. Eliphaz accuses Job of believing that God is so transcendent that he cannot see sins on earth: "You say, 'What does God know? Can he judge through the thick darkness? Thick clouds are a covering to him, so that he does not see. He walks on the vault of the sky.'" Similarly, the Psalmist declares that the wicked say, "'How does God know? Is there knowledge in the Most High?'"[2] Although Eliphaz cannot produce evidence of Job's sins, he is undeterred. Nothing will convince him that those who suffer are innocent. Job is a hypocrite. Eliphaz argues that God sees what is hidden from humans. Eliphaz warns: "Will you keep the old way, which wicked men have trodden?" Will Job continue his sinful life, walking the evil path? Life as a path or way is a principal metaphor of Hebrew wisdom literature. The way of wisdom and righteousness is contrasted with the way of foolishness and wickedness. According to the Book of Proverbs, "Whoever walks in integrity walks securely, but whoever takes crooked paths will be found out."[3] Rebutting Job's complaint that God allows the wicked to flourish, Eliphaz insists that they are "snatched away before their time," the foundations of their lives washed away.

Eliphaz proceeds to parody Job's previous speech, turning his own words against him. He associates Job with the wicked, who believe that they sin with impunity. Job claimed that the wicked see no profit in serving God, saying to him "Depart from us."[4] Echoing Job's words, Eliphaz places him among the wicked who say to God: "Depart from us. What can the Almighty do for us?" Eliphaz agrees that God, the cause of everything, provides the wicked with prosperity. But their prosperity is temporary, for they inevitably suffer God's judgment. Distinguishing himself from the wicked, Eliphaz sarcastically uses Job's exact words: "The counsel [plans]of the wicked are far from me."[5] But Eliphaz is convinced that he, not Job, avoids the ways of the wicked. Job had asked: "How often is it that the lamp of the wicked is put out?" Eliphaz counters that the wicked cannot escape destruction. Implying that Job is among the wicked, Eliphaz celebrates the certainty of their untimely demise:

"The righteous see it, and are glad. The innocent ridicule them, saying, 'Surely those who rose up against us are cut off. The fire has consumed their remnant.'" Eliphaz's claim that the righteous rejoice at the destruction of the wicked echoes the Psalmist's gruesome prediction: "The righteous shall rejoice when he sees the vengeance. He shall wash his feet in the blood of the wicked."[6]

So Job is a great sinner, according to Eliphaz, dangling over the precipice of destruction. Having maligned Job's character, Eliphaz attempts to mollify his message by offering the usual platitudes. He claims that because Job still lives, there is hope. Eliphaz makes a last plea to Job to repent before it is too late. Turn to God "and be at peace. Thereby good shall come to you. Receive instruction from his mouth, and lay up his words in your heart. If you return to the Almighty, you shall be built up." Job must turn from sin and direct himself towards God. Having earlier characterized his own words as "consolations from God,"[7] Eliphaz considers his counsel as expressing God's wish. Job's sins stem from an inordinate desire for material gain. To be restored, Eliphaz argues, Job must "put away unrighteousness" by relinquishing his love of wealth. Although Job has been reduced to poverty, Eliphaz believes that his greed persists. But if Job casts his gold and silver "in the dust," God will be his treasure, as Eliphaz claims God to be for himself. We recall that the name Eliphaz in Hebrew means, "My God is pure gold." If Job places God above material wealth, Eliphaz assures: "Then you will delight yourself in the Almighty, and shall lift up your face to God." Job's prayers will be answered: "You shall make your prayer to him and he will hear you. You shall also decree a thing, and it shall be established to you." Through Job's intercession, the downtrodden will be saved: "Light shall shine on your ways. When they cast down, you shall say, 'be lifted up.' He will save the humble person." Job will also become a mediator between God and human sinners. Eliphaz claims that Job, upon his repentance, will be transformed by God into a savior of others. Indeed, Job "will even deliver him who is not innocent. He shall be delivered through the cleanness of your hands." But if Job were guilty of the great sins Eliphaz imputed to him, he would be beyond divine help. Moreover, Eliphaz's pious advice fosters the religion of self-interest that the Satan attributed to Job. If Job repents, Eliphaz argues, he will have much to gain from God.

## Chapter 23   Job: God Remains Hidden

ELIPHAZ HAS VICIOUSLY ATTACKED JOB, identifying him as a wicked person who has committed crimes against humanity. Job now delivers a moving monologue, meditating on the prospect of confronting God in court. We have seen Job display the full spectrum of emotional responses, from anger to hope to despair, characteristic of many people facing death. Through Job, we experience vicariously the emotions of an innocent sufferer protesting God's injustice. At this point, Job's anger at his friends abates. We recall his stipulating two conditions which God must meet in order for him to receive a fair trial. First, God must release the "rod" of affliction from him, at least temporarily. Second, God must no longer terrify him. These conditions being met, Job believes that he could argue his case successfully in God's court. But God ignores Job's earnest pleas. Eliphaz's frontal assault on his integrity weighs heavily upon him. Rather than responding to Eliphaz, Job returns his attention to God. He laments that God has given him no choice but to continue his protest: "Even today my complaint is rebellious. His hand is heavy in spite of my groaning." If God would only give him a hearing, Job is confident that he would be vindicated: "Oh, that I knew where I might find him! That I might come even to his seat!" But God remains silent and hidden.

Job's despair changes briefly to hope as he visualizes, as he did in an earlier speech, a scene in which he presents his legal case against God. We recall the emotionally charged conclusion Job had reached previously, expressing confidence that he would be vindicated through the agency of a redeemer, if not before death, then certainly afterward. Now Job focuses on achieving justification before death. Never again will he introduce the ideas of a mediating umpire, heavenly witness or vindicator to argue on his behalf.[8] Job has decided to dispense with an intermediary and boldly argue his case alone. He overcomes his fear that he would be unable to confront God and speak coherently, but resort instead to pleading for mercy.[9] He is now prepared to approach God in full confidence. Earlier, he claimed that God could choose to be plaintiff or defendant. Job fantasizes finding his way to God's court and arguing his case as the accusing plaintiff: "I would set my cause in order before him, and fill my mouth with arguments. I would know the words which he would answer me, and understand what he would tell me." Job and God would have a meaningful dialogue. Job would receive a fair trial. He would articulate persuasive arguments in his defense. God would not overwhelm him with his power: "Would he contend with me in the greatness of his power? No, but he would listen to me." God will dispense justice from his court: "There the upright might reason with him, so I should be delivered forever from my judge." God the judge will see that he has treated Job unjustly and will publicly vindicate him. Job's relationship with God will be restored.

But Job's mood suddenly darkens as he ruminates on the prospect of his trial. His conflicting emotions are reflected in his attitude toward God. In his darkest moments, Job sensed God's stifling presence, his intrusive scrutiny, and begged to be left alone to die. When emboldened to continue his quest for vindication before dying, Job laments God's absence. Job is convinced that his suffering results from a terrible miscarriage of justice, rectifiable only if God can be summoned to court. Yet God remains hidden. Job searches for him at all points of the compass: "If I go east, he is not there; if west, I cannot find him. He works to the north, but I cannot see him. He turns south, but I cannot catch a glimpse of him." Job speaks for the countless many who cry out to God to relieve their misery. Nowhere can God be seen. Job wrestles with an invisible adversary. As Martin Buber wrote, "Job struggles against the remoteness of God, against the deity who rages and is *silent,* rages and 'hides his face,' that is to say, against a deity who has changed for him from a nearby person into a sinister power."[10] According to the friends, God hides his face because Job is a sinner. The Psalmist relates how the self-righteous pour scorn upon the sufferer, jeering "Where is your God?"[11] But from Job's perspective, God hides his face only to enhance his suffering.

Although God is silent, Job maintains that his integrity will ultimately be vindicated. Job pursues God as aggressively as God seems determined to avoid him. While Job cannot see God, he knows that God sees him. Eliphaz accused Job of keeping to the way trodden by the wicked.[12] But Job insists that God knows that he is righteous. Notwithstanding his attack on divine justice, Job believes that once in court, a fair trial will successfully conclude his wrestling with God: "He knows the way that I take. When he has tried me, I shall come out like gold." Angered by God's surveillance, trying to catch him sinning, Job now focuses on God's knowledge of his innocence. Job reaffirms his life of integrity: "My foot has held fast to his steps. I have kept his way, and not turned aside." Job's words reflect the sentiment of the Psalmist: "My steps have held fast to your paths. My feet have not slipped."[13] Eliphaz exhorted Job to repent, laying up God's words in his heart, but Job asserts that he has never departed from God. We recall that Job declared if he dies, even without being vindicated, his one consolation would be that he never denied "the Holy One." [14] Job affirms his unfailing adherence to God's moral law: "I have not gone back from the commandments of his lips. I have treasured up the words of his mouth more than my necessary food." The bitter irony is that while Job never turned from God, God turned from Job.

From optimism, Job's mood sinks again to abject despair. Regardless of his integrity, Job laments that his lawsuit will fail. Almighty God cannot be compelled to act justly: "He stands alone, who can oppose him? What his soul desires, even that he does." Job echoes his earlier lament about God's tyrannical power: "Who can hinder him? Who can ask him, 'What are you doing?'"[15] God's purposes cannot be thwarted. He is an absolute ruler, accountable to no one. Job cannot fathom why God is determined to destroy him. God has implemented sinister designs against him, and he fears that worse may come: "He performs that which is appointed for me. Many such things are with him." Job's fear is palpable: "I am terrified at his presence. When I consider, I am afraid of him. For God has made my heart faint. The Almighty has terrified me. Because I was not cut off before the darkness, neither did he cover the darkness from my face." The despairing Job regrets that God neither took his life prior to his calamity, nor did God shield him when it came. Job's whole life is now darkness.

## Chapter 24   Job: God is Contradictory

IN THE MIDST OF DESPAIR, Job renews his complaint about the prosperity of the wicked. Earlier, he reflected on the unjust plight of the poor at the hands of the corrupt rich and powerful. He argued that God not only permits the wicked to succeed, he actually favors them. A just God would not allow the wicked to commit their crimes. If God enforces retributive justice, as the friends argue, why do the wicked succeed? Job laments: "Why are not times laid up by the Almighty" for judgment? Why do not those who know him see his days?" God fails to fulfill his duty as moral governor of the universe. According to the wisdom tradition, the wicked should suffer God's wrath. Nevertheless, Job argues, the expectation of the righteous that God punishes their oppressors is unfulfilled. The righteous ask, when will the wicked reap the bitter harvest they have sown? Job's personal suffering has made him more sympathetic to all suffering humanity. Injustice reigns in a world supposedly ruled by a righteous God. One might consider Job's litigation a class-action suit against God on behalf of the countless multitudes who suffer innocently.

Job vividly depicts the heinous social crimes committed by the wicked, subverting the basis of society. According to the modern Catholic theologian, Gustavo Gutierrez, the poet "put into the mouth of Job the most radical and cruel description of the wretchedness of the poor that is to be found in the Bible."[16] While Job, the product of a hierarchical society, never questions the economic inequality that fosters many social abuses, he believes that the wealthy have a moral responsibility to assist the poor.   Job concentrates on the innocent victims of the wicked, society's poor and helpless. Job's friends are blind to social injustice. They hold that people get what they deserve. As long as suffering is viewed as the result of sin, victims of injustice will be blamed rather than the root social causes. Nevertheless, moral responsibility was not entirely shirked. Ancient Near Eastern society, including Israel, regarded the protection of the disadvantaged—orphans, widows, and the poor—as a moral obligation established by God.[17]

Yet Job argues that the wicked oppress the disadvantaged without punishment. They appropriate the land of others, illegally removing boundary stones. They seize the flocks of the poor. They drive the needy out of the way. They deprive widows and orphans of their means of subsistence. The orphan's donkey is stolen and the widow is forced to surrender her ox as a pledge for a loan. The wicked push the needy from the road and force them to go into hiding from their oppressors. Like beasts, the destitute must search the barren wilderness for food to feed their children. These starving poor are reduced to gathering fodder in the fields and gleaning what remains in the vineyards of the wicked. The poor lack protection from nature. Inadequately clothed, they freeze at night. "Wet with the showers of the mountains," they must "embrace the rock for lack of a shelter." Fatherless children are seized from their mothers as payment to rich creditors. Children "go around naked without clothing," carrying bundles of grain for the landowner, and yet they starve. They press out olive oil and trod winepresses for greedy landowners, and yet they go thirsty. The evil of the wicked blights not only the rural country, but also the cities, to which many uprooted poor flee in search of subsistence, but to no avail. Job reaches an emotional climax as he lays blame not on society, but on an indifferent absent God: "The soul of the wounded cries out" to heaven, but God ignores their dismal plight. The Psalmist cries: "Wake up! Why do you sleep Lord? Arise! Do not reject us forever. Why do you hide your face, and forget our affliction and our oppression."[18] Where is the God of compassion, the God who heard the desperate cries of his suffering people and delivered them from Egypt?[19]

The prevalence of social injustice demonstrates to Job that the world is fundamentally unjust. The moral order is reversed as the innocent suffer and the wicked prosper. Even those wicked who are ultimately punished thrive much longer than justice demands. Once again, the theodicy question arises. If God is, by definition, perfectly good and just, why do so many innocent people suffer? Why is God blind to the plight of the wretched people of the earth? The God who is the enemy of Job, is the enemy of all humanity. Like Job, many victims of the Nazi Holocaust looked in vain for God, who remained hidden and silent. The Psalmist cries: "My God, my God, why have you forsaken me? Why are you so far from helping me? Our fathers trusted in you. They trusted and you delivered them. They cried to you and were delivered. They trusted in you and were not disappointed."[20] Job's anguish is enhanced because God hides his face.

The oppressed of society have more to fear than economic exploitation by the greedy rich and powerful. They become victims of evil criminals who act under the cover of darkness, undermining the security of life, family, and property. Although the Ten Commandments are not referred to in the Book of Job, the wicked violate God's law, including the sixth, seventh, and eighth commandments of the Decalogue. Using contrasting images of light and darkness, metaphors for righteousness and wickedness respectively, Job depicts the criminal as hiding in the night. Criminals "who rebel against the light, who do not know its ways nor stay on its paths," defy God's law without punishment: "The murderer rises with the light. He kills the poor and needy. In the night he is like a thief." To the murderer is added the adulterer, and possibly the rapist: "The eye of the adulterer watches for the twilight, saying, 'No eye shall see me.' He disguises his face." To the murderer and the adulterer is added the thief: "In the dark they dig through houses. They shut themselves up in the daytime. They do not know the light." For the dawn is like death to them.

Many critics believe that some upcoming words ascribed to Job in this speech on the fate of the wicked belong to his friends, either to Bildad, who has an unusually brief speech in the third cycle, or to Zophar who has no speech at all.[21] Many presume that an early scribe might have confused a number of verses, assigning them to the wrong speaker, or intentionally moved verses from the friends to the mouth of Job in order to make him appear less heretical. The apparent textual anomaly has induced some critics and translators to redistribute portions of the ancient Masoretic text, a precarious venture, assigning portions of Job's words to the friends. Yet there is no scholarly consensus on the proper textual rearrangement. Robert Gordis, translator of the Book of Job, observes: "All proposed restorations, of which there have been many, are necessarily tentative and uncertain."[22] At the same time, the ancient Greek Septuagint and the Aramaic Targum have the same arrangement as the Masoretic text, which is the basis for our analysis.[23]

Assuming the words to be Job's, he now describes the ultimate downfall of the wicked, ostensibly contradicting his earlier speeches, where he lamented the success of the wicked. Nevertheless, Job may not be as inconsistent as he appears. While he protests that retribution has been misapplied in his case, and that God often punishes arbitrarily, Job never repudiates the retribution doctrine outright.[24] While many righteous suffer and many wicked prosper, Job never claims that the world is entirely devoid of justice. To argue that the righteous always suffer and the wicked always prosper would supplant the simplistic doctrine of the friends with another simplistic doctrine.[25] Nor does Job claim that the righteous never prosper and the wicked never suffer. Job had already argued that God destroys the blameless and the wicked alike.[26] Nevertheless, Job is troubled by the apparent arbitrariness and belatedness of God's judgment. He does not adopt a rigid stance like the friends. If he were to deny divine retribution absolutely, he would sabotage his legal case. If he believes that God never acts justly, defending his integrity would be in vain. He could never win vindication. Job would have simply despaired and resigned himself to his fate.

The apparent conflict in the text stems from the real conflict within Job and perhaps the poet as well. Job is experiencing cognitive dissonance, a mental conflict stemming from holding incongruous beliefs simultaneously. Job's life-long belief in divine retribution conflicts with his new realization of the extent of widespread innocent suffering. Notwithstanding his observation that the wicked often prosper, Job cannot discard his hope that God will ultimately show his benevolent and just side. This tension in Job's mind is reflected in the two parts of his speech, the first outlining the triumph of the wicked, the second their inevitable downfall. In the second part, Job might be unconsciously displacing his rage at God, transferring his anger to wicked humans who are less threatening. This displacement might explain the contradictory nature of Job's depiction of the wicked, first as flourishing, and now receiving their just punishment. Angry at God for behaving wickedly towards him, Job directs his rage at the wicked. At the same time, the latter part of Job's speech might also reflect his view of how God ought to behave towards the wicked. Job is torn between his conception of the God who now afflicts him unjustly and the God who treated him justly throughout much of his life.

Although troubled by God's inexplicable failure to always hold the wicked accountable, Job has a glimmer of hope, stemming from his residual belief in divine retribution, that the wicked will receive from God the punishment they deserve, even if belated. The wicked are ephemeral "foam on the surface of the waters." The land they own is cursed and laborers shun their vineyards. As heat melts the snow, "so does Sheol those who have sinned." Their own mothers will forget them and the worms of death will feast on them. As we have noted, without a belief in immortality, many in the ancient world sought to live on in the memory of posterity. But the wicked, Job affirms, are consigned to oblivion, "no more remembered. Unrighteousness shall be broken as a tree." The wicked may enjoy temporary security, but the eyes of a punishing God "are on their ways. They are exalted; yet a little while, and they are gone." They are "cut off as the tops of the ears of grain."

Job brings his speech to a climax with a defiant challenge to all three friends— Eliphaz, Bildad, and Zophar: "If this is not so now," he declares, "who will prove me a liar, and make my speech worth nothing?" Job is referring to his entire speech. In the first part, he argued that the wicked prosper; in the second part that the wicked eventually fall. Job knows that the friends will not deny that the wicked eventually suffer. Strict believers in divine retribution, the friends would agree with the second part, but they could not accept the contradictory nature of God's treatment of the wicked. Believing in an absolutely just God, the friends insist that the righteous are always rewarded and the wicked are always punished. In contrast, Job argues that God's moral government of the world is arbitrary. If divine retribution would operate as it should, the wicked would never prosper. Job yearns for a consistent God. Confident in his depiction of God's paradoxical nature, Job dares the friends to refute him.

## Chapter 25    Bildad: No Person is Righteous

BILDAD DOES NOT RESPOND TO JOB'S CHALLENGE to refute him on the contradictory nature of God. Instead, he calls attention to God's power and human frailty. This is Bildad's last speech, and very short. It also concludes the friends' case against Job, for Zophar will have no third speech. Many critics argue that at this point the text reflects the poet's signal that the friends' case has disintegrated. They failed to convince Job of God's absolute justice. They presented the retribution creed again and again, but their case weakened while Job's grew increasingly stronger. Their vicious calumny merely emboldened his resolve to be vindicated. Their verbal assault upon Job demonstrates the dangers of a rigid orthodoxy that seeks to stifle dissent. In desperation, Bildad makes a final attempt to deliver a knockout blow. Job lamented that God remained hidden, preventing him from having a fair trial. He also confessed his trepidation, conceding that no human can oppose God, who "stands alone, and who can oppose him? I am terrified at his presence."[27] Bildad's tactic is to exploit Job's knowledge of God's awe-inspiring power and majesty in comparison to the fragility of human beings. At the same time, Bildad will again attack Job for having the hubris to attempt litigation against God.

Bildad commences his speech abruptly. Dispensing with the usual opening insult, he launches into a doxology, praising God's omnipotence: "Dominion and fear are with him. He makes peace in his high places." How dare Job presume to challenge God? God is sovereign, ruling over heaven and the entire cosmos. His power inspires awe in heaven and on earth. God is the *mysterium tremendum*, the transcendent being before whom humans shrink in terror. Aiming to subdue Job, Bildad fires a series of rhetorical questions. Evoking the motif of the warrior God, Bildad's first question extols the countless members of God's angelic army: "Can his armies be counted?" Bildad recalls Job's fear that God regards him as his enemy and besieges him with an invincible force. Bildad proceeds with his praise of God by posing a second question: "On whom does his light not arise?" Bildad proclaims that God's power sustains the entire cosmos. Divine light, like the sun, shines throughout the world, ruling and sustaining all of creation. But Job never denied God's power. He yearns for a God who is benevolent and just.

Bildad next attempts to strike at the heart of Job's legal defense with additional rhetorical questions. The first deliberately repeats Job's early question: "How can man be just with God?"[28] As we have seen, Job never claims to be absolutely sinless, but he does claim that his calamity outweighs any sin he might have committed. Bildad argues that Job's legal quest is doomed not only because no human can challenge God but, more importantly, no human is sinless before God. Job, therefore, cannot claim his innocence. Stating the essence of Eliphaz's belief, Bildad asks his final question: "How can he who is born of a woman be clean?" Using light as a metaphor for moral purity, Bildad affirms that even the moon and the stars cannot compare with the effulgence of God. If the moon and the stars are impure in God's eyes, "how much less man, who is a worm."

The view of humanity throughout the Book of Job is nothing short of dismal. Humans are sinners, doomed to suffer, living from the cradle to the grave in constant fear of God. If humans are so despicable, what does this say about their Creator? Throughout the entire book, Job is the sole positive inspiration, with his integrity intact, tenaciously defending his innocence. Bildad reflects the anti-humanism that detracts from religion. He asks, how dare Job, a contemptible human, challenge God's justice? How dare any human consider himself righteous before God? Having solemnly reduced human beings to contemptible creatures, unworthy of God's solicitude, Bildad closes the case for the friends. They will speak no more.

Determined to defeat Job, the cunning Bildad overstated his argument. He exalts God by condemning humanity. Convinced that Job is guilty of hubris, challenging God's justice, Bildad reduces the human race to worms. By introducing the theme of human depravity, Bildad wants to undermine Job's self-esteem and confidence in his integrity. But if human beings are degraded in God's eyes, how would Bildad reconcile this belief with the idea that God created humans in his own image, endowing them with dignity? The vehement Bildad unwittingly subverts the Eighth Psalm. We have seen how Job parodied this Psalm by lamenting that God pays inordinate attention to human beings, menacing them with surveillance. According to Bildad, human beings are vermin, worthless in the eyes of God. Like Bildad, the Psalmist looks into the heavens, marveling at God's creation of the moon and the stars: "What is mankind that you are mindful of them, human beings that you care for them?" Unlike Bildad, the Psalmist, as noted earlier, praises man as God's special creation: "You have made them a little lower than the angels and crowned them with glory and honor. You made them rulers over the works of your hands. You put everything under their feet."[29] Bildad fancies that he can crush Job's dignity, inducing him to relinquish his lawsuit and repent for his sins. Bildad's admonition is simple: Job, a miserable worm, cannot challenge Almighty God. Representing the rigid force of orthodox religion, the friends seek to crush any dissent.

## Chapter 26   Job: God Is Inscrutable

HEARING HIMSELF, AND ALL HUMANITY, denigrated as a miserable worm, for the first time Job refuses to allow a friend to finish. He abruptly cuts off Bildad.  Job will not be intimidated into forsaking his integrity. The friends have nothing more to add to the debate, which has ended in a stalemate. Both sides remain unconvinced. The three friends are inflexible in defending the unwavering rectitude of God. Job is inflexible in defending his integrity. He will continue to affirm his innocence, his rhetoric rising to lyrical heights.

Departing from his usual practice of replying to the friends together, Job responds to Bildad alone. With biting sarcasm, Job reproaches Bildad: "How you have helped him who is without power! How you have saved the arm that has no strength! How you have counseled him who has no wisdom, and plentifully declared sound knowledge!" Bildad's advice has been feckless. Thinking himself wise, he has failed to support Job in his vulnerable condition. Nor has he the wisdom or knowledge to help Job comprehend his suffering. Continuing his sarcasm, Job interrogates: "To whom have you uttered words? Whose spirit came out of you?" Bildad's speech is so far off the mark that it could not have been meant for Job. Who gave Bildad his worthless words? At a loss for an original final argument, Bildad merely parroted Eliphaz's claim that no human can be just before God.[30]

Summarily dismissing Bildad, Job now offers his own doxology. Job never questioned God's omnipotence, but he does challenge God's justice and goodness. Echoing his previous speeches, Job highlights God's destructive as well as his creative power.[31] Job knows the power and majesty of God as much as the friends do. Anticipating God's great speeches at the end of the book, Job celebrates the deity's rule over the entire cosmos. This includes the heavens, the earth, the sea and the underworld. Nothing in the universe is hidden from God, including Sheol, the abode of the dead, believed to lie under the sea. "The departed spirits tremble," declares Job, for Sheol "is naked before God," exposed completely to his penetrating surveillance. With beautiful poetry, Job affirms God's wondrous power, echoing parts of the creation story in Genesis. Out of the void, God creates the sky and the earth: "He stretches out the north over empty space, and hangs the earth on nothing." Ancient cosmologists regarded the northern sky as the dwelling of God, who at creation stretched out heaven like a tent and suspended the earth over empty space. The notion that the earth floats in a void contradicted the ancient cosmological view that the earth is supported by pillars. Job also marvels at God's control of the meteorological order: "He binds up the waters in his thick clouds," and clouds do not burst under their weight. "He encloses the face of his throne, and spreads his cloud on it." Recalling Genesis, Job then describes how God created the horizon and separated night from day: "He has described a boundary on the surface of the waters, and to the confines of light and darkness." God's awesome power is manifest, but is God just?

Having praised God's creative power, Job reiterates the theme of his previous doxology, God's destructive power.[32] Unlike the friends, Job's suffering made him more aware of God's awesome threatening side: "The pillars of heaven tremble and are astonished at his rebuke. He stirs up the sea with his power, and by his understanding he strikes through Rahab," the sea monster. "By his Spirit the heavens are garnished. His hand has pierced the swift serpent." In ancient cosmology, the pillars of heaven refer to the mountains at the horizon believed to be the foundations of God's abode.[33] The ancients believed that when God expressed his wrath through deafening peals of thunder, the mountains shook. The Psalmist proclaims: "The earth shook and trembled. The foundations also of the mountains quaked and were shaken, because he was angry." [34] Job also introduces the Canaanite mythological sea monsters Rahab and Leviathan, personifications of primeval chaos. Job concludes by admitting that all he has said regarding God's creative and destructive powers is "but the outskirts of his ways. How small a whisper do we hear of him! But who can understand the thunder of his power?" Job's doxology conveys only an infinitesimally small fraction of God's awesome wisdom and power, which is beyond human comprehension. If only Job could have heard in the small whisper the reason for his suffering. Anticipating God's speeches to come, Job praises God's power, but not his justice. Would this God whose power pervades the entire universe grant Job a fair trial?

## Chapter 27   Job: I Maintain My Integrity

IT IS NOW ZOPHAR'S TURN to respond to Job. But he does not speak. The friends have exhausted their arguments, unable to penetrate Job's steadfast resistance. Zophar would have nothing constructive to offer. Seeing that no friend ventures to answer him, Job resumes his discourse. He now makes a courageous decision. Dismissing the friends, Job is poised to mount a major legal offensive. He will aim to provoke God to grant his right to a fair trial.[35] He will not depend on the fantasy of an umpire, a witness, or a vindicator. He is prepared to meet God face-to-face in court, either as defendant, if God presents charges against him, or as plaintiff, if God condescends to be questioned. Job proceeds to his extensive pre-trial preparation—ranging over five chapters in the book, trusting that he will live to see his vindication. Job's risky challenge to God is the boldest of the Hebrew Bible and one of boldest of any character in the history of Western religion.

As if standing to testify before a court, Job begins his speech with a solemn oath, swearing to his innocence and identifying God as his legal adversary. God has deprived him of his "right." With great courage, Job swears before God that he will adhere to his integrity, always speaking truth to divine power: "As God lives, who has taken away my right, the Almighty, who has made my soul bitter," as long as "my life is still in me, and the spirit of God is in my nostrils, my lips shall not speak unrighteousness, neither shall my tongue utter deceit." The phrase "as God lives" means that Job is as certain of the truth of his words as he is of the existence of God. Paradoxically, Job's oath is in the name of the God he accuses of committing injustice, not only against him, but also against all who suffer innocently. Whatever role God compels him to play, either plaintiff or defendant, Job swears to tell the truth. Because God is the sovereign authority, Job believes he has no other recourse but to appeal to his legal adversary, God himself. Similarly, the *Koran* exclaims: "There is no refuge from God but unto Him."[36]

Notwithstanding the illogic of his legal procedure, Job remains hopeful that he will succeed in vindicating himself. Addressing the friends, he swears, "Far be it from me that I should justify you," by falsely admitting any sin. He refuses to compromise his integrity by confessing sins without evidence of guilt. He must be true to himself; he will not lie to escape his torment. Reaching an emotional climax, Job vows, "Until I die, I will not put away my integrity from me. I hold fast to my righteousness, and will not let it go." Not even the Psalms can equal the depth of feeling expressed by Job's speeches. Job's adherence to his integrity echoes the Prologue's description of his character.[37] The question in heaven is whether Job will maintain his integrity in the face of overwhelming suffering. Job's question on earth is whether God himself has integrity. Confronted by implacable opposition from his friends and the silence of God, Job has been driven to rely on his conscience, an impregnable citadel. God could ravish his body, friends and neighbors could pummel him with shameful accusations, but no one, not even God, could compel Job to deny his conscience. Despite his physical and emotional agony, he has grown progressively stronger. Elie Wiesel captures the essence of Job's heroism: "Job personified man's eternal quest for justice and truth. Thanks to him, we know that it is given to man to transform divine injustice into human justice and compassion."[38] Humans must compensate for God's moral deficiency. Job adheres to his conscience: "My heart shall not reproach me so long as I live."

By making God the guarantor of his oath to tell the truth, Job hopes to force a trial before the heavenly tribunal. According to ancient legal procedure, once a defendant swears to his innocence, the plaintiff is obligated to supply evidence of guilt or drop the charges. Job aims to compel God to recognize his right to habeas corpus and present the charges against him. Having sworn to God to tell the truth, Job would suffer death were he to speak falsely. At the same time, if God endorses Job's testimony, he would be admitting that he committed a grave injustice. If God fails to produce evidence against him, Job will win his lawsuit by default. His integrity will be vindicated.

After swearing to his innocence, Job's mood swings again like a pendulum from hope to indignation. He had sternly warned the friends that traducing his character will bring God's wrath upon them.[39] Job now summons God to punish the friends. When Job expressed confidence that he would be vindicated because no "godless" person would dare come before God, the friends associated him with the godless.[40] According to Job, not he but they are wicked. The friends painted lurid pictures of the fate of the wicked, cruelly alluding to Job. Now it is Job's turn to draw an equally lurid picture of the fate of the wicked, in which the friends should recognize themselves. Job continues to displace his rage at God, employing the wicked as his substitute target. If God is ultimately just, the friends ought to suffer the fate of the unrighteous wicked, their desperate cries ignored by God: "Let my enemy be as the wicked. Let him who rises up against me be as the unrighteous. For what is the hope of the godless, when he is cut off, when God takes away his life? Will God hear his cry when trouble comes on him? Will he delight himself in the Almighty and call on God at all times?"

The friends betrayed Job by denying his innocence and maligning his character. Instead of acting as witnesses on his behalf, defending his integrity, the friends have become his accusers. Hebrew scripture condemns bearing false witness. According to Deuteronomy, a person who gives false testimony against another must suffer the punishment "as that witness intended to do to the other party…Show no pity: life for life, eye for eye, tooth for tooth, hand for hand, foot for foot." [41] This is the *lex talionis* punishment Job wishes God to inflict upon his friends. If they had been truthful, they would have admitted failure to understand Job's suffering. Instead, without a shred of evidence, they accuse him of serious sins. Certain of their own righteousness, the friends assume they are morally superior, urging Job to compromise his integrity. While Job remained true to himself, they were untrue to themselves and to Job. Turning their own words against them, Job details the fate that the friends have earned for themselves by bearing false witness against him. They should suffer the dire fate that they assigned him. God has not heeded Job's cries, may he not heed theirs. Eliphaz had counseled Job that if he repented he would find "delight in the Almighty."[42] Job wishes that his friends will find no delight in God, who will unleash his wrath upon them.

Job warns of God's punitive power: "I will teach you about the hand of God," he declares. "That which is with the Almighty I will not conceal. You have seen it yourselves; why then have you become altogether vain," spewing foolish words? The friends have told Job of God's plan for the wicked. But they, not Job, are the wicked. Driven by anger and despair, Job might have imagined himself directing the hand of God to inflict upon the friends the suffering that they saw descending upon him. Maligning his character unjustly, they deserve severe punishment.

Job has already matched the rhetoric of the friends in describing the horrific fate of the wicked.[43] One can imagine the friends shuddering while listening to Job reiterate the litany of punishments meted out by God to the godless. Job thrashes the friends with their own whips. He circles back to Zophar's second speech, replicating the friends' words on the miserable fate of the wicked. While Job had lamented that too often the righteous suffer and the wicked prosper, he returns to his conviction that God ultimately destroys them: "This is the portion of a wicked man with God," Job alleges, the "heritage" he receives from the "Almighty." The wicked man's children are destined for starvation and violent death: "If his children are multiplied, it is for the sword. His offspring shall not be satisfied with bread. Those who remain of him shall be buried in death." His widow shall welcome his death, making "no lamentation." The wicked man's wealth passes to the deserving righteous: "Though he heap up silver as the dust, and prepare clothing as the clay; he may prepare it, but the just shall put it on, and the innocent shall divine the silver." The prosperity of the wicked is fleeting: "He builds his house as a moth," like a makeshift shack built by a watchman. The prosperity of the wicked man is only temporary. In the end, he cannot escape God's wrath. Sudden death awaits him: "He lies down rich, but he shall not do so again. He opens his eyes, and he is not." Having characterized the friends as wicked, they should expect destruction from God.

Job continues his onslaught. The friends had lectured him repeatedly on the terrors that afflict the wicked. May these terrors afflict each friend, as he suffers the storm of God's wrath, sweeping him away like a tornado to sudden untimely death: "Terrors overtake him like waters. A storm steals him away in the night. The east wind carries him away, and he departs. It sweeps him out of his place. It hurls at him, and does not spare, as he flees away from his hand." The east wind, the sirocco, blows fiercely from the desert, often bringing havoc. The storm is a traditional biblical symbol of the destruction that results from God's punishment.[44] Job concludes his curse with a prediction that the friends will suffer the humiliation he has undeservedly endured. As the wicked person flees from the divine whirlwind that will destroy him, the community shall rightly condemn him: "Men shall clap their hands at him" in derision, "and shall hiss him out of his place." Clapping and hissing were common expressions of scorn and ridicule.[45] Although God may not punish the wicked immediately, they never know their day of reckoning.

The friends introduced no new arguments in the third cycle of speeches, but threw all caution aside by bluntly accusing Job of specific sins. The absence of evidence did not deter them, for they merely argued from the effect, Job's suffering, to the cause, Job's supposed sins. Meanwhile, Job continues his desperate search for God, his elusive legal adversary who hides his face. At this point, Job would have found bitter irony in the Psalmist's confident declaration: "Yahweh is near to all those who call on him, to all who call on him in truth."[46] Finally, aiming to compel God to respond to his grievance, Job swears to his integrity, calling upon God to punish him severely if what he says is not true. Job will defend his integrity until his dying breath.

His friends having withdrawn from the dialogue, Job is confident that he has made progress in preparing for his trial. Undeterred in his effort to secure vindication, his fear of God diminishes. His integrity is more important than life itself. He has taken a solemn oath affirming his innocence, calling upon God as his witness. He has sworn to tell the truth. He has sworn never to relinquish his integrity. And he hopes to have undermined his friends as potential hostile witnesses. His next step will be to reaffirm his character as a blameless servant of God, accused of sins he never committed.

# HYMN TO WISDOM

## Chapter 28   Job: Where Shall Wisdom be Found?

JOB'S NEXT SPEECH presents a problem for commentators. With the advent of biblical scholarship in the nineteenth century, commentators maintained that the Bible should be read like any other book— critically. This approach led to the discovery that some parts of the Book of Job, such as the Hymn to Divine Wisdom and the speeches of Elihu which come later in the book, are interpolations, and not part of the original text. Yet it is possible that the interpolations were also composed by the Job poet in a later stage of his life. Like Goethe with *Faust* and Walt Whitman with *Leaves of* Grass, the poet might never have been able to distance himself from his sublime work of art and the profound issues it raises. The canonical text of the Hebrew Bible was established between the fifth and the tenth centuries AD by a group of rabbinic scholars and scribes, known as the Masoretes, derived from the word *masora,* meaning tradition. Arguing along lines similar to G. K. Chesterton, we hold that like Canterbury Cathedral, the Book of Job, even with later additions and modifications, has a an organic unity.[1] Rather than indulge in speculative reconstruction, we consider the received canonical text as an artistic unity that warrants close analysis. Generations of readers have either been unaware or unconcerned that the Masoretic text contains interpolations and possibly dislocated verses. The text is also marred by some corruptions as it was transmitted by generations of copyists. Such corruptions are either accidental, owing to scribal error, or deliberate, the text altered to conform more closely to orthodox belief. But to truncate the canonical text by surgically removing possible later additions, or to re-arrange verses allegedly displaced, tarnishes a text that, whatever transformations it has undergone, has taken on a life of its own. In this book, therefore, we honor the received canonical text.[2]

In the absence of incontrovertible evidence to the contrary, we treat the Hymn to Divine Wisdom as the words of Job himself. Over centuries, countless readers have followed the canonical text, which ascribes the words to Job. Having completed the rousing affirmation of his integrity and condemned his friends to the doom of the wicked, Job moves to a beautiful monologue on wisdom. The acrimonious debate with the friends has ended, allowing Job a moment for calm reflection. With magnificent poetry, he praises the wisdom of God. Job's hymn expands upon what he has already said of God's wisdom and power. Job has proclaimed that humans can grasp but a fragmentary whisper of God's ways.[3] Job also distinguishes between God's wisdom and the limited wisdom accessible to humans. The debate between Job and the friends is essentially a debate about wisdom. Who possesses true wisdom, the friends or Job? We have seen that, applying the traditional wisdom to Job, the friends insist that he deserves his calamity. But Job's experience of innocent suffering belies the accepted retribution teaching. If the doctrine of retribution is false, how can Job's innocent suffering be explained? The three friends having been silenced, Job considers the path before him. The explanation for his suffering can come only from God. Job's hymn will play an important role in his trial preparation, as he will define human wisdom, ironically associating it with his own righteous character.

A monologue designed to be heard by God, Job's hymn is an implicit critique of the spurious wisdom the friends put forth as the ways of the deity. At the same time, in defining human wisdom, Job will once again affirm his integrity as he prepares to meet God. Job begins surprisingly by celebrating the marvelous technological achievements of humanity, particularly in the field of mining. The subject of mining is especially appropriate, as the search for wisdom is analogous to the human quest for precious metals (gold, silver, iron and copper) and gemstones beneath the surface of the earth. While Bildad denounced humans as mere "worms," Job celebrates their intelligence, inventiveness and courage. He paints an artful picture of miners prospecting for the earth's rich resources: "There is a mine for silver and a place for gold" to be refined. Iron is extracted from the earth, and copper is smelted out of ore. Guided by lights, miners put "an end to darkness," penetrating deep into the earth, searching for precious stones in desolate places, "away from where people live." While farmers till the land above, below the surface, intrepid miners "swing back and forth," suspended by ropes, as they cut shafts deep into the earth. The earth, from whose surface comes food, is "turned up as it were by fire," as miners "cut out channels among the rocks," extracting precious metals. No animal is privy to the miner's underground world. The falcon, renowned for its acute vision, swoops down from the sky to snatch its prey. Yet it is unaware of the hidden path to treasures that lie deep within the earth. The "fierce lion" rules its habitat, but it prowls far above the miner's realm. The miners work tirelessly, cutting into rock, burrowing at the base of mountains, and scanning rivers in search of treasures: "The thing that is hidden," the miner "brings out to light."

Having celebrated humanity's technological achievements, Job inquires rhetorically: "Where shall wisdom be found? Where is the place of understanding?" Wisdom and understanding are virtually synonymous in wisdom literature.[4] Despite their technological prowess, extracting riches from beneath the earth, humans cannot find true wisdom. If humans had true wisdom, they would be able to comprehend God's plan for the universe as well as its organizing principles. Such wisdom cannot be discovered among humans in "the land of the living." Nor can wisdom be found within the vast subterranean watery abyss known as the deep from which emerge the seas and the oceans.[5] "The deep," says, 'It is not in me'; the sea says, 'It is not with me.'" Wisdom cannot be found, nor can any human comprehend its supreme worth. Wisdom is not a commodity that can be purchased: "It cannot be gotten for gold, neither shall silver be weighed for its price. It cannot be valued with the gold of Ophir [famous for its wealth], with the precious onyx, or the sapphire. Gold and glass cannot equal it, neither shall it be exchanged for jewels of fine gold. The topaz of Ethiopia shall not equal it, neither shall it be valued with pure gold." Similar to the modern exploration of outer space, humans have exhibited prodigious technological and scientific skill, but the wisdom that would disclose the meaning of innocent suffering escapes them.

Job repeats the two-question refrain: "Where then does wisdom come from? Where is the place of understanding?" Wisdom cannot be found either on the surface or beneath the earth or in the sky: "It is hidden from the eyes of all living, and kept close from the birds of the sky." Nor can wisdom be found in the underworld, which has merely heard about it second hand: "Destruction and Death say, 'We have heard a rumor of it with our ears.'" If true wisdom cannot be found on earth, in the sky, or in the underground of Sheol, where can it be located? God alone knows the place of wisdom: "God understands its way, and he knows its place." In the Book of Proverbs, wisdom is personified as a woman, generated by God before he created the world.[6] Job does not explicitly say that God produced wisdom; nevertheless, he believes that wisdom was present at the world's creation. According to Job, only the omniscient God can locate wisdom, "for he looks to the ends of the earth, and sees under the whole sky." Having found wisdom, God used it to create the universe: "He establishes the force of the wind. He measures out the waters by measure. When he made a decree for the rain, and a way for the lightning of the thunder; then he saw it, and declared it. He established it, and searched it out." With his omniscience and omnipotence, God demonstrated the full range of his creative activity. He searched, looked, saw, measured, decreed, and declared. According to the Book of Proverbs, "By wisdom the Lord laid the earth's foundations, by understanding he set the heavens in place." [7] God's transcendent wisdom is reflected by the created order of the universe. Such wisdom is beyond Job, the friends, and all human beings.

After his paean to God's wisdom, Job concludes by raising the possibility of human wisdom. Until the poem's conclusion, "wisdom" is preceded by the definite article, hence *the* wisdom, which refers to the wisdom of God.[8] To speak of God's wisdom, as did Job, is to see as through a glass darkly. God's wisdom is inaccessible to humans. Even Zophar had affirmed that wisdom has "two sides," one manifest, the other hidden.[9] Humans can access a limited, practical wisdom, related to moral conduct. This is wisdom without the definite article. Having distinguished between divine and human wisdom, Job brings his poem to a climax. Human scientific and technological progress does not bring the true wisdom which lies in moral conduct. The modern era, having witnessed the horrors of two world wars and the destructive potential of nuclear war, cannot automatically equate science with wisdom. In conformity with the wisdom tradition, Job holds that humans are wise when they obey God's will, acting morally in all circumstances. According to Job, God revealed this limited wisdom to humans: "To man he said, 'Behold, fear of the Lord is wisdom. To depart from evil is understanding.'" Human wisdom is ethical. Those who fear God are religiously devout; those who shun evil abide by the moral law. The Hebrew wisdom literature also reflects this teaching. The Wisdom Teacher counsels his son in Ecclesiastes: "Fear God and keep his commandments; for this is the duty of all mankind."[10]

Ironically, Job's definition of human wisdom, fearing God and shunning evil, reflects God's description of Job's character in the Prologue: "He is blameless and upright; a man who fears God and shuns evil."[11] In his concluding speeches, Job will present the details of his righteous character, fundamental to his legal defense. Neither Job nor the friends possess God's absolute wisdom; but Job possesses human wisdom. He is wiser than the friends in perceiving the fallacy in the rigid doctrine of retribution. Like the miner, Job is searching for treasure. But the treasure he seeks is more precious than gold. He seeks the higher wisdom that will shed light on the dark mystery of innocent human suffering. Only God can provide the answer. Job's doxology reflects the biblical teaching that God alone in his infinite wisdom knows how the universe is constructed and interrelated. But in praising God's wisdom, Job significantly says nothing about divine justice. Does justice exist in the world God created?

# JOB'S SUMMATION

## Chapter 29   Job: I Recall My Happy Past

HAVING CELEBRATED GOD'S INFINITE WISDOM and defined human practical wisdom, Job waits for a reply. But his friends remaining silent, Job continues his monologue. In a beautiful and moving lament, he recalls his idyllic past, when he lived in fellowship with God. Job presents a review of his life as if it were a legal brief in his case against God. Given the opportunity to appear before the heavenly tribunal, Job's monologue would be his closing argument. He intends to prove that God has unjustly ruined his life, reducing him to poverty and destroying his esteemed reputation. His former happiness and prosperity are evidence of his righteous life, fearing God and shunning evil.

Job's mood shifts from the optimism of his doxology to profound depression as he faces a painful death. He pours out a lament, perhaps in the hope that God is listening. Job begins by recalling his prosperous past, "when the Lord gave." Then the sudden tragic reversal came, destroying Job's entire world. He has already endured months of agony. With great emotion, he cries: "Oh that I were as in the months of old, as in the days when God watched over me: When his lamp shone on my head, and by his light I walked through darkness." King David enjoyed the same divine favor: "You, Lord, are my lamp; the Lord turns my darkness into light."[1] If Job experienced dark times in the past, God always supported him. But where is God now? Job depicts the idyllic past when he was blessed with domestic happiness and material prosperity: "I was in the ripeness of my days, when the friendship of God was in my tent, when the Almighty was yet with me, and my children were around me." But Job's innocent suffering shattered his view of life. The God who watched over him, providing a protective hedge in the Prologue, has been supplanted by a malicious watcher God who murders Job's children and spies on him, hoping to catch him in sin.[2]

Supplementing the sparse details of Job's life that we learn from the Prologue, Job describes the honored position he held in society because of his righteousness. His household was presumably located near the city. Throughout the ancient Near East, including Israel, legal and commercial business was conducted at the city gate and the public square.[3] Job's wisdom and righteousness earned him considerable public esteem. He embodied to the fullest virtues hailed by the ancient wisdom tradition. Whenever he entered the city and took his honored seat as a judge or magistrate in the public square, everyone, young and old, rich and poor, weak and powerful, greeted him with profound respect. Job probably sat in this place when the successive messengers arrived with the horrific news of his calamities, culminating in the deaths of his children. He now recalls: "When I went out to the city gate, when I prepared my seat in the street, the young men saw me and hid themselves. The aged rose up and stood. The princes refrained from talking, and laid their hand on their mouth. The voice of the nobles was hushed, and their tongue stuck to the roof of their mouth. For when the ear heard me, then it blessed me; and when the eye saw me, it commended me." The deference Job earned reflected the values of his culture. He apparently held a prominent position as a judge in the city's court. In adjudicating disputes, his impartial decisions and prudent counsel manifested righteousness. Serving as a judge made Job intimately familiar with ancient legal procedure, especially the rights of the accused, which became the background for his quest for a trial before God. Job could readily identify with those falsely accused, encouraging them to resist oppression from evil doers who abuse their power. Having defended the rights of the poor and disadvantaged, Job was prepared to defend himself when God violated his rights.

As a judge, Job became champion of the underprivileged and promoter of the public welfare. Implicitly refuting Eliphaz's unsubstantiated accusation that he committed sins against humanity,[4] Job avers that he was honored because "I delivered the poor who cried, and the fatherless also, who had no one to help him." Throughout the ancient Near East, wealthy and powerful individuals who assisted the downtrodden received great esteem. Helping the underprivileged reflected Job's practical wisdom, revering God and shunning evil: "The blessing of him who was ready to perish," either from neglect or oppression, "came to me." Job assisted the widow, making her "heart sing for joy" because of his compassionate aid. Job used his influential position in society to embody justice: "I put on righteousness, and it clothed me. My justice was a robe and a diadem." There seemed no end to Job's acts of charity: "I was eyes to the blind and feet to the lame," guiding and protecting them. "I was a father to the needy," providing for them. Job's beneficence was not limited to fellow citizens, but extended also to strangers: "The cause of him who I did not know, I searched out." As a judge, Job crushed the wicked with the arm of the law, rescuing innocent victims: "I broke the jaws of the unrighteous, and plucked the prey out of his teeth." A paragon of righteousness, Job's reputation was well-deserved. The Book of Proverbs declares: "Whoever pursues righteousness and love finds life, prosperity and honor."[5] As an agent of impartial justice, always responsive to the needs of his community, Job wished to receive the same justice from God.

Reflecting on his past, Job's poignant words bring to mind the words of the poet Dante that there is no greater sorrow than to recall a time of joy when in misery. Believing in divine retribution, Job expected God to recompense him with a long, fruitful life and a peaceful death. He would thrive like a tree, a symbol of fertility, with deep roots and extensive branches, kept fresh throughout the night by dew as the warm air cools: "I said, 'I shall die in my own house. I shall number my days as the sand. My root is spread out to the waters. The dew lies all night on my branch. My glory is fresh in me. My bow is renewed in my hand.'" Job believed that his honor as well as his "bow" of strength and vitality would never fail him while he fostered justice. Instead, Job now faces a premature painful death, not at home surrounded by his family, but prostrate on the dirty ash-heap, wasting away, stripped of his glory as a righteous man.

Before concluding his sad remembrance of things past, Job returns to his description of the position of great honor he once held in society. His sage advice benefited all: "They waited for me as for the rain. Their mouths drank as with the spring rain." Despite his position of authority, Job was a friend to all, encouraging, strengthening and comforting others. His was the face of righteousness, reflecting the benevolence of God: "I smiled on them when they had no confidence. They did not reject the light on my face." An enlightened and charismatic leader and judge, guiding the community on a just course, his counsel was heeded like the law. His statesmanship earned him the status of royalty within his community: "I chose out their way, and sat as chief. I lived as a king in the army, as one who comforts the mourners." Job ends with an ironic barb directed at his friends who failed to console him in his grief. He lived "as one who comforts the mourners." Significantly, in lamenting his lost past, Job ignores his material prosperity—his great wealth, his huge flocks and numerous servants. Instead, he concentrates on his beloved family life and his benevolent service to his community as a voice for the disadvantaged and a beacon of justice. But his world has been overturned. Now in the position of a mourner, he is totally isolated. Betrayed by the friends and community that once revered him, and apparently forsaken by God, Job endures his agony alone.

There is an apparent contradiction between Job's impeccable virtue and his detailing the honors he received from the community. Does this reflect a lack of humility unbefitting a servant of God? Job stresses the honor bestowed upon him by society because of his practical wisdom. To focus upon his honor is not a sign of overweening pride, but a reflection of his self-worth. According to the doctrine of divine retribution, the righteous should enjoy God's favor. Job's belief in his self-worth enabled him to challenge God.

His unwavering belief in his innocence, supported by the testimony of his conscience, gives him the strength to persist in defending his integrity against the false accusations of his friends. Created *imago dei*, in God's image, Job could not deny his self-worth. He could not lie to himself and to God by confessing sins he did not commit. Admitting falsely to sin would be to admit that he deserved his suffering. It would also make him complicit in the deaths of his ten children, for their loss was also viewed as a result of his sin.

But Job does not exaggerate his righteousness. His friends accuse him of sins against humanity. His community regards him as a hypocritical sinner. With his integrity at stake, Job appropriately reviews the course of his entire life. He hopes to submit his virtuous life as evidence in his trial against God. Moreover, Job credits God, who until now had blessed and watched over him, with the benefits and honors he had received from society.[6] Job catalogues his righteous deeds, not from inordinate pride, but from the satisfaction that he lived as God wished.

## Chapter 30   Job: I Lament My Present

HAVING DESCRIBED THE LIFE HE ENJOYED, when God gave him prosperity, Job now highlights his catastrophic reversal of fortune, when God took everything away. This would constitute essential evidence in Job's closing argument against God. Once revered as the "greatest" person of the East,"[7] Job is reduced to a miserable social pariah, regarded as the enemy of God. The prevailing retribution creed, we have noted, led people to reason from the effect to the cause. When Job was prosperous, people assumed he was righteous. Now that he suffers, afflicted with gruesome sores and impoverished, they assume that he is a sinner. Job's depiction of his tragic fall elicits empathy. His words read like a funeral dirge given for a man who, after enjoying years of happiness and prosperity, is dying in ignominy. Job's life before and after his affliction reflects his experience of the two faces of God.

Before his catastrophe, Job experienced the God of justice and benevolence who rewards the righteous, and whom Job hopes will ultimately vindicate him; but now suffering innocently, he is experiencing what he believes to be a demonic predator afflicting him unjustly.

Applying once again Elisabeth Kübler-Ross' flexible model of the emotional stages of a person with a terminal illness, Job's mood shifts from bitter anger to depression, and his monologue becomes a lament of his present condition. We have noted that Job's culture prized honor and shunned public disgrace. Although reviled as a sinner by people of all ages in his community, Job is especially mortified by the scorn he now receives from the younger generation, adding to his emotional agony. While in former times, the youth treated him with the utmost respect, moving aside out of deference whenever he entered the public square, they now insult him: "Those who are younger than I have me in derision, whose fathers I would have disdained to put with my sheep dogs." His taunters are shameful vagabonds, the dregs of society. "Gaunt from lack and famine," they roam the desolate wastelands. Homeless scavengers, they live on desert leaves and roots, "driven out from among men," shouted at like thieves. Ostracized from society, they are forced to hide and "dwell in frightful valleys, and in holes of the earth and of the rocks." Their dissolute lives reduce them to beasts, braying like donkeys, huddled among the bushes. These men who ridicule Job, "are children of fools, children of base men," who are "flogged out of the land." In the past, Job had assisted such miserable people out of compassion, but now relegated unjustly to the community's ash-heap in disgrace, he seethes with righteous indignation. He feels lacerated by the insults flung upon him by vulgar youth: "Now I have become their song. I am a byword to them." Blind to Job's righteousness, they mock him throughout the community as a wicked sinner: "They abhor me; they stand aloof from me, and do not hesitate to spit in my face." And why is Job so vulnerable to their abuse? Because God has turned from Job, he is vulnerable to the vulgar youth who "have thrown off restraint." Job's abusers believe that God sanctions their actions.

Indeed, Job imagines that God enlisted these youths into his army, ready to attack. Whereas previously Job depicted himself as a king sitting among his troops,[8] he now imagines himself a city besieged by an overwhelming army of detractors. In a previous speech, he envisioned God using troops to besiege him.[9] With a vivid extended metaphor, Job returns to this theme with a nightmarish scenario. Wicked rabble youths launch a vicious attack on his right flank: "They thrust aside my feet. They cast up against me their ways of destruction." Job is trapped. "They mar my path," cutting off all means of escape. With their vastly superior forces, "they set forward" Job's destruction, while he lay "without anyone's help." The situation is hopeless. The nightmare reaches a terrifying climax. Concentrating their forces, the enemy invaders breach Job's wall, gaining access to the city: "As through a wide breach they come. In the middle of the ruin they roll themselves in." Once revered for his righteousness, Job is now condemned as a hypocrite. Deprived of his honor and security, he is despondent: "Terrors have turned on me. They chase my honor as the wind. My welfare has passed away as a cloud."

Job's horrifying nightmare represents his greatest fear. The torment inflicted upon him by God has destroyed his righteous reputation and brought him to the brink of death. Having enjoyed God's favor in the past, Job laments, "now my soul is poured out within me. Days of affliction have taken hold on me." Job's physical pain is relentless: "In the night my bones are pierced in me, and the pains that gnaw take no rest." With lurid imagery, Job depicts God as a violent thug, grabbing him by the neck, like a choking collar, and flinging him to the ground, as unimportant as the ashes on which he sits: "He has cast me into the mire," Job laments. "I have become like dust and ashes." God has brutally degraded Job into an insignificant creature, deprived of dignity, awaiting death.

In the last segment of his speech, Job's mood alters from rage and fear to depression as he reflects on his fate. Not having addressed God directly for some time, Job laments that God has become his malicious enemy. Job had persisted in appealing to God to relieve his undeserved suffering. He had pleaded with God to grant him a legal hearing so that he would know the charges against him. Yet God remains hidden; a sign of divine anger. Job is deeply hurt by his belief that God has abandoned him. Job's sentiment is echoed by C. S. Lewis, devastated by the death of his wife. When one is happy, says Lewis, and one has no sense of needing God, one will be welcomed by him with open arms. "But go to Him when your need is desperate, when all other help is vain, and what do you find? A door slammed in your face.... After that, silence....The longer you wait, the more emphatic the silence will become." For Lewis, as for Job, the real danger is not ceasing to believe in God, but "of coming to believe such dreadful things about Him. The conclusion I dread is not 'So there's no God after all,' but 'So this is what God's really like. Deceive yourself no longer.'"[10]

So what does Job conclude about God? Using a theme from the psalms of lamentation, he utters another desperate plea, hoping to provoke God to respond. What Job says to God is what he imagines he would say if he were granted a fair trial. He is submitting his indictment, stating the crimes God has committed against him. If Job survives to see a trial, God will be the defendant, charged with tyrannical injustice. Might does not make right. Though God sees Job's anguish, he hides his face when Job rises in desperate prayer: "I cry to you, and you do not answer me. I stand up, and you gaze at me." God has turned against his faithful servant, subjecting him to tyrannical abuse: "You have turned to be cruel to me. With the might of your hand you persecute me." God treats Job like rubbish, tossed helplessly in the wind: "You lift me up to the wind, and drive me with it. You dissolve me in the storm." Why does God treat Job so cruelly? Job is convinced that God intends to kill him. "I know," he cries despondently, "that you will bring me to death, to the house appointed for all living." What Job fears is that he will die without having the opportunity to defend his integrity in a trial with God.

Job cannot comprehend why God ignores his cries. How could God be so cruel and unjust, continuing to abuse him? Unlike God, Job has shown compassion for the weak and unfortunate, responding to their desperate needs. Why does God not show him the same compassion? "Did I not weep for him who was in trouble? Was not my soul grieved for the needy?" Indeed, Job practiced the virtues of justice and benevolence expected of God. Job again seeks to bargain with God, calling upon him for vindication. Job led a righteous life, but God's justice has failed: "When I looked for good, then evil came. When I waited for light, there came darkness." During his prosperity, God had been Job's lamp and light, helping him walk through darkness. Now God has plunged Job into utter darkness. Faced with the prospect of imminent death, Job's mental turmoil is excruciating: "My heart is troubled, and does not rest. Days of affliction have come on me." Stripped of his dignity, Job has put on the black sackcloth of mourning: "I stand up in the assembly and cry for help." Once revered in the city's assembly, his cries for justice go unanswered. Before retiring to the ash-heap, Job might have defended his innocence before the assembly at the city gate, but to no avail. A social pariah, abandoned by his friends and condemned as a sinner by his community, Job is a "brother to jackals" and a companion to ostriches, creatures who haunt desolate areas and utter plaintive cries. Meanwhile, Job's physical pain intensifies each day: "My skin grows black and peels from me." Job's only prospect is death. The joyful music of his days of prosperity has become the grieving music of a dying man: "My harp has turned to mourning, and my pipe into the voice of those who weep."

# Chapter 31   Job: I Take an Oath of Innocence

AFTER SUBMITTING IN EVIDENCE the damage that God has unjustly inflicted upon him, Job's mood rises to courageous determination. He visualizes presenting to the divine tribunal a sworn affidavit containing the record of his righteous life. We recall his impassioned declaration: "Until I die I will not put away my integrity."[11] Job will make a final effort to compel God to hear him. This step in his trial preparation is the most heroic. Job devises a brilliant legal stratagem. Assuming the role of defendant, he will take a solemn oath of innocence, consisting of a series of conditional curses upon himself, swearing that he is blameless and invoking God to strike him dead if he does not tell the truth. In the ancient world, curses were taken seriously. They were believed to have the power to bring about the intended effect. Exculpatory oaths were a common legal procedure in the ancient Near East.[12] The Babylonian Code of Hammurabi and the Egyptian Book of the Dead contain such oaths. The Hebrew legal code also included the oath of innocence.[13] Ordinarily, a person accused of a crime was brought before the local elders. After hearing the charges and examining the evidence, a verdict was reached.  But in the absence of conclusive evidence or witnesses, accused persons could swear to their innocence, making God the judge. These oaths became public legal documents, signed by the accused. If the accused swore falsely, God was expected to punish them sternly for their perjury.

Job's oath of innocence is powerful testimony to support his case against both his friends and God. Job submits his upright character in evidence to show that he does not deserve the suffering inflicted upon him. He will make a compelling, if belated, reply to Eliphaz's accusation that he is a grave sinner. The oath reflects Job's confidence that if God grants him a fair trial, he will be acquitted. Only a person convinced of his innocence would call upon himself the wrath of God. Job's challenge is bold. God can no longer remain silent. In effect, Job's self-imprecations say to God, "Strike me dead if I lie about my righteous life; acquit me if I tell the truth."

In preparing his defense, Job was at a disadvantage. As the defendant, he has a right to know the charges against him, but God has refused to reveal them in a formal indictment. Complicating the issue, Job also regards himself as the plaintiff, suing God for unjust treatment. In the absence of any word from God, Job's only alternative as a defendant is to supply a negative confession, a catalogue of possible sins he could have committed to merit his suffering and disavow each of them. The oath of innocence formula he employs may be stated succinctly: "If I have committed the crime, may this happen to me." Using the customary conditional oath formula, Job begins each of sixteen avowals with an "if," referring to the possible sin. While oath takers usually left unspecified the dreaded punishment that should ensue if they fail to tell the truth, Job audaciously utters the full oath, including the conditional curse or consequence five times. The curse would bring irreparable damage to his integrity, his material goods, his marriage, his physical body, and the fertility of his land. Job's sense of justice calls for God to inflict punishment, even death, if he is guilty.

Job is so confident in his integrity that he fears no dire consequences. Imagining that he stands before the heavenly tribunal, he provides a list of possible sins, private and public, in thought as well as deed. He presents his *apologia pro vita sua*, an eloquent defense of his entire life, the basis for which he is hailed in the Prologue as a "blameless and upright" person. Having examined his conscience, his belief in his innocence remains unwavering. While the friends grew increasingly vituperative in their speeches, eventually abandoning their self-appointed role as God's defenders, at this final stage Job has attained the quiet dignity of one confident in his cause. If God grants him a legal hearing, Job believes that he will be exonerated.

The litany of sins Job avoided reflects an advanced moral code, including not only actions, but also the thoughts and motivations that precede them. Commentators have praised Job's oath of innocence, one calling it the "code of a man of honor," another "a highpoint of Old Testament ethics....refining and deepening" the ethics of Wisdom literature.[14] The moral values ascribed to Job by the poet surpass any other in the Hebrew Bible or ancient Near Eastern literature, prefiguring the morality of Jesus' Sermon on the Mount. While the Ten Commandments are stated negatively, what one should not do, Job's ethics imply positive actions. His oaths underscore that all actions, whether righteous or wicked, are rooted in the mind.[15] In the Prologue, Job offered sacrifices for his sons in case they had "sinned and cursed God in their hearts." Job's integrity encompasses thoughts as well as actions.

The sins Job disavows relate to the temptations typical of a rich and powerful patriarch. He commences with the virtue of chastity, disavowing the sin of lust: "I made a covenant with my eyes," not to "look lustfully at a young woman." Job made a solemn pledge, a binding mental agreement, presumably as a young man, not to look upon young women as mere objects of sensual pleasure. The eyes are the instrument by which temptation enters the mind, after which comes the thought, then the deed. Lust is condemned in the Hebrew Bible. Armed with the power and wealth of a patriarch, with many female servants, Job was in a position to exploit sexually the women of his household. Civil order depends upon the control of sexual gratification and violent selfish behavior. Unless basic instincts are regulated, especially in patriarchs like Job, society would degenerate into anarchy. Lust, Job affirms, deserves God's severe punishment in accord with the principle of retribution. Wavering again on the fate of the wicked, Job now reaffirms that they cannot escape divine judgment. He poses two rhetorical questions: "What is the portion from God above, and the heritage from the Almighty on high? Is it not calamity to the unrighteous?" Job contends that the omniscient God sees his every thought and action and knows that he is not wicked: "Does he not see my ways, and number all my steps?" Job is still hopeful that God will act justly and apply the principle of retribution correctly to him.

Job then disavows the sin of falsehood or deceit, calling down a curse upon himself if he lied. He challenges God to weigh him on the scales of divine justice to determine whether he is righteous or wicked: "If I have walked with falsehood, and my foot has hurried to deceit, let me be weighed in an even balance, that God may know my integrity." Job believes that if God judges him fairly, he will be acquitted. Adhering to justice, Job always spoke the truth and was scrupulously honest in his business dealings. The stability of society depends upon truth-telling and honest commercial transactions. With a solemn self-curse, Job declares: "If my step has turned out of the way, if my heart walked after my eyes, if any defilement has stuck to my hands, then let me sow, and another eat. Let the produce of my field be rooted out." If Job were guilty, God would be just in punishing him by having his livelihood destroyed. But Job is innocent, and yet he has suffered the complete loss of his material prosperity as if he were a wicked sinner.

Next Job disavows the sin of adultery, a grave sin in the ancient Near East. Adultery was a capital crime in Israel, punishable by death.[16] Job presents the sin, followed by the self-curse that would activate the principle of talion, "an eye for an eye, and a tooth for a tooth."[17] Job vows: "If my heart has been enticed by a woman, and I have laid wait at my neighbor's door, then may my wife grind grain for another, and let others sleep with her." As with the other sins, adultery begins in the heart. Job's focus on the interior source of sexual ethics anticipates the words of Jesus, who declared: "You have heard that it was said, 'You shall not commit adultery.' But I tell you that anyone who looks at a woman lustfully has already committed adultery with her in his heart."[18] Committing adultery was not only a sin, but also a threat to the family, the basis of society. Accordingly, Job avers that if he has been unfaithful in marriage, his wife should become another man's property, the word "grind" either a reference to having his wife become a lowly slave, grinding another man's grain, or a euphemism for sexual subjugation to other men. If he committed this sin, Job believes that such harsh divine punishment would be justified. Because patriarchal society regarded a wife as a man's property, adultery was considered a violation of the right of property. Hence, if Job committed adultery, his wife would unfairly bear the brunt of the punishment. But Job swore fidelity to his wife, declaring that if he committed adultery, it would be "a heinous crime" to be "punished by the judges. It is a fire that consumes to destruction, and would root out all my increase." Fire symbolizes God's wrath. According to Deuteronomy, God rebuked the sinful Israelites, proclaiming: "A fire is kindled in my anger that burns to the lowest Sheol, devours the earth with its increase, and sets the foundations of the mountains on fire."[19]

Job now disavows sins of social injustice. As a wealthy patriarch, Job could have abused members of his large household, relying on favorable rulings from the court. Yet he denies mistreating people or trampling upon their rights. Job dealt justly with his household servants, even if they had a grievance against him. He did not misuse his legal power to oppress those in his power. God enjoined the Israelites from Mount Sinai: "You shall not deny justice to your poor people in their lawsuits."[20] Job affirms his adherence to God's law: "If I have despised the cause of my male servant or of my female servant, when they contended with me, what shall I do when God rises up?" Job vows that if he acted unjustly toward his servants, he deserves divine punishment. Regardless of social class, Job and his servant are equal in the eyes of God: "Did not he who made me in the womb make him?" Regarding his servants as human beings, Job believes that they are entitled to dignity and rights. His solemn oath that he never abused a servant is an indirect appeal to God to look mercifully upon Job, God's loyal servant. The root of Job's social ethic, which exceeds the Mosaic code, is his understanding of a common humanity.[21] According to the Book of Proverbs, "The rich and the poor have this in common. Yahweh is the maker of them all."[22] While Job did not oppose human servitude, prevalent in his day, his integrity prohibited him from regarding his servants as exploitable chattel property.

Job was not only just, but also compassionate. Implicitly refuting the charges of Eliphaz that he sinned against his fellow humans,[23] Job disavows committing sins against the poor, widows, orphans and strangers. He devoted his life to acts of charity, caring for the poor, feeding the orphan, clothing the naked, and soothing the grief of widows. He calls upon God to punish him if he has failed to embody compassion and righteousness: "If I withheld the poor from their desire, or caused the eyes of the widow" to weep from neglect, or if I have "eaten my morsel alone," not sharing it with the orphan who regarded me as a father," may God punish me. "If I have seen any perish from want of clothing, or that the needy had no covering" and their hearts did not bless me for warming them "with my sheep's fleece; if I have lifted my hand against the fatherless, because I saw my help in the gate, then let my shoulder fall from the shoulder blade and my arm be broken from the bone." Job never used his influence at the city gate to win a favorable verdict against the fatherless. If he failed to perform these right actions, Job calls upon God to rip his arm from his body. By summoning God's wrath upon himself if he neglected his duty to fellow humans, Job shows the strength of his commitment to social justice.

At this point, Job reveals a surprising reason why he devoted his life to avoiding serious sins: "For calamity from God is a terror to me." Job would dread to stand guilty before God: "Because of his majesty, I can do nothing" to offend him. Job's reason would have interested the Satan. We presume that the Satan is privy to the dialogue between Job and the friends, and is waiting to hear Job's reaction to God. We recall the fundamental question raised by the Prologue: Is Job's piety pure or self-interested? The Satan's challenge to God is that Job has an ulterior motive for piety. Deprived of his livelihood, family and health, the Satan alleges, Job will curse God directly to his face, revealing that his piety is selfish, conditional upon God's favor. Yet the traditional doctrine of retribution actually fostered a selfish piety. If God unfailingly rewards virtue with prosperity and punishes wickedness with calamity, humans are likely to be virtuous in order to gain God's blessings. While Job is pious not solely for his advantage, he expects God to recompense him. To this extent, Job's faith is conditional. Ironically, though righteous, Job now suffers "calamity from God." Instead of acting solely out of love of virtue for its own sake, Job appears to have acted from expectation of reward and fear of punishment. Like the piety of most of the devout, Job's piety stems from some degree of self-interest. In lamenting his downfall, Job declared that because of his righteous life, he looked for good and light, but evil and darkness came.[24] The *Babylonian Talmud* records that Rabbi Johanan argued that Job's piety was based on fear rather than love of God.[25] God himself is to blame for causing such dread in people.

From sins of social injustice, Job moves to the interior sins of an excessive love of riches and idolatry. He could have used his wealth selfishly, worshipping Mammon and power. But Job swears that he never did. If he made gold his security instead of God, if he believed that his great wealth came from his own hand rather than God, Job would deserve God's punishment. Job also disavows the common pagan practice of idolatry, worshiping luminous celestial bodies as gods: "If I have seen the sun when it shined, or the moon moving in splendor, and my heart was secretly enticed, and my hand threw a kiss from my mouth" to express veneration, "this also would be an iniquity to be punished by the judges; for I should have denied the God who is above." Canaanites worshipped the pagan fertility god, Baal, by kissing his image.[26] According to Deuteronomy, idolatry, including worship of the sun, the moon, or the stars, was punishable by death.[27] But Job professes to be loyal to the supreme God, Creator of the universe. As we have noted, although Job was a Gentile, the Hebrew Bible, as well as rabbinical literature, depict him as a servant of the Hebrew God.[28]

Proceeding with his disavowals, Job passes to the sins of exulting over the suffering of an enemy, failing to feed the hungry members of his large household, and turning away strangers in need. "If I have rejoiced at the destruction of him who hated me, or lifted up myself when evil found him," or wished him dead with a curse, then, Job implies, he would deserve God's punishment. While Job's past life demonstrated magnanimity towards his enemies, we recall that, in the depth of his despair, rejected by his friends, Job did wish upon them the punishment due the wicked.[29] But the Epilogue will demonstrate that Job harbors no ill-will towards his friends. Indeed, he will rescue them from the wrath of God.[30] Job's repudiation of vindictiveness towards enemies marks a progression from the ethics of the ancient Near East. Job had lamented that God hides his face, treating him as an enemy.[31] In contrast, Job vows that he was never unkind to his enemies.

Job then calls a curse upon himself if members of his household have ever found him refusing food and shelter to a stranger or wayfarer: "Who can find one who has not been filled" with Job's food? "The foreigner has not camped in the street, but I have opened my doors to the traveler." Next, Job disavows the sin of hypocrisy. The product of an honor and shame culture, a person in Job's exalted position might have been tempted to disguise transgressions. Indeed, his friends accused him of secret sins. Contrasting himself to Adam of Genesis, Job vows that he never concealed sins in his heart out of fear of being condemned by his community: "If, like Adam, I have covered my transgressions, by hiding my iniquity in my heart, because I feared the great multitude, and the contempt of families terrified me, so that I kept silence," then, Job implies, he would deserve God's punishment. Job desperately wants vindication, but he will not sacrifice his integrity. He refuses to betray his moral values, values endorsed by the just God that he had believed in his entire life. Confessing sins he did not commit, merely to gain God's favor, as his friends urged, would make Job a greater hypocrite than persons who hide iniquity under the appearance of righteousness.

Job had proclaimed earlier that no godless person need fear God. In his defense, he has submitted his detailed oath of innocence, repudiating a range of sins, both personal and social, including lust, deceit, adultery, injustice to servants, ignoring the needs of the poor, violence against the vulnerable, materialism, idolatry, rejoicing over the fall of his enemies, refusing hospitality to strangers, and moral hypocrisy. Job's oath encompasses both sins of commission and sins of omission. His disavowals constitute a rebuke of God, whom he believes is unjustly treating him as a sinner. Having sought in vain to bargain with God, Job believes that his righteous life should be vindicated. As the Prologue testifies, Job is the epitome of righteousness. He has been just to his servants, but God has been unjust to him, his most righteous servant; Job has been faithful in his marriage, but God has been unfaithful to him; and Job has been compassionate toward the poor, treating them with dignity, but God has abused him.

Overflowing with emotion, Job interrupts his self-imprecations and cries out his final appeal to God: "Oh, that I had one to hear me!" Buoyed by confidence in his integrity, he throws down the gauntlet before God, demanding a speedy trial. Certain of victory, Job is ready to affix metaphorically his signature to his sworn affidavit, defending his innocence. According to ancient legal procedure an oath of innocence must be signed. Job exclaims defiantly: "Behold, here is my signature, let the Almighty answer me." The Hebrew letter appearing in the text is "taw," meaning "mark" or signature. In the ancient period, "taw," the final letter in the Hebrew alphabet, was written in the form of the English X, and appeared at the end of various legal documents. It is fitting that Job concludes his final speech with the last letter in the Hebrew alphabet. His signature proclaims his integrity. Wrestling with God, Job is indomitable. The frail Job, treated by God as if he were an insignificant "driven leaf," or "dry stubble,"[32] is prepared to storm heaven for justice.

Breaking from the traditional lament, which usually concludes with a humble plea for divine help, Job takes the offensive. He will provoke God to indict him. Job gives God an ultimatum: "Let the accuser write my indictment." To justify afflicting Job, God must produce evidence that he committed grave sins. Job demands that God, his accuser, "hear" and "answer" him with a list of the charges against him as defendant. Job is so confident in victory that he would display God's indictment of him proudly like a badge of honor or a royal crown for all to see. For the indictment will be free of any legitimate charges: "Surely I would carry it on my shoulder; and I would bind it to me as a crown." Earlier, Job lamented that God had "stripped me of my glory, and taken the crown from my head."[33] Later, he declared that once God "has tried me, I shall come out like gold."[34] Now concluding his defense, Job envisions a great triumph, his crown of honor restored. Overcoming his fear, he has issued God a verbal summons to reveal himself. Facing God in the heavenly court, Job will "declare to him the number of my steps," his life of impeccable rectitude. With Promethean dignity, Job will present the record of his life to God, not meekly like a wretched sinner, but boldly like a "prince." Job will speak truth to divine power.

Having uttered these provocative words, Job's emotions subside enough to permit him to complete his negative confession. While these additional verses might appear anti-climactic, coming directly after Job's passionate challenge to God, they reflect the mood swings of a man confronting death. Job concludes his declaration of innocence by disavowing one final sin: violating the land. As Gustavo Gutierrez aptly puts it: "Not only did Job deal justly with the poor; he also practiced a kind of ecological justice toward the earth, mother of life and source of food for the poor."[35] Job personifies the land as crying out for vengeance against those who sin against her: "If my land cries out against me and its furrows weep together; if I have eaten its fruits without money, or have caused its owners to lose their lives, let briers grow instead of wheat and stinkweed instead of barley." The land would cry out if Job cultivated it out of greed for wealth, or seized it from its rightful owner, or consumed its produce without compensating the farmers in his employ. If guilty, Job would deserve God's punishment, making his land unfertile, producing weeds and thorns instead of a bountiful harvest. But Job has been a faithful steward of the land gifted him by God. Curiously, Job does not include blasphemy among the sins he disavows. He has blasphemed God repeatedly throughout the dialogue. Omitting blasphemy might indicate that the poet did not consider Job's language sinful but justified. Job speaks the truth about God.

At this point, the narrator declares: "The words of Job are ended." He has concluded his oath of innocence, the closing argument he would make before God's court. The tension built up throughout the dialogue is now released, as Job awaits his fate. We have referred to Job's suffering as analogous to a person facing death. After an initial denial of what actually happened to him, Job's emotions oscillated between denial, anger, hope and depression. He tried to bargain with God to postpone death until his integrity is vindicated. Job now reaches the final stage of dying— acceptance. According to Kübler-Ross, the person who reaches the stage of acceptance "will contemplate his coming end with a certain degree of quiet expectation."[36] Having presented the record of his moral life in evidence, Job has the serenity of a clear conscience, confident that he will be vindicated after death if not before. He is prepared to accept death with the knowledge that his integrity has remained unblemished.

## A Hero of Integrity

JOB HAS ADHERED TO HIS INTEGRITY throughout his ordeal. Rejected by friends and society, and unheeded by God, following his conscience and speaking the truth in defense of his innocence has given Job's life added significance. Psychologist Viktor Frankl held that the search for meaning is a fundamental human aspiration. Having lost everything— his children, his prosperity, and his honor— Job's quest for vindication gave purpose and hope to his life. While he could not undo the terrible calamity that befell him, he could choose how to respond. Philosopher Friedrich Nietzsche observed: "Those who have a *why* in life can bear almost any *how*."[37] Job had a choice to make. The retribution doctrine assumes that sufferers are responsible for their tribulations. Job can either accept his affliction as God's just punishment for sins he is unaware of committing, or he can follow his conscience and protest his innocence. Refusing to surrender his inner spiritual freedom, Job chooses to protest, wrestling with God to vindicate his integrity. He defends values that make his life meaningful: truth, justice, and compassion. Job is the greatest symbol of innocent human suffering in world literature. Nietzsche, no stranger to suffering, declared: "Profound suffering makes you noble; it separates."[38] Job is the Bible's greatest rebel, a source of inspiration for those who strive to maintain their moral convictions in the face of adversity. Job gives voice to the anguish of the afflicted who struggle to comprehend their suffering while God hides his face.

Kierkegaard captures the nobility of Job. The young man declares in *Repetition*: "The secret of Job, the vital force, the nerve, the idea, is that Job, despite everything, is in the right….Job continues to take the position that he is in the right. He does it in such a way that he thereby witnesses to the noble, human, bold confidence that he knows what a human being is, knows that despite his being frail, despite his withering away like a flower, that in freedom he still has something of greatness, has a consciousness that even God cannot wrest from him even though he gave it to him."[39] In defense of his integrity, Job battled God, his friends, and the wisdom tradition. Job had come to realize that the prevailing theology contradicted human experience. His body wracked with pain, he transforms the ash-heap into a forum to challenge God's justice and to highlight the problem of innocent suffering. Notwithstanding Job's blasphemies, even pious readers find it difficult not to admire his valiant struggle.

Throughout the dialogue with his friends, Job, confronted by what he believes to be a terminal illness, undergoes remarkable growth. At the same time, the rhetoric of the friends diminishes in effectiveness as it becomes more strident. Rather than buckle under the friends' verbal assault, the dying Job summons inner resources. Although the dialogue lacks the action of an epic or a stage play, we follow the progress of Job's inner spiritual struggle against forces beyond his control. Job has discovered a power in himself that he had hitherto attributed to God alone. When Job began his quest, he was a passive sufferer, cursing the day of his birth and pleading with God to let him die. But he soon rose from the ashes of desolation and conceived the outrageous idea to challenge God in court, suing the Almighty for failing to act justly. No character in the Hebrew Bible matches Job in boldness. At first insecure, fearful that he would be unable to confront God face-to-face, Job imagines receiving assistance from various heavenly intermediaries— first a mediating umpire, then a witness, and finally a vindicator— in his lawsuit. But he soon dismissed the idea of intermediaries as mere fancies of his desperate imagination. Then, when all seemed lost and he was most isolated, Job summoned his courage and decided to plead his case alone before God, even if it killed him.

Here Job is at his noblest, an inspiration to all those who struggle for justice against seemingly overwhelming power. People of integrity refuse to compromise their values in the face of public opposition. Job's integrity prevents him from denying his innocence in order to restore his relationship with God, as his friends urge. Throughout his affliction, he never loses his integrity, speaking directly and honestly not only to his friends but also to God. True to his conscience, Job is undaunted before the omnipotence of God. Maligned by public opinion, he remains adamant in his pursuit of justice from God. Job's speeches exhibit a formidable eloquence, their pathos unequalled anywhere else in the Bible. Under the shadow of death, with no hope of a life beyond the grave, Job's quest for vindication ironically keeps him alive.

But Job's vindication raises a troubling question about God. If Job is acquitted, God must admit that he afflicted an innocent man unjustly. To say that Job's suffering is a test of faith does not justify God's action. God knows that Job is righteous. If Job suffers innocently at the hand of an unjust God, so have all innocent sufferers of the world. God is caught in a dilemma: If Job is just, God is not just. If Job is not just, God was wrong about Job, and the Satan wins the challenge. Job's virtue would be demonstrated to be selfish.

Having rested his case, Job's fate is in God's hands. Job stakes everything on his integrity. He has lived by his exemplary code of ethics. He embodies the practical human wisdom of fearing God and shunning evil. Taking an oath of innocence, Job the defendant called upon God to respond as his accuser. Wrestling with God, Job will not relent until God either acquits or kills him. The Book of Job has arrived at its crisis. The friends, reduced to silence, have despaired of saving Job from divine wrath. Their staunch defense of the doctrine of strict and perfect retribution has not prevailed. Will God remain hidden and silent? Will God now destroy Job with a thunderbolt from heaven? Will God fulfill Job's quest for vindication? We await God's response.

"The Wrath of Elihu" (1825)

By William Blake

# ELIHU SPEAKS

## Chapter 32   Elihu: I Will Defend God

AT THIS POINT, THE OMNISCIENT NARRATOR interjects to inform readers that the three friends "ceased to answer Job because he was righteous in his own eyes." They realized that they could not convince Job that he is a serious sinner who must repent. Job rejected their false retribution theology, adhering to the testimony of his conscience that he is innocent. If Job is self-righteous, as the friends claim, he is guilty of the sin of foolish pride. The Book of Proverbs declares: "Do not be wise in your own eyes. Fear Yahweh, and depart from evil."[1] But what the friends, and many commentators, call pride is really Job's determination to defend his integrity against all odds. The friends make no reply to Job's oath of innocence, probably considering it additional blasphemy from a wicked hypocrite.

With the friends silenced, one might expect God to speak. Job has challenged him to appear with a formal indictment. Instead, a young man abruptly enters the scene. The narrator introduces him as Elihu, son of Barakel the Buzite, of the family of Ram. Elihu is not mentioned in the Prologue. Unlike Job and the three friends— Eliphaz, Bildad, and Zophar— he has a Hebrew name. Elihu had listened as a bystander to their dialogue. The word that best characterizes him is "angry." The omniscient narrator tells us that Elihu is angry at Job because he "justified himself rather than God." Indeed, Job's arguments made him appear right and God wrong. If God punished an innocent man, God is not just. Elihu is also angry with the three friends because they condemned Job without convincing him of his guilt. For Job to declare God unjust is in itself, according to Elihu, a grave sin. But the friends, despite their professed wisdom, were unsuccessful defenders of the Israelite wisdom tradition. As far as Elihu is concerned, the friends have been routed and retreated ignominiously from the battlefield. If Job refuses to repent and appeal to God's mercy, the entire dialogue was fruitless. Unless Job is decisively defeated, the theology of retribution and belief in a just God will be undermined.

Elihu must have been as shocked as the friends while listening to Job defend his integrity by cursing God. Until now, Elihu had remained silent. Because he is the youngest, he had allowed the three friends to address Job first. According to ancient custom, the aged, given their years of experience, were presumed to have wisdom. But when the third cycle of the dialogue was abruptly terminated, Bildad giving a very short speech and Zophar none at all, Elihu could not contain himself. The narrator relates: "When Elihu saw that there was no answer in the mouth of these three men, his wrath was kindled." Elihu concluded that only he could defeat Job.

Because the friends failed to make a cogent case, Elihu takes up their task of constructing a theodicy, a vindication of God's justice. The name Elihu means "He is my God." Indeed Elihu intends to speak for God. Elihu delivers four speeches over six chapters, aiming to vanquish the defiant Job and coerce him to drop his lawsuit against God and repent.[2] Elihu's role is analogous to what is now called *amicus curiae*, literally a "friend of the court." This person is not a party to the lawsuit, but having a strong interest in its outcome, petitions the court for permission to file a brief on behalf of a party. The brief expresses views on the subject matter of the lawsuit. Such briefs are often submitted in cases involving issues of important public concern.

While not a party in the legal dispute between Job and God, Elihu believes that he has a compelling interest in the case. Job's blistering assault upon God's justice threatens the belief in the moral government of the world. The dispute between Job and God should be the concern of all humankind. While Elihu does not have express permission from God's Supreme Tribunal to file an *amicus curiae* brief, his upcoming allegation that his words are divinely inspired will imply that he has God's approval to argue on his behalf. Elihu expects his speeches to break the deadlock in the dispute and decide the case in favor of God.

Most commentators consider Elihu's speeches not part of the original book, but an ancient interpolation by a different poet who believed that Job's friends failed to defend God adequately. Nevertheless, Elihu's speeches are an organic part of the canonical Masoretic text. A number of commentators treat Elihu as an officious intruder who detracts from God's speeches. Yet Elihu's speeches demonstrate an eloquence and beauty of their own, enhancing the Book of Job. Elihu might not have appeared in the original dramatis personae, but for centuries he has played a prominent role in the Book of Job. Hence, we shall interpret the speeches as integral to the narrative. Medieval Jewish commentators, including Gersonides, believed Elihu's speeches to be the most compelling thus far in the Book of Job.[3] Like the Hymn to Divine Wisdom, Elihu's contribution is important in analyzing the dispute between Job and the three friends. Elihu's speeches may be considered the oldest commentary on the dialogue of the Book of Job. The speeches point backward and forward. Backward, as Elihu adverts to what Job and the friends have said, providing a review of salient points and offering a view of suffering more nuanced than the strict retribution creed; and forward, as Elihu partly anticipates God's speeches from the whirlwind.

Elihu initiates his discourse by addressing the friends. His first objective is to defend his right to speak. Because he is young and they are old, he had hesitated: "I held back, and did not dare show you my opinion." According to custom, Elihu had deferred to his elders, for age "should teach wisdom." But listening to the failed dialogue between Job and the friends made Elihu realize that age does not necessarily bring wisdom. Assessing the friends, Elihu alleges that they do not "understand justice." Despite his youth, he claims a right to speak because "there is a spirit in man, and the breath of the Almighty gives them understanding." While he might merely be saying that all humans, regardless of age, can attain wisdom, Elihu believes that he has attained superior wisdom that qualifies him to teach. Often criticized by commentators as an impetuous young man, Elihu reveals more of his individual character than do Job's friends.

Elihu explains to the friends the reason for his intervention. "Listen to me," he enjoins, "I also will show my opinion. I waited for your words and I listened to your reasoning while you searched out what to say. I gave you my full attention. But there was no one who convinced Job, or answered his words, among you." Elihu assumes that Job could have been easily refuted. He rebukes the friends for retreating before the battle is won, making God appear guilty. Elihu infers that the friends must have rationalized that the wisest course was to let God finish the fight. Elihu warns: "Beware lest you say, 'We have found wisdom; God may refute him, not man.'" The young Elihu insists that he will succeed where the friends failed. Attentive to their dialogue, he has had sufficient time to reflect on what he will say. He pledges not to repeat the feckless speeches of the friends. He is confident of success because Job "has not directed his words against me; neither will I answer him with your speeches." Elihu promises to introduce more compelling arguments. Rather than focusing on Job's alleged sinful actions, Elihu will concentrate on Job's sinful language.

Having stated his intention, Elihu soliloquizes on his mission. Speaking about the friends in the third person, he muses: "They are amazed. They answer no more." Words fail them. Elihu insists that he must fill the intellectual vacuum left by the inept friends: "Shall I wait, because they do not speak, because they stand still, and answer no more? I also will answer my part, and I also will show my opinion." Reverting to his claim to superior wisdom, Elihu insists that divine inspiration compels him to argue God's case: "I am full of words. The spirit within me constrains me. My breast is as wine which has no vent; like new wineskins it is ready to burst." Elihu can no longer contain himself: "I will open my lips and answer." The Job poet appears to be parodying the prophet Jeremiah, who could not refrain from proclaiming the words of God: "If I say," Jeremiah declares, "'I will not mention his word or speak anymore in his name, his word is in my heart like a fire, a fire shut upon in my bones. I am weary of holding it in; indeed I cannot.'"[4] Having defended his right to speak, Elihu alleges that he aims to discover the truth. Remembering Job's early concern that the friends would be biased in favor of God,[5] Elihu professes to be completely impartial: "I do not know how to give flattering titles." In his assumed role as a friend of the court, Elihu declares that if he fails to be objective, God "would soon take me away." Elihu will not flatter Job or merely insinuate his guilt. Nor will he tolerate what he considers Job's self-righteous defense. Despite his lofty claims, Elihu's opening statements, indicating his determination to prove Job wrong and God right belie his objectivity. He has already decided that Job is guilty.

## Chapter 33   Elihu: I Rebuke Job

ELIHU BEGINS HIS PARTISAN LEGAL BRIEF by introducing himself in the guise of an objective judge. The three friends remain at the ash-heap to hear his discourse. His exordium is designed to make Job receptive. Unlike the friends, Elihu addresses Job by name. He entreats Job to heed his arguments: "Job, please hear my speech, and listen to all my words." Having restrained himself for so long, Elihu is anxious to unleash his verbal torrent: "I have opened my mouth. My tongue has spoken in my mouth." He assures Job that he will speak the truth: "My words shall utter the uprightness of my heart. That which my lips know they shall speak sincerely." To gain an advantage over Job, Elihu adverts to his earlier claim to special authority. Although a mortal, given life by God's breath, Elihu claims divine inspiration, instilling in him wisdom lacking in Job and the friends: "The Spirit of God has made me, and the breath of the Almighty gives me life." Assuming this privileged authority, Elihu invites Job to a legal debate, confident that he will prevail. "If you can, answer me," Elihu challenges, "set your words in order before me, and stand up." As God's self-appointed legal spokesperson, Elihu has assigned Job the place of the defendant. Elihu affirms that like Job he is a mere human: "I am toward God even as you are. I am also formed out of the clay." Mindful of Job's early lament that his fear of God would prevent his arguing before a heavenly court,[6] Elihu insists that Job need not fear him: "My terror shall not make you afraid, neither shall my pressure be heavy on you." Elihu expects to convince Job of his guilt in a secure earthly forum, enabling him to escape a harrowing confrontation before God's tribunal. Ironically, Elihu will attempt to terrify and pressure Job to repent.

Having completed his lengthy opening statement, Elihu begins his argument for God. After listening to the dialogue between Job and the friends, Elihu believes that he can state the essence of Job's case. While the friends had, for the most part, merely alluded obliquely to Job's contentions, usually long after he uttered them, Elihu will try a different tactic. He will assemble some of Job's most offensive charges and challenge him to address them. Elihu apparently expects that when confronted with his blasphemies, Job will realize the danger of pursuing a lawsuit against God. Elihu is not deterred by the lack of evidence that Job committed sinful actions. Elihu apparently believes that the blasphemies Job committed after suffering constitute *prima facie* evidence that he had sinned before his calamity. Elihu proceeds, therefore, by addressing Job's claims and accusations against God: "You have spoken in my hearing. I have heard the voice of your words, saying, 'I am innocent, neither is there iniquity in me. God finds occasions against me. He counts me as his enemy. He puts my feet in the stocks. He marks all my paths.'" Elihu's summary of Job's complaint is substantially true, but contains just enough distortion to appear to weaken Job's case. Job did indeed protest his innocence time and again;[7] he also accused God of treating him as an enemy,[8] imprisoning him in the stocks like a criminal; and he did accuse God of malevolently watching his every move in order to catch him in a transgression. Yet Job never declares himself completely sinless,[9] maintaining only that his "prayer is pure."[10] Job held only that his affliction exceeds any sins he could have possibly committed.

Job's accusations against God, Elihu maintains, "are not just, for God is greater than man. Why do you strive against him, because he does not give account of any of his matters?" By greatness Elihu refers to God's power, wishing to convince Job of the futility of his lawsuit. God and Job are not equals; no human can hold God accountable. God would never condescend to be subjected to legal cross-examination. God does not speak like a human to another human. But if Elihu had listened carefully to Job's speeches, as he claims to have done, he would have heard Job concede these points: "God is not a man, as I am," Job declared, "that I should answer him, that we should come together in judgment."[11] Indeed, Job had despaired of successfully confronting God in court.[12]

Job lamented repeatedly that God is silent, refusing to listen to his pleas. Nevertheless, Elihu rebuts, God has indirect ways of communicating to humans: "God speaks, though man pays no attention." God has responded to Job, but he fails to recognize the divine teaching. While the friends held that penitent sinners must initiate their restoration by appealing to God, Elihu insists that God himself reaches out to call sinners to repentance. The shrewd Elihu remembers Job's lament that God afflicted him with tormenting dreams and visions.[13] According to Elihu, God may send dreams to sinners to warn them to repent or suffer an early death: "In a dream, in a vision of the night, when deep sleep falls on men, in slumbering on the bed," God "opens the ears of men, and seals their instruction" on their minds. God terrifies and instructs a human to overcome his "pride," thus saving "his soul from the pit and his life from perishing by the sword." The Hebrew Bible and other ancient literature regard dreams as a means by which the gods speak to humans. Elihu wishes Job to interpret his dreams as merciful divine admonitions, urging him to abandon his pride, the source of all sin.

God may warn and instruct the sinner in another way. Seeking to justify Job's physical suffering, Elihu maintains that affliction can serve a good purpose. God may impose suffering on sinners as a warning to stimulate them to examine their lives. This idea of remedial suffering is Elihu's principal contribution to the debate between Job and the friends. Eliphaz had alluded briefly to remedial suffering when he told Job that God wounds in order to make a person whole.[14] According to the Prologue, suffering is a test of faith. This idea is absent from the poetic dialogue, where the friends argue that suffering is only a consequence of sin. Elihu goes beyond the friends in claiming that suffering can also be a sign of God's mercy. In doing so, Elihu offers Job a way to extricate himself from his conflict with God. The friends maintain that Job suffers because he is a wicked sinner. But Job insists that his suffering is innocent, for he examined his life and sees no serious transgressions. Elihu sees a way to resolve the dispute. While the friends have forsaken Job as a wicked sinner, Elihu seeks to pave the way for Job's restoration. Elihu will argue that Job is not wicked, but nevertheless suffers because of sins he committed. Elihu thus revives the distinction Eliphaz made in his first speech between a righteous repentant sinner and a wicked unrepentant sinner. Being righteous does not preclude sin. Unlike the friends, Elihu will not impute wicked sins to Job. Nevertheless, he urges him to repent for his blasphemous words. If Job can be convinced that his suffering is not punishment for wickedness, but God's effort to correct him, he might repent and regain divine favor.

A determined theodicist, Elihu aims to construct a stronger defense of God's justice. Human suffering, Elihu contends, does not detract from God's goodness. Contrary to the rigid doctrine of retribution, suffering can be beneficial, a reflection not of God's wrath, but of his mercy. The righteous are afflicted for their higher good. Suffering can be educational, a means by which God disciplines and morally reproves sinners in order to bring them to repentance. With a transparent allusion to Job, sitting emaciated on the ash-heap in the presence of the friends, Elihu elaborates on the remedial benefits of suffering. A righteous sinner "may be chastened with pain on his bed, with continual strife in his bones, so that his life abhors bread, and his soul dainty food. His flesh is so consumed away, that it cannot be seen. His bones that were not seen stick out." Like Job, this sinner is on the verge of death: "His soul draws near to the pit." By repenting the sinner avoids a premature death.

The notion of salutary educational suffering is found in the wisdom literature. The Psalmist confesses: "Before I was afflicted, I went astray; but now I observe your word....It is good for me that I have been afflicted, that I may learn your statutes."[15] In modern times, C. S. Lewis wrote that affliction can bring a person closer to God: "Pain insists upon being attended to. God whispers to us in our pleasures, speaks to our conscience, but shouts in our pain; it is His megaphone to rouse a deaf world."[16] Hence, Elihu is saying to Job: Accept your affliction as a sign of God's beneficence. God is shouting at you through your pain. Woe to you if you remain deaf to God. If you could view your suffering as a means to salvation, you could embrace it as meaningful.

The second century Christian theologian Irenaeus presented a slightly modified form of educational suffering. According to Irenaeus, humans are created in God's "image," but not in God's "likeness." As incomplete beings, humans must strive to become a finite likeness to God. By sending challenges that humans must confront, God assists in perfecting them morally. According to Irenaeus, human life ought to exhibit progressive development from immature creatures to the finite moral perfection intended by God. The world, with its trials and tribulations, is the place for humanity to fulfill its transcendent destiny. Experiencing both good and evil in life, one learns to pursue virtue and avoid vice. According to the modern British theologian John Hick, the world may be viewed as a place of "soul-making," with humans free to use evil and suffering to strengthen and develop character.[17] Therefore, Job's suffering, according to Elihu, can have moral and spiritual value.

Elihu promised to improve on the friends' arguments, making Job realize the futility of his lawsuit. He attempts to do so by supplementing the retribution doctrine with his positive view of suffering. Suffering is still punitive, but if sufferers can see their pain as a means of spiritual growth, they might be restored. Yet Elihu repeats the error of the friends. He takes a general principle that might have some validity, and applies it to the wrong person. Job cannot accept his tribulation as God's means to his moral improvement. There is also the issue of proportionality. Much human suffering is disproportionate to the possible degree of moral improvement. Catastrophic evils such as earthquakes, wars, and massive slaughter cannot be justified on the grounds that they perfect human character. If God intends horrible suffering as a discipline to heal wayward humans, the medicine is worse than the disease. Significantly, in outlining for Job the ways in which God speaks to humans for their benefit, Elihu says nothing of an inner voice that we call conscience. Often viewed as the voice of God, conscience, as we have argued, is the immoveable basis for Job's legal attack on God.

The experience of suffering, Elihu insists, might be an occasion for God to provide a sinner with extraordinary grace. God will sometimes dispatch: "an angel, an interpreter, one among a thousand, to show to man what is right for him." Owing to the intervention of God's messenger the sinner repents, sparing himself from premature death. Elihu is exploiting Job's earlier pleas for a mediator, a witness or a redeemer to make his case before God.[18] But whereas these figures of Job's fancy would act for him in opposition to God, Elihu's messenger will reconcile him with God. On behalf of the repentant sinner, Elihu explains, this messenger will say to God: "'Deliver him from going down to the pit, I have found a ransom.'" Once Job is ransomed by his repentance, he will receive the glorious restoration promised by the friends. Elihu proffers the dying Job the tantalizing prospect of having his skin healed as he regains his youthful health and vigor. The repentant sinner's "flesh shall be fresher than a child's. He returns to the days of his youth."

Like a skillful attorney, Elihu seeks to take advantage of his knowledge of Job's desperate quest for vindication. Circling back to Job's emotional declaration that a redeemer will ultimately come to his defense, and that he will "see God" on his side, "not as a stranger," but as a friend,[19] Elihu assures that the repentant sinner is restored: "He prays to God and he is favorable to him. He sees God's face with joy. He restores to man his righteousness." The Psalmist declares: "Yahweh is righteous. He loves righteousness. The upright shall see his face."[20] According to Elihu, the penitent sinner shows remorse by publicly confessing: "I have sinned, and perverted that which is right, and it did not profit me. God has redeemed my soul from going into the pit. My life shall see the light." Is this messenger from God an angel, charged like the Satan with a specific service, or could a mortal play the role? Having claimed divine inspiration, Elihu might believe himself to be God's messenger. The Hebrew Bible records instances of humans as God's envoys.[21] Elihu reiterates that God in his mercy gives the sinner more than one opportunity to repent: "God does all these things, twice, even three times, with a man, to bring back his soul from the pit, that he may be enlightened with the light of the living."

Before concluding this portion of his legal polemic, Elihu addresses Job and again tells him to heed the words of his speech to come: "Mark well, Job, and listen to me. Hold your peace, and I will speak." Before proceeding, Elihu again bids Job to respond: "If you have anything to say, answer me. Speak, for I desire to justify you. If not, listen to me. Hold your peace, and I will teach you wisdom." Assuming Job's guilt, Elihu has exhorted him to repent, holding over him the threat of death. Elihu's remedial view of suffering is not applicable to Job, for he is innocent of sin. Consequently, Elihu fails to advance the argument beyond the narrow confines of the friends. Neither Elihu nor the friends understand that Job values his integrity more than his life. If God spoke to Job in dreams, it was merely to enhance his affliction and frighten him into dropping his legal case. If God afflicted Job, it was not for his edification, but a glaring example of arbitrary divine power. If God sends a messenger to interpret the suffering, Job, adhering to his integrity, would refuse to repent for sins he did not commit.

## Chapter 34   Elihu: God is Just

AFTER EXPLAINING THE MEANS GOD USES to communicate with sinners, warning them to repent, Elihu, God's self-appointed messenger, probably expected Job to reply. But Job is silent, having confidently rested his case. Hence, Elihu resumes his legal discourse by again summoning the friends to heed his wisdom. Elihu opens with sarcasm directed at the friends: "Hear my words, you wise men. Give ear to me, you who have knowledge." As Elihu presents himself, he is the wise man, gifted with wisdom. Having belittled the wisdom of the friends, Elihu presumes to teach them, as well as Job, the proper understanding: "For the ear tries words as the palate tastes food." The ear of understanding should assist them to distinguish the wise from the unwise, the true from the false, just as the tongue can distinguish between good and bad taste. Elihu then summons the friends to join him in determining a just resolution to Job's case: "Let us choose for us that which is right. Let us know among ourselves what is good." Elihu will argue that the resolution Job intends is neither right nor good. Elihu expects that the friends, associating themselves with his wisdom, will concur.

Elihu resumes his strategy of quoting Job's own words against him. He begins by focusing on Job's lawsuit: "Job has said, 'I am righteous. God has taken away my right. Notwithstanding my right, I am considered a liar. My wound is incurable, though I am without disobedience.'" While Job never claimed to be perfect, he did claim to be essentially righteous.[22] We have seen him swear to his innocence multiple times. Elihu is also correct in saying that Job accuses God of denying him justice.[23] And Job's friends did consider him a liar in defending his integrity.[24] The friends insist that God would never afflict an innocent person.

After reminding the friends of Job's complaints, Elihu cannot restrain his indignation at Job's language. His rhetorical question is a stern rebuke: "What man is like Job, who drinks scorn like water?" Here Elihu echoes Eliphaz's condemnation of the wicked person who "drinks up evil like water?"[25] According to Elihu, Job's multiple blasphemies deserve severe condemnation. These blasphemies, Elihu charges, place Job among the godless: "He goes in company with the workers of iniquity, ands walks with wicked men. For he has said, 'It profits a man nothing that he should delight himself in God.'" Job never used these precise words, but he did condemn God for destroying the righteous and the wicked regardless of merit. Like the friends, Elihu cannot produce evidence that sin is the source of Job's suffering. But Elihu will not follow the friends and accuse Job of being a wicked sinner. Instead, Elihu focuses on Job's blasphemous words uttered in reaction to his plight. Nevertheless, Elihu, like the friends, evades the central issue: God's horrendous action against Job, a righteous man.

Having maligned Job's character, Elihu defends the character of God. He again calls Job and the friends to attention: "Listen to me, you men of understanding. Far be it from God that he should do wickedness, from the Almighty, that he should commit iniquity." Injustice is contrary to God's perfect character. Had Elihu been privy to the events in heaven depicted in the Prologue, would he still defend God as just? A devout believer, Elihu cannot conceive of God committing injustice. Job's suffering cannot be innocent. Evil and injustice are incompatible with God's nature. God rewards the righteous and punishes the wicked according to perfect justice. Echoing Bildad,[26] Elihu declares: "God will not do wickedly, neither will the Almighty pervert justice." To prove his point, Elihu stumbles into a *non sequitur*, inferring God's absolute justice from his absolute power. He poses two rhetorical questions about God:

"Who put him in charge of the earth? Who has appointed him over the whole world?" According to Elihu, God's omnipotence makes him just. Job's lawsuit, accusing God of injustice, could never succeed. Job has no legitimate grievance. He must defer to God's omnipotence. The Creator sustains all life and could easily destroy all humanity: "If he set his heart on himself, if he gathered to himself his spirit and his breath," undoing the creation of humanity, "all flesh would perish together, and man would turn again to dust." As absolute sovereign of the universe, God does whatever he wills.

Elihu then expands his spurious attempt to vindicate God's justice on the basis of his omnipotence. Elihu insists on Job's rapt attention: "If you have understanding, hear this; listen to the voice of my words." For Elihu, if God is not just, the moral universe would be completely overturned. Responding to Job's attack on God's justice, Elihu poses two rhetorical questions: "Shall one who hates justice govern? Will you condemn him who is righteous and mighty?" Job has already answered these questions in the negative. Job never denied God's omnipotence, but his experience and his observation of prevalent innocent suffering led him to doubt divine justice.

Continuing his argument, Elihu declares that divine justice is absolutely impartial. As ruler of the world, God treats everyone equally, whether rich or poor, powerful or weak, "for they all are the work of his hands." God will not permit the rich and powerful to abuse other humans. He brings wicked kings and nobles to judgment. With an implied response to Job's lament that God permits the wicked to flourish, Elihu rebuts that the wicked, regardless of social status, inevitably suffer divine wrath: "In a moment they die, even at midnight. The people are shaken and pass away. The mighty are taken away without a hand." The wicked might prosper temporarily, but when they least expect it, they are struck dead, not by a human hand, but by the hand of God. Contrary to his initial claim, Elihu uses arguments of the friends, reiterating their depiction of the fate of the wicked.

God's absolute justice, Elihu argues, is guided by his omniscience: "His eyes are on the ways of a man. He sees all his goings." Nothing can be hidden from God: "There is no darkness, nor thick gloom." In his summation, Job lamented his unjust suffering, asking of God: "Does he not see my ways and number all my steps?"[27] Elihu's declaration implies that God has indeed observed Job's ways and treated him accordingly. Job had also lamented that evil doers such as the murderer, the adulterer, and the thief are able to commit their sins under the cover of darkness.[28] Elihu rebuts that there is no way for the sinner to escape God's scrutiny: "There is no darkness, nor thick gloom, where the workers of iniquity can hide themselves."

Seeking to sabotage Job's effort to litigate, Elihu insists that God's omniscience makes it unnecessary for him to make any legal inquiry: "He does not need to consider a man further that he should go before God in judgment. He breaks in pieces mighty men in ways past finding out." Deploring the success of the wicked, Job asked why God does not set a time to judge them.[29] Elihu rebuts that God does not need to summon the wicked to judgment. Their punishment is swift: "God destroys the wicked "without inquiry" and "sets up others in their place." Like the friends, Elihu alludes to Job as he describes how God destroys evildoers: "He takes knowledge of their works. He overturns them in the night, so that they are destroyed." Because they turn from good toward evil, God makes them an example to all: "He strikes them as wicked men in the open sight of others, because they turned aside from following him, and would not pay attention to any of his ways." To Job's lament that God ignores the plight of the poor and the needy, Elihu rebuts that God does heed their cries for relief from the wicked rich and powerful: "They caused the cry of the poor to come to him. He heard the cry of the afflicted." To Job's lament that God is hidden and silent at his time of great need, Elihu counters: "If he gives quietness, who can condemn him? When he hides his face, who can see him?" Elihu implies that, even when silent, God's justice prevails. Although humans cannot see God, his benevolent providence watches over the world, nations as well as individuals, insuring that "the godless man may not reign," and that "there be no one to ensnare the people."

Concluding this section of his theodicy, Elihu presents a hypothetical case of a repentant sinner. With an obvious allusion to Job, he suggests: "Has any said to God, 'I am guilty, but I will not offend any more. Teach me that which I do not see. If I have done iniquity, I will do it no more?'" But in conscience, Job knew that he had not offended God. To confess sins he did not commit would compromise his integrity. Job seeks vindication, not forgiveness. Bildad had reproved Job as wishing to overturn the moral order of the universe to suit his whim.[30] But Elihu insists that Job cannot dictate justice to God. Job's day of reckoning draws near. Only he can make the decision to drop his suit and repent: "You must choose," insists Elihu, "and not I."

Turning to the three friends, Elihu solicits their concurrence while the dying Job listens from the ash-heap: "Men of understanding will tell me, every wise man who hears me: 'Job speaks without knowledge. His words are without wisdom.'" Elihu's professed impartiality is a pretense. He had promised Job that he would secure his vindication, but he wants Job to forsake vindication and repent. As the narrator's introduction indicated, Elihu's ruling passion is anger. He is an angry young man. His anger is born of fear, for Job represents a potent threat to his moral world view. Elihu tried to restrain himself, but he now unleashes his rage. Bringing his indictment to a crescendo, Elihu concludes with the cruel wish that as long as Job refuses to repent, God should inflict the harshest punishment. As if addressing God, Elihu apostrophizes: "I wish that Job were tried to the end, because of his answering like wicked men." Thomas Aquinas illuminates this verse: "That is, let his defect be shown to him through scourges *to the very end*, that is, to the point that he recognizes that he is unjust, or *to the very end*, to the death." [31] According to Elihu, Job is doubly guilty. He is not only a grievous sinner, but also a defiant rebel against divine authority, clapping his hands in mockery: "He adds rebellion to his sin. He claps his hands among us, and multiplies his words against God." Elihu recognizes what many orthodox commentators do not: Job is guilty of blasphemy. But when the righteous Job blasphemes God, he speaks the truth. Elihu believes that as long as Job persists in his blasphemy, he sinks deeper and deeper into wickedness. Like the friends, Elihu fails to understand that Job will not be intimidated. Adhering to his conscience, Job refuses to escape suffering by betraying his integrity.

## Chapter 35   Elihu: Job is Self-Righteous

WITHOUT GIVING JOB A CHANCE TO REPLY, Elihu launches into his third speech. His principal objective remains to convince Job to drop his lawsuit against God. Like the friends, Elihu does not seek to comfort Job in his suffering. He focuses again on Job's impious speech. Elihu questions him directly: "Do you think this to be your right, do you say, 'My righteousness is more than God's?'" Job's lawsuit implies his own innocence and God's guilt. According to Elihu, Job acts as if God regards him as a personal rival who must be defeated. Elihu's question also accuses Job, ironically like the Satan, of self-interested piety. Elihu portrays Job as asking how he benefits from not sinning. Indeed, Job's speeches implied that a life of righteousness or wickedness makes no difference to God. If God does not punish the wicked, there is no benefit in acting virtuously. In times of great tribulation, many ancient Israelites echoed Job's concern, wondering whether they served God in vain. Cynicism about the rewards of a religious life is reflected in the book of the prophet Malachi, when God rebukes the Jews: "You have said, 'It is vain to serve God;' and 'What profit is it that we have followed his instructions. ... Now we call the proud happy; those who work wickedness are built up; they tempt God, and escape.'"[32] Elihu next addresses not only Job, but also the friends, since he has found their arguments for God's justice deficient: "I will answer you, and your companions with you." Having listened to Job and the friends expound the retribution dogma repeatedly, Elihu believes that their emphasis upon rewards and punishments might lead to the conclusion that God is benefited or harmed by human virtue and vice. But nothing can add or detract from God's essential perfection. We recall Job's lament that God pays too much attention to humans in an effort to catch them in sin.[33] On the contrary, Elihu argues, God has no such trivial concerns.

Elihu seeks to give Job a sense of his insignificance. He summons Job to gaze at the sky above the land of Uz and contemplate God's transcendent realm: "Look to the heavens, and see. See the skies, which are higher than you. If you have sinned, what effect do you have against him? If your transgressions are multiplied, what do you do to him? If you are righteous, what do you give him? What does he receive from your hand?" Job had made this point earlier, asking how, even if he did sin, could he hurt God.[34] Elihu repeats the argument of Eliphaz that God is too exalted to be affected by human conduct. Perfectly self-sufficient, righteous and wicked actions neither benefit nor detract from God. Hence, Elihu contends, God has no interest in being partial.

Believing that he has vindicated God's justice, Elihu addresses Job's complaint that God neglects the plight of the oppressed.[35] Elihu responds that God distinguishes between the righteous oppressed and the wicked oppressed before deciding to intervene. God ignores the cries only of wicked sinners who refuse to pray with humility and sincere devotion: "No one says, 'Where is God my Maker, who gives songs in the night, who teaches us more than the animals of the earth, and makes us wiser than the birds of the sky?'" The unrepentant wicked do not deserve relief from suffering. They ignore God, who alone can save. In the night of their sorrow and spiritual darkness, the repentant will sing joyous songs praising God, their deliverer. The Psalmist prayed: "Yahweh will command his loving kindness in the daytime. In the night his song shall be with me: a prayer to the God of my life." [36] According to Elihu, unlike the animals of the earth, who merely cry out in pain, God has endowed humans with the wisdom to turn their cries into prayers, songs of deliverance. Unless the oppressed offer sincere prayers, God will not respond: "They cry, but no one gives answer because of the pride of evil men. Surely God will not hear an empty cry. Neither will the Almighty regard it." For Elihu, if God ignores Job, the fault is not with God. Job is proud. If God disregards the insincere pleas of the wicked, "how much less," Elihu insists, when you say "you do not see him" and that "the cause is before him, and you wait for him!" How much less God will respond when Job attacks his justice, declaring that he has presented his case and awaits God's answer.

At this point, Elihu's effort to still distinguish Job from the wicked is a distinction without a difference. As Elihu closes his third speech, he addresses the friends, while Job listens: "Job opens his mouth with empty talk. He multiplies words without knowledge." Job's only wise option is to overcome his pride. He should repent and withdraw his lawsuit.

## Chapter 36   Elihu: God Enforces Retributive Justice

REALIZING THAT JOB REMAINS UNCONVINCED, Elihu delivers the fourth and final speech of his theodicy. He seeks to intimidate Job whose time is running out. If Job continues to reject God's message in his suffering, he will be consigned to the fate of the wicked, those who flagrantly offend God. Sensing Job's impatience, Elihu beseeches him to forbear as he presents the remainder of his legal brief: "Bear with me a little, and I will show you; for I still have something to say on God's behalf." As God's spokesman, Elihu continues to argue that Job has not been treated unjustly. He has no legal case. God's government of the world is perfectly just. Once, again, he attempts to base his arguments on the highest authority. His words, he boldly proclaims, convey a message inspired by God: "I will get my knowledge from afar, and will ascribe righteousness to my Maker. For truly my words are not false.

One who is perfect in knowledge is with you." The twelfth-century Rabbi Abraham Ibn Ezra interpreted "from afar" to mean coming from God, who is far above.[37] As God's presumptive spokesperson, Elihu professes to speak the truth, based upon his "perfect" knowledge of the issue between God and Job. Since Elihu will later ascribe "perfect knowledge" to God, he apparently wishes to associate himself with divine wisdom.[38] To dispute God's representative is to dispute God himself.

Elihu begins by emphasizing again God's omnipotence: "God is mighty, and does not despise anyone. He is mighty in strength and understanding." As creator and ruler of the world, God has no motive to behave arbitrarily. All humans, rich as well as poor, are judged according to their character and actions. God cannot be deterred from implementing strict retributive justice, punishing the wicked and rewarding the righteous. Elihu denies Job's charge that God permits the wicked to prosper and ignores the plight of the innocent: "He does not preserve the life of the wicked, but gives the afflicted their right. He does not withdraw his eyes from the righteous, but with kings on the throne, he sets them forever, and they are exalted." Job must have found ironic Elihu's claim that God exalts the righteous, enthroning them like kings. In Job's view, the eyes of God are not those of a benevolent creator but of a malicious "watcher of men" who wishes to destroy him.[39]

Returning to his argument that suffering can benefit righteous sinners, Elihu again alleges that God sends affliction to awaken them to repent, ask for forgiveness, and mend their errant ways. Alluding to Job's accusation that God imprisons him with suffering, Elihu argues that it is intended as disciplinary warning. If humans are "bound in fetters" by affliction, God is showing them "that they have behaved themselves proudly. He also opens their ears to instruction, and commands that they return from iniquity." Job should therefore accept his affliction gratefully, Elihu alleges, as a message from God that he ignores at his peril. Job had demanded that God provide him with an indictment, detailing his sins. According to Elihu, Job need only examine his sinful life to discover the source of his torment.

Once the righteous experience remedial suffering, they have a fateful choice: accept their affliction as God's merciful discipline, ask for forgiveness, and return to virtue, or reject God's summons and bear the fate of the wicked— untimely death, devoid of the insight that their suffering was intended to teach. Obviously wishing that Job be considered among the righteous sinners, Elihu presents the alternatives open to him: "If they listen and serve God they shall spend their days in prosperity and their years in pleasures. But if they do not listen, they shall perish by the sword; they shall die without knowledge." If righteous sinners repent, their prosperity will be restored. If they reject God's mercy and continue to sin, they will suffer the sword of divine judgment. The worst thing in life, Elihu implies, is not suffering, but failing to learn its lessons.

Instead of accepting affliction as salutary discipline, the incorrigibly wicked project their anger upon a just God: "Those who are godless in heart cherish anger. They do not cry for help when he binds them." With an apparent allusion to Job's loss of honor, Elihu avers that the godless die prematurely, "among the unclean." On the other hand, God delivers righteous sinners "by their affliction, and opens their ear in oppression." Elihu's message is that unless Job listens to God's call to repent, he will be condemned with the wicked. Instead of responding with angry blasphemy, Job must accept God's chastening recall to virtue. Addressing Job directly, Elihu explains: "Yes, he would have allured you out of distress, into a wide space, where there is no restriction. He is wooing you from the jaws of distress to the spacious place free from restriction. That which is set on your table would be full of fatness." Metaphors of spaciousness and tables laden with food are found in wisdom literature as expressions of God's redemptive action.[40] Elihu still fails to understand that Job does not wish his prosperity restored. He wants God to vindicate his integrity.

But Elihu does not want to hear Job defend his integrity. Desperate to convince Job of his guilt, Elihu's rhetoric reaches an angry crescendo. He accuses Job of self-righteousness, obsessively charging God with neglecting to judge the wicked: "You are full of the judgment of the wicked. Judgment and justice take hold of you." Elihu implies that Job is consumed by a sinful thirst for wealth and power that could never relieve Job's suffering: "Would your wealth sustain you in distress, or all the might of your strength?" Neither riches nor power can save Job from God's judgment. Elihu warns Job that his stubborn refusal to repent will lead only to his death: "Do not desire the night, when people are cut off in their place." For death can come suddenly in the night, foreclosing Job's final opportunity to restore his relationship with God. Continuing his offensive, Elihu warns Job to cease impugning God's justice and accept his affliction as merciful divine discipline: "Take heed, do not regard iniquity; for you have chosen this rather than affliction." According to Elihu, the unrepentant Job teeters on the brink of disaster.

Elihu now regales Job with a description of God's awesome omnipotence, which Job has already acknowledged. Elihu proclaims: "Behold, God is exalted in his power." Responding to Job's defiant resistance, Elihu inquires: "Who is a teacher like him?" God teaches through dreams and afflictions. Instead of accepting his calamity as a merciful discipline, Job maligns God, accusing him of misgoverning the world. Anticipating God's speeches from the whirlwind, Elihu believes that the magnificence of creation should teach Job not to question divine justice. Humans cannot hold the omnipotent God accountable: "Who has prescribed his way for him? Or who can say, 'You have committed unrighteousness?'" As absolute sovereign, God is subject to no higher law or power. Job's attempt to sue God is, therefore, a futile impious act of defiance. Rather than attacking Almighty God, Elihu exhorts, Job should "magnify his work, whereof men have sung. All men have looked on it. Man sees it afar off." Continuing his doxology, Elihu proclaims: "Behold, God is great, and we do not know him. The number of his years is unsearchable." No human can comprehend God's inscrutable ways; his eternal duration is beyond human reckoning. How can Job have the impudence to believe that he can sue God? Unless Job drops his litigation, he will suffer the miserable fate of the wicked.

Elihu believes that humans can perceive God's omnipotence and wisdom through his wondrous works. He proceeds to foreshadow God's upcoming speeches from the whirlwind by showing the Creator's providential meteorological activity. One of Elihu's important roles in the Book of Job, as we explained, is to point both backward and forward. Backward, as he reminds us of Job's early arguments, and forward, as he prepares the way for God's dramatic entrance. As Elihu speaks, he senses a gathering storm. God sends the rain essential to human survival: "He draws up the drops of water, which distill in rain from his vapor, which the skies pour down and which drop on man abundantly." Hearing a crash of thunder echo across the Uz sky, Elihu, Job and the three friends look upward. Elihu exclaims: "Can any understand the spreading of the clouds, and the thunder of his pavilion?" God directs the thunder and lightning, expressions of divine anger and judgment: "Behold, he spreads his light around him. He covers the bottom of the sea. For by these he judges the people. He covers his hands with the lightning, and commands it to strike its mark." Nature reflects God's providence, sustaining the righteous and vanquishing the wicked.

## Chapter 37  Elihu: Behold God's Awesome Majesty

THE CRASHING PEAL OF THUNDER heralds God's approach. As the tempest grows ever near, Elihu cannot contain himself, his heart racing as he hears God's thunder and sees his lightning flash. Elihu cries: "At this my heart trembles, and is moved out of its place." Forecasting God's appearance from the whirlwind, Elihu describes the coming ominous storm, preparing us for the imminent theophany. Storms were associated with theophanies, notably at Sinai, when God revealed himself to Moses and the Israelites.[41] The sudden onset of dark clouds, crashing thunder and lightning flashing across the sky were seen as manifestations of God's power, terrifying humans, threatening them with annihilation. The biblical scholar Walther Eichrodt explains the role of the thunderstorm in the Israelite religion: "From the earliest to the latest times the God who hastens both to judgment and to succor is envisaged in the thunderstorm, riding upon the storm-clouds as if in a chariot or on a charger, causing his voice to resound in the thunder, hurling lightning as his arrows or spears, shooting forth fire from heaven as his burning breath or tongue of flame. In the snorting of his anger he sends down the lashing rain; with his fist he smites in the hail or the shattering storm." [42]

As the storm gathers over the land of Uz, Elihu entreats Job and the friends to observe God's awesome majesty in nature. God's voice is a thunderous roar, symbolizing a power that no human dare challenge. Divine lightning precedes the deafening thunder clap. Elihu exhorts: "Hear, hear the noise of his voice, the sound that goes out of his mouth. He sends it out under the whole sky, and his lightning to the ends of the earth. After it a voice roars. He thunders with the voice of his majesty. He does not hold back anything when his voice is heard." The God who speaks from the heavens is unfathomable: "God thunders marvelously with his voice. He does great things, which we cannot comprehend." God is Lord of nature: "He says to the snow, 'fall on the earth;' likewise to the shower of rain." When God manifests in winter storms and torrential rains, humans as well as animals marvel as they seek shelter. He stops all people from labor, so they can marvel at his handiwork: "The animals take cover and remain in their dens." The storm gains force, as God unleashes fierce winds from heaven's chamber: "Out of its room comes the storm, and cold out of the north. The tempest comes out from its chamber, the cold from the driving winds." God's chilling winds, rain and snow cause everything to freeze: "By the breath of God, ice is given, and the width of the waters is frozen."

Rain clouds, permeated by God's lightning, cover the earth: "He loads the thick cloud with moisture. He spreads abroad the cloud of his lightning. It is turned around by his guidance, that he may do whatever he commands them on the surface of the habitable world." For Elihu and the ancient Israelites storms were viewed as instruments of God's providence and retributive justice: "Whether it is for correction, or for his land, or for loving kindness," Elihu declares, "God causes it to come."

Elihu remains hopeful that he can finally persuade Job to withdraw his lawsuit. For the last time, he exhorts Job to consider the power of God: "Listen to this, Job. Stand still and consider the wondrous works of God." With a series of rhetorical questions, foreshadowing God's speeches from the whirlwind, Elihu urges Job to listen to reason. To underscore Job's ignorance of God's wondrous works, Elihu interrogates sarcastically: "Do you know how God controls them, and causes the lightning of his cloud to shine? Do you know the workings of the clouds, the wondrous works of him who is perfect in knowledge?" Humans can observe the wonders of nature, but they are unable to comprehend how and why they work as they do. We have seen Elihu allege that because he speaks for God, he is "perfect in knowledge,"[43] the same words he now applies to God himself. Elihu explains that God controls the winter cold as well as the summer heat. As Job sits in his mourning sackcloth on the ash-heap, Elihu taunts: "You whose clothing is warm, when the earth is still by reason of the south wind, can you, with him, spread out the sky, which is strong as a cast metal mirror?" Can Job, like God, form the heavens as a great dome reflecting the sunlight like a mirror? Can Job generate the hot wind that blows over the desert of Arabia? Because Job lacks God's power, he cannot question God's justice.

Elihu addresses Job's lawsuit with bitter sarcasm. Job had boldly declared that if God produces the indictment he calls for, he would wear it as a badge of honor.[44] Elihu asks Job to consider whether mere humans, their minds dark to the secrets of the divine, could possibly arraign God: "Teach us what we shall tell him, for we cannot make our case by reason of darkness." How could a human possibly confront God in court? Elihu warns Job not to persist in demanding "I would speak" to God in person. This would be tantamount to suicide: "Should a man wish that he were swallowed up?" What Elihu does not know is that if Job were swallowed up, the outcome of the wager between the Satan and God could never be determined.

To impress upon Job the inaccessibility of God to humans, Elihu compares the deity to the sun: "Now men do not see the light which is bright in the skies, but the wind passes, and clears them." Once God's tempest subsides, and the clouds disperse, the sun, symbol of the divine, reappears. Unwittingly, Elihu has begun to raise the curtain for God's dramatic appearance from the whirlwind. Job should fear the resplendent God emerging from his abode in the north: "Out of the north comes golden splendor. With God is awesome majesty." This parallels the prophet Ezekiel's vision of God coming from the north in a windstorm with an immense cloud and flashing lightning.[45] Once the wind disperses the clouds, Elihu observes, no human can stare directly at the bright sun. Even more so, they cannot gaze at the radiance of God.

Elihu brings his legal brief to a close, reaffirming his principal contentions. God is both omnipotent and just. Contrary to Job's contention, God does not oppress the righteous: "We cannot reach the Almighty. He is exalted in power. In justice and great righteousness, he will not oppress. Therefore men revere him." With a final censure of the dying Job, Elihu alleges that God ignores the self-righteous who arrogantly presume to be "wise of heart." Elihu angrily rests his case. Will Job rescind his lawsuit against God?

**Yahweh Speaks to Job**

God to Job: "Will you condemn me that you may be justified?" Job 40:8

# YAHWEH SPEAKS FROM THE WHIRLWIND

## Chapter 38   God: Behold My Wisdom and Power

THE BOOK OF JOB NOW REACHES ITS MAJOR CLIMAX. After the lengthy dialogue between Job and his friends, and Elihu's defense of God, Job remains relentless. He will not withdraw his demand that God present him with an indictment and grant him a fair trial. Job is confident that his integrity will be publicly vindicated. Hearing Job malign his character and disparage his government of the world, God must respond. God's integrity has been challenged as never before. He has been silent during the dialogue between Job and the friends. Indeed, he has not spoken since his fateful exchange with the Satan in the Prologue God has heard Job disparage his character and management of the world. He has heard the friends defend him on the basis of the moribund doctrine of retribution. And he has listened as Elihu attempted to defend him by appealing to divine omnipotence and majesty. But Job remains adamant in affirming his innocence and defending his integrity.

The way the poet frames the dispute between Job and the friends, Job and God cannot both be right. If Job is right, God is wrong. His own integrity at stake, God must mount his own defense. Having been confined to a number of cameo appearances in the Hebrew Bible, God finally speaks, compelled by Job to break his silence. The Job poet might have intended God's delayed response not merely for dramatic effect, holding off the appearance of a principal character until the book reached a climactic moment. The poet might also have sought to emphasize that God hides his face from so many who suffer innocently. Many sufferers plead with God in vain.

The lengthy descriptions of God's power and wisdom given by the friends and Elihu have done nothing to pierce Job's spiritual armor. His oath of innocence, constituted a compelling challenge to God. According to the ancient legal procedure, unless Job is presented with evidence of his crimes, there is no case against him. If Job is vindicated, God would be guilty of punishing his righteous servant unjustly. God cannot reveal the cruel wager that he made with the Satan that began Job's innocent suffering. Were Job to learn the real cause, he might renounce God and die. God is in a quandary. Admitting his injustice to Job, would reveal a fatal flaw in God's character. Such an immoral God has no integrity.

God must intervene for another important reason. We recall the substance of the Satan's challenge in the Prologue. The Satan affirmed that Job's piety was merely rational self interest. Without God's hedge of protection, Job would curse him directly "to his face." The Satan is certain that Job would curse God while somehow in his presence. In the context of the Book of Job, there are different ways to curse God. First, one can curse God in one's mind or heart. The Prologue relates that Job regularly offered sacrifices on behalf of his sons on the mere chance that they "sinned and cursed God in their hearts." God can also be cursed with words. Despite his unjust suffering, the Job of the Prologue does not curse God; as the narrator declares, Job "did not sin with his lips."[1] But as time passed, Job had irreverent thoughts about God as he sat mourning with his friends. These irreverent thoughts grew into angry words, first in the form of his curse upon the day of his birth. Throughout the poetic dialogue, Job sins with his lips, cursing or blaspheming God again and again. As his rage intensified, Job's language became increasingly blasphemous, accusing God of being a malicious predator who laughs at the suffering of the innocent. We have noted that in the ancient world, texts were read aloud rather than silently. One can imagine the shock and terror of early audiences if they listened to a reading of the blasphemies of Job. Would listeners sympathize with Job? Would readers even dare to utter Job's blasphemies? For God hears everything. While Job curses God repeatedly, until now, he has not had an opportunity to do what the Satan said he would do: Curse God directly to his face.[2]

Cursing God "to his face" means more than cursing him in his absence, but explicitly in a direct face-to-face encounter. The Israelites did not believe that God literally had a face, and the poet would never commit the sacrilege of attempting to give him one. As Job had lamented, God is "not a man, as I am, that I should answer him, that we should come together in judgment."[3] Nevertheless, one might curse God in the midst of an encounter similar to that vouchsafed to other biblical figures. If Job were to curse God in such an encounter, he would indeed curse God "to his face." When Job defends himself against the friends, asking "would I lie to your face?" he refers to their immediate physical presence before him.[4] When Job challenges God's justice, he hopes to meet God in court, "to defend my ways to his face."[5] References to blaspheming God directly in the Hebrew Bible never quote the offending words.[6] To do so would be blasphemy itself. Conjecturing what Job might say to curse God to his face, it might be something to this effect: "I am your most righteous servant, whom you betrayed by afflicting me unjustly. You are neither just nor benevolent." Reversing his "may the name of the LORD be praised" of the Prologue, Job would declare: "May the name of the Lord be cursed." The ultimate irony is that God, sovereign of the universe, depends upon the response of Job. Should Job curse God in his presence, the Satan will be victorious and God's judgment of Job's integrity would be proven false. The Satan will have demonstrated his superior knowledge of human nature.

God will speak to Job directly, not through mediation such as in a vision or dream. God will grant Job's wish that they speak face-to-face. According to Deuteronomy, "there has not arisen a prophet in Israel like Moses, whom Yahweh knew face-to-face."[7] Job will be granted the same privilege as Moses. But God's words to Job will be the voice of reprimand. He will thrash Job with a torrent of more than seventy resounding rhetorical questions, hurled like divine thunderbolts. We have seen the importance of the rhetorical question in the Book of Job. The three friends and Elihu use the device to insinuate Job's guilt. Job uses the device to probe the mystery of his suffering and to defend his integrity. God will now use the device to magnify Job's ignorance and impotence. A rhetorical question often makes a statement in the guise of a question. Each question God poses to Job can only be met with a negative reply. God aims to show Job that his case is insignificant in light of the divine plan for the universe, of which Job is abysmally ignorant.

God will resort to the ploy of many advocates with a weak case. He creates a diversion. Instead of addressing the question of divine justice, God will rebuke Job for hubris. But Job's pursuit of justice is not generated by self-centered pride, but integrity. Robert Gordis correctly notes: "Whatever may have been the case with the Greeks, it was not an act of hubris, or insolence or arrogance, for a Hebrew to demand justice of his God: The patriarch Abraham, whose faith was exemplary, voiced the challenge, 'Shall not the Judge of all the earth do right?'"[8] Critics who accuse Job of sinful pride because he insists on his righteousness and challenges God's justice do so only by ignoring the Prologue and siding with the friends. Declared righteous by God himself in the Prologue, it is not pride but disillusionment with God, whom he trusted to be just, that motivates Job. A God reputed to be just who betrays a loyal servant should be challenged. A God who ignores the pleas of suffering humanity should be compelled to speak. It is easy for those who have never suffered to accuse rebelling victims like Job of egoism and self-pity. Such accusations merely compound the injustice.

As Elihu concludes his vivid depiction of the storm, God suddenly appears in its midst, similar to the *deus ex machina* of Greek tragedy. The narrator announces: "Then Yahweh answered Job out of the whirlwind." God seizes center stage in the drama. Job's provocations, including his oath of innocence, have compelled the hidden God, *deus absconditus,* to become the revealed God, *deus revelatus*. Job is vouchsafed a theophany as God reveals himself. God does not appear in human-like form, but only as a voice. Unlike the "gentle whisper" heard by Elijah at Mount Horeb, Job hears God's voice within a raging tempest. It is perhaps the most dramatic episode involving God in the entire Bible. When God appeared on Mt. Sinai amid thunder and lightning, the Israelites "trembled with fear." They implored Moses: "'Speak to us yourself and we will listen. But do not have God speak to us or we will die.'...The people remained at a distance, while Moses approached the thick darkness where God was."[9] Job is among the few individuals in the Hebrew Bible, including Abraham, Moses, Isaiah, and Jeremiah, to experience a theophany. But Job's experience of the Hebrew God is significant for two reasons. First, Job is not an Israelite, but a Gentile; and second, God reveals more of his character than ever before or later in Hebrew scripture. The God who addresses Job directly is Yahweh, God of Israel who admitted that he afflicted Job "without any reason."[10]

The poetry placed in the mouth of God, startling in its beautiful imagery, surpasses any other in the Hebrew Bible. As Robert Alter observes, "With God's speech as the climax of the book, the Job poet takes a risk that only a supreme artist confident in his genius could do. He had already created for Job the most extraordinarily powerful poetry to express Job's intolerable anguish and his anger against God. Now, when God finally speaks, the poet fashions for Him still greater poetry which thus becomes a poetic manifestation of God's transcendent power."[11] Despite their beauty, God's speeches lack the honesty, the passion and, shall we say, the humanity of those of Job. The words fashioned by the poet are not literally God's words, but the product of the poet's genius. Because no human can resolve the mystery of innocent suffering, we cannot expect the Job poet to do so. Creating God's speeches was the poet's greatest challenge. Rather than provide a definitive answer to suffering, the poet chose to compose speeches that, while unsurpassed in the Bible for their beauty, are necessarily ambiguous.

Yet the ambiguity still haunts us. Instead of having God give an unequivocal answer, the poet summons us to form our own conclusions on the issues of innocent suffering and the nature of God.

From the whirlwind, God begins by rebuking Job: "Who is this who darkens counsel by words without knowledge?" God knows well that it is Job! Had Job the strength to speak from his heart, he might have answered: "It is I, Job, a human being, created in your image and endowed with dignity and worth, your devoted servant whom you afflict unjustly." According to the Oxford English Dictionary, "counsel" was early defined as a private or secret design or purpose. God's ways are secret. Although not stated in the text, we assume that the three friends and Elihu are present, listening in terror as God speaks directly to Job. God accuses Job of ignorance, darkening the divine purpose unfathomable to humans. Job lamented that the universe lacks a coherent moral purpose and that God is neither just nor benevolent. God aims to reprove Job for his ignorance and compel him to rescind his lawsuit. In several speeches, Job claimed knowledge about himself and God. Job insisted that God knows that he is not wicked.[12] Job alleged that God hid in his heart a sinister plan to trap him in sin.[13] Job claimed to know that he is righteous and that God has treated him unjustly.[14] Job knew that the friends argued falsely on God's behalf.[15] Job affirmed that he knows that he will ultimately be vindicated. In each instance, Job is correct. He knows the truth of his innocence, and so does God. Cruelly, God will ignore Job's knowledge of the truth, focusing instead on what is beyond human comprehension: the complexity of the universe.

Taking the offensive, God throws down the gauntlet, challenging the heroic Job to combat: "Brace yourself like a man," he taunts. Another popular rendition is: "Gird up your loins like a man," referring to tucking the ends of one's robe into a belt, allowing for freedom of movement for running, fighting, or wrestling.[16] This wrestling was also a court procedure in ancient Israel, the phrase "girding one's loins" used in a legal sense. The dispute was decided in favor of the victorious wrestler.[17] With God's challenge to Job, demanding that he gird up his loins, the poet depicts an absurd image. For the duration of the dialogue, Job has been wrestling with a hidden God. Ironically, God now wants to wrestle with Job. One imagines a physical battle between Titans. A ninth-century Byzantine illuminator at Saint John Monastery, Patmos depicted Job tightening his belt as he prepares to wrestle with God.[18] But the wrestling will obviously not be physical, but a challenge to Job's knowledge and ability.

There could be no greater mismatch, the dying Job against the Almighty deity. The absurd image reveals God as an unsympathetic cosmic tormentor. God treats Job not as a frail human, but like a competing deity challenging his sway over the universe. We recall Job's early lament to God: "Am I a sea, or a sea monster, that you put a guard over me."[19] For Job to answer God's questions, he must have the wisdom and power of a deity. The Hebrew God is a jealous God, a rival of the many pagan gods. Issuing the commandments to the Israelites on Mount Sinai, God declared, "I am the Lord your God....You shall have no other gods before me."[20] God speaks through his prophet, the second Isaiah: "Is there a God besides me? Indeed there is not."[21] Yet Job's speeches question God's integrity and challenge divine authority.

Defiant and courageous, Job sought relentlessly to interrogate God, "let the Almighty answer me."[22] Job pleaded with God for a trial, crying: "Call, and I will answer; or let me speak, and you answer me."[23] Of the two options offered by Job, God chooses the former. Adopting Job's legal language, God seizes the role of the accusing plaintiff and summons Job to respond: "I will question you," God commands, "then you answer me." God does not come with the indictment Job had demanded. No list of sins will be provided. Nor will God address Job's innocent suffering. If anyone obscures God's plans, it is God himself, not Job. God will not debate with Job, but bludgeon him with rhetorical questions. God responds as if it is beneath his dignity to explain why he permits innocent suffering and submit himself to cross-examination by a human.

The emaciated Job will be interrogated as if he is on the witness stand in the divine court instead of sitting on the ash-heap. Throughout his two speeches, spanning four chapters, God never condescends to mention Job's name, the object of his tirades. Essentially, God will ask Job: Can you do what I have done? Do you understand what I understand? Have you been where I have been? But what God asserts about himself, no human would deny. Indeed, throughout his speeches Job affirmed God's superior power and wisdom in creating the cosmos. Moreover, despite God's rebuke, Job never claimed to possess superior knowledge. What he did know conformed to the wisdom teaching that a just God rewards the virtuous and punishes the wicked.

God begins with cosmogony. According to ancient Near Eastern thinking, the world comprises three levels: the heavens, the earth, and the underworld. In resounding poetic cadences, God challenges Job's knowledge of cosmogony, taking him on a journey through his vast creation, reflecting providential design. God depicts the origin of the earth, a majestic display of his creative wisdom. He asks Job sarcastically: "Where were you when I laid the foundations of the earth? Declare, if you have understanding." Comparing himself to a master builder and his creation of the earth to constructing a magnificent building, God continues his sarcasm: "Who determined its measures, if you know? Who stretched the [measuring] line on it? Whereupon were its foundations fastened? Or who laid its cornerstone, when the morning stars sang together, and all the sons of God [angels] shouted for joy?" God was the earth's designer, surveyor and builder. The earth was revered as God's temple, eliciting a chorus of celebration from the animated stars and the heavenly host of angels, praising God as the Creator. Magnificent human constructions later drew a similar response. The laying of the foundation of the Second Temple in Jerusalem was greeted by joyous shouts, festive music and choirs singing the praise of God.[24]

When the Temple of Solomon was completed, singers, accompanied by musicians, raised their voices honoring God.[25] If such edifices constructed by humans deserve celebration, how much more does God's construction of the earth. Everything in creation proceeds according to a master plan incomprehensible to humans. Without knowledge of how the earth was created, Job cannot challenge God's plans.

From the creation of the earth, God transitions to the origin of the sea, tossing another derisive rhetorical question at Job: "Who shut up the sea with doors, when it broke out of the womb, when I made clouds its garment, and wrapped it in thick darkness, marked out for it my bound, set bars and doors, and said, 'Here you may come, but no further. Here you proud waves shall be stayed?'" God echoes Genesis, when, on the second day of creation, he declared: "Let the waters under the sky be gathered together in one place, and let the dry ground appear."[26] With beautiful imagery, God compares the birth of the sea out of the void to the birth of a child, the Creator as midwife and the clouds serving as its clothing, covering it tenderly in darkness. God also separated the sea from the land, established its limits, the shores and cliffs, and commanded when its waves must break. In ancient Near Eastern mythology, the sea was personified as the primeval chaos monster that God overcame during the creation. Job would obviously reply to God's rhetorical question that he lacks the power to control the chaotic sea.

From the creation of the earth and sea, God asks Job whether he can command the day to follow the night. Job had seen the sun rise in the morning, but he lacks God's power to summon the morning light. According to Genesis, God said: "'Let there be light,' and there was light. God saw that the light was good, and he separated the light from the darkness. God called the light 'day' and darkness he called 'night.'"[27] In ancient times, without the knowledge of science, people believed that God spoke the word for the miracle of each day to come into existence. God mocks Job by reminding him constantly that he lacks the power to do what only an omnipotent being can do. He pounds Job with another sardonic rhetorical question: "Have you ever commanded the morning in your days, and caused the dawn to know its place; that it might take hold of the ends of the earth, and shake the wicked out if it?" The image of the dawn taking the earth by the edges is that of the morning light stretching out across the earth, covering it like a blanket or garment. Hidden during the night, with the coming of dawn, the earth is "changed as clay under the seal," and things stand out like a multi-colored garment. Daylight exposes evildoers—murderers, robbers, and adulterers—who rely on the cover of night darkness to commit their crimes. God is asking Job whether he is capable of controlling the wicked. Significantly, God does not say that the wicked are destroyed; they are merely limited and controlled, like the chaotic sea. Although God tells Job that the wicked are exposed and hindered, he evades Job's complaint that they too often prosper.

God continues to highlight Job's vast ignorance. God rules the entire universe—including the earth and the stars, the seas and the underworld. He asks Job to consider the primordial ocean, the source of the sea. Does he know the depths of the sea? "Have you entered into the springs of the sea? Or have you walked in the recesses of the deep?" Going further, God asks Job whether he has seen the depths of the underworld, beneath the earth. Has Job experienced death? "Have the gates of death been revealed to you? Have you seen the gates of the shadow of death?" In Babylonian myth, Ishtar, goddess of love and war, descended to the underworld, passing through its gates, and returned successfully. If Job could journey to Sheol while alive, he would see the gates through which the spirits of the dead pass, never to return to this life. Of course, Job has not visited the underworld. Unlike Ishtar, he has not passed through its gates. God's questions about the underworld are poignantly ironic since Job, his festering skin rotting away, seemed to be at death's gate. Indeed, the specter of death haunted him from the beginning of his terrible ordeal.

Directing attention again to the earth, God professes that Job's vision is so limited that he cannot possibly fathom its size: "Have you comprehended the earth in its width?" It is obvious that Job, or any human, could not possibly have this knowledge. Unlike God, he could not survey the earth, observing all its aspects. Job has not explored the unfathomable waters or seen and returned from the abode of the dead. Nor can he grasp the magnitude of the entire earth. Yet God persists in his mockery: "Declare, if you know it all." God asks Job if he can comprehend the mystery of light and darkness: "What is the way to the dwelling of light? As for darkness, where is its place, that you should take it to its bound, that you should discern the paths to its house?" Only one able to comprehend such mysteries can guide them to the place where they perform their work. Only if Job existed at the time of creation and possessed God's knowledge, could he comprehend the size of the earth. With biting irony God declares: "Surely you know, for you were born then, and the number of your days is great!"

God now directs Job's focus from cosmogony to meteorology. The ancients believed that God kept the snow and hail in warehouses, ready to be emptied at his will, especially as instruments of judgment. God interrogates Job: "Have you entered the treasuries of the snow, or have you seen the treasuries of the hail, which I have reserved against the time of trouble, against the day of battle and war?" Scripture relates that God frequently used hail to quell Israel's enemies. In the Book of Exodus, hail was the seventh plague God sent against the Egyptians to compel the Pharaoh to release God's people from bondage.[28] God also hurled a destructive shower of hailstones to enable the Israelites to defeat the Canaanites and conquer the Promised Land.[29]

Of course, Job is not aware of the warehouses of snow and hail. Nor does he know the origins of rain, lightning and the east wind. God continues his barrage of rhetorical questions: "By what way is the lightning distributed, or the east wind scattered on the earth? Who has cut a channel for the flood water, or the path for the thunderstorm; to cause it to rain on a land where no man is; on the wilderness, in which there is no man; to satisfy the waste and desolate ground, to cause the tender grass to grow?" God sends life-supporting rain even to barren deserts, uninhabited by human beings to provide food for wild animals. Even natural phenomena not directly related to humans have a place in divine providence. Job does not have knowledge of the elements: "Does the rain have a father? Who fathers the drops of dew? Out of whose womb came the ice? The gray frost of the sky, who has given birth to it? The waters become hard like stone, when the surface of the deep is frozen." Of course, God is the source of all. He is both the begetting father and birthing mother to the wondrous meteorological phenomena.

Passing briefly from meteorology to cosmology, God bids Job to gaze at the stars in the heavens, made on the fourth day of creation. He commands Job to consider the magnificent constellations of stars that spangle the heavens, from the Pleiades and Orion to the Great Bear or Big Dipper and the Little Bear or Little Dipper. Has Job knowledge of astronomy? Can he control celestial phenomena? Again, the answer is no. Humans cannot comprehend God's laws regulating the heavenly bodies and the seasons: "Can you bind the cluster of the Pleiades, or loosen the cords of Orion? Can you lead the constellations out in their season? Can you guide the Bear with its cubs? Do you know the laws of the heavens?" No. Job obviously has neither the ability nor the understanding to control the heavens. Under God's management, the stars were believed to influence earthly affairs. God asks Job whether he can establish heaven's "dominion over the earth." God wants Job to recognize that, lacking divine knowledge and power, he cannot challenge divine justice.

Continuing to display the splendor of his creation, God returns to meteorology and asks Job: "Can you lift your voice to the clouds, that abundance of waters may cover you? Can you send out lightnings, that they may go? Do they report to you, 'Here we are?' " According to Genesis, God's control of the rain enabled him to wipe out the entire world except Noah and the inhabitants of the ark during the Great Flood. Humans marvel at the awesome power of nature, but lack the wisdom to comprehend its mysteries. God asks Job: "Who has put wisdom in the inward parts," the secret workings of nature? "Who has given understanding to the mind?" Humans cannot grasp the workings of nature: "Who can number the clouds by wisdom? Who can pour out the bottles of the sky," watering the parched earth after a drought, "when the dust runs into a mass, and the clods of earth stick together?"

Having taken Job on an imaginary tour of the heavens, the earth, and the underworld, God proceeds to show his power over the animal kingdom. He presents a menagerie of wild animals for Job to consider. God continues to follow the question format, mocking Job: "Do you know?" "Can you?" In each case, Job must plead either ignorance or impotence.  God supplies animals, such as the fierce lion and the scavenging raven, with the skill to hunt prey to eat: "Can you hunt the prey for the lioness," God asks Job, "or satisfy the appetite of the young lions, when they crouch in their dens, and lie in wait in the thicket? Who provides for the raven his prey, when his young ones cry to God, and wander for lack of food?" Again, Job must plead impotence. But the image recalls Job's lament that God stalked him like a predatory lion. That both the lion and the raven are predators implies that God's providence has established an amoral natural order, as animals struggle to survive in a world divided between predator and prey. Ironically, God asserts that he responds to the cries of hungry young ravens. Yet Job had lamented that God neglects the cries of the innocent hungry humans.

## Chapter 39   God: Behold My Animal Creation

AFTER THE LION AND THE RAVEN, God moves to the wild mountain goat and the doe. The Prologue indicates that Job had owned flocks. He knew something about the lives of domesticated animals. But he is totally ignorant of their wild counterparts: "Do you know the time when the mountain goats give birth? Do you watch when the doe bears fawns? Can you number the months that they fulfill? Do you know the time when they give birth?" Like most people of his day, Job was unfamiliar with the intimate details of how these animals reproduce and bear their young. He knew nothing of their period of gestation or how the mothers delivered their offspring. But the mysteries of nature fulfill a divine plan. Under God's providential eye, nature provides for the renewal of life. God explains: "They bow themselves, they bear their young. They end their labor pains. Their young ones become strong. They grow up in the open field. They go out, and do not return again." After being properly nurtured, the young instinctively leave home to continue the life cycle independent of human beings. God wishes to show Job that he is ignorant of how and why basic animal behavior is established by divine providence. Nature functions well without human assistance or interference.

Expanding his zoological picture gallery, God asks Job to consider the freedom of the wild donkey: "Who has set the wild donkey free? Who has loosened the bonds of the swift donkey, whose home I have made the wilderness, and the salt land his dwelling place?" Only God could create the wild donkey with its freedom and habitat. Unlike his domesticated counterpart, a beast of burden, the wild donkey lives free from human domination, happy to roam the desolate lands that are its home. Away from the bustling town, the wild donkey does not have to listen to a human driver, whipping and shouting commands to carry heavy loads: "It scorns the tumult of the city, neither does he hear the shouting of the driver. The range of the mountains is his pasture. He searches after every green thing." But Job already knows that wild animals can survive happily without human domination.

God continues by referring to the wild ox, known for its prodigious strength. God submits a series of rapid rhetorical questions, each with the implied emphatic "No" for an answer: "Will the wild ox be content to serve you? Will he stay by your feeding trough?" Even if Job could manage to secure a wild ox, it would refuse to serve him: "Can you hold the wild ox in the furrow with his harness? Will he till the valleys after you? Will you trust him because his strength is great? Or will you leave to him your labor? Will you confide in him, that he will bring home your seed, and gather the grain of your threshing floor?" Unlike the domesticated ox, castrated to make it more docile, the wild ox cannot be controlled by humans. Unlike its tame equivalent, the unruly wild ox cannot be harnessed to a plow or a cart. It cannot be constrained in a stall to be fed at night according to human schedule. Job lacks, therefore, the power to subject the wild ox to his will.

The next vignette features the ostrich, an odd looking gangly bird that has wings but cannot fly: "The wings of the ostrich wave proudly; but are they the feathers and plumage of love?" To the ancients, the ostrich seemed to not properly care for its young, leaving them exposed to predators. Unable to fly like other birds, the ostrich "leaves her eggs on the earth, warms them in the dust, and forgets that the foot may crush them or that wild animals may trample them." According to folklore, the ostrich is unaware of consequences: "She deals harshly with her young ones, as if they were not hers. Though her labor is in vain, she is without fear." If her offspring die, she seems unmoved by the fact that her efforts to reproduce have been wasted. The ostrich behaves this way because "God has deprived her of wisdom, neither has he imparted to her understanding." Nevertheless, although unfathomable to humans, the inane ostrich is part of God's plan. The creator has apparently compensated the ostrich for its lack of sense by making it one of the swiftest animals, faster than a horse: "When she lifts herself on high, she scorns the horse and his rider."

Now God provides a magnificent vignette of the war horse, deservedly hailed as one of the most beautiful sections of the Book of Job. Unlike the other animals in God's tour, the war horse is domesticated, trained for battle. Its strength, speed and courage make it arguably the most noble of animals. But the awesome war horse is never completely under human control. Returning to the question format, God asks Job if he could create such a majestic creature. Consider the horse as it readies for charge in battle. A cavalryman upon it, armed with bow and arrows, spear and lance. The neighing horse leaps up with the man in the saddle. The horse strikes the earth with his front hooves in anticipation of the attack. The trumpet signals the charge, the commanders shout orders, and the fearless horse is unleashed, galloping so fast that it seems to devour the ground. All this is beautifully portrayed by the poet: "Have you given the horse might? Have you clothed his neck with a quivering mane? Have you made him to leap as a locust? The glory of his snorting is awesome. He paws in the valley, and rejoices in his strength. He goes out to meet the armed men. He mocks at fear and is not dismayed. Neither does he turn back from the sword. The quiver rattles against him, the flashing spear and the javelin. He eats up the ground with fierceness and rage. Neither does he stand still at the sound of the trumpet. As often as the trumpet sounds he snorts, 'Aha!' He smells the battle afar off, the thunder of the captains, and the shouting."

God's final two vignettes feature the hawk and the eagle, birds of prey. God inquires whether Job has instilled wisdom in these birds: "Is it by your wisdom that the hawk soars, and stretches her wings toward the south? Is it at your command that the eagle mounts up, and makes his nest on high? On the cliff he dwells, and makes his home on the point of the cliff and the stronghold." Flying through the sky, the eagle spots its prey from a great distance, swooping down for the kill. And after a battle, the unburied bodies of the human dead become the eagle's food: "His young ones also suck up blood. Where the slain are, there he is." God has instilled in all animals their patterns of behavior and their instincts to survive. Violence and bloodshed are integral to God's creation. While the animals presented to Job, except for the horse, were independent and uncontrolled by human beings, this is not true today. We know much more about the animal kingdom than a person in Job's time. Nevertheless, our dominion over the earth has taken on grotesque proportions. In the name of human progress, the habitats of wild animals are being destroyed, threatening many with extinction.

Just as Job lacks the ability to understand the mysteries of the heavens, the earth, and the underworld, he lacks the ability to understand or control nature. According to Genesis, humans are given dominion over the animal kingdom, created to serve them.[30] God now tells Job that there are important aspects of creation beyond human control. But Job never denied God's power. Nor did he claim to know the secrets of cosmogony, astronomy, meteorology, and the animal world. The principal message of God's speeches is that everything conforms to the divine plan. This seems to imply that even innocent suffering must be part of God's providence.

## Chapter 40   Job: How Can I Answer God?

CONFIDENT THAT HIS GRANDIOSE DISPLAY of the universe and his pageant of animals have humbled Job, God speaks directly to him, again without using his name: "Shall he who argues contend with the Almighty?" Job is challenged to reply. Does he dare continue his lawsuit, accusing God of injustice? We recall Job's challenge to God: "Let the Almighty answer me. Let the accuser write my indictment!"[31] But God will not allow his judgment to be questioned. Job, not God, must defend himself: "He who argues with God, let him answer."

Job now has his opportunity to respond to God. What words could the poet possibly place in the mouth of Job, finally face-to-face with God? Job never doubted his relative unimportance in the vast universe. But how can a human respond to a theophany, the voice of God rebuking him? Job is reeling from God's barrage of accusatory rhetorical questions. Each question must have seemed like crashing peals of thunder. Whereas God "spoke to Moses face-to-face, as a man speaks to his friend,"[32] God speaks to Job as a threatening adversary. Instead of addressing Job's suffering, God pounds his chest in triumph, crushing Job with his stentorian harangue. In his darkest hour, Job had anticipated his tongue-tied reaction: "Though I were righteous, I would not answer him....For he breaks me with a storm."[33] Is this the God of justice that Job believed in all his life prior to his calamity? Or is this a God of sheer power, determined to vanquish the slightest challenge to his authority? Perhaps God waits with apprehension for Job's reaction. God has not given him a reason not to curse him. But if Job does curse him, now that they are face-to-face, what would be the consequence? The Satan would win the challenge presented in the Prologue, and God would be compelled to admit that no human loves him out of pure disinterested faith. Has God done anything to merit such faith from Job?

In an early optimistic mood, Job expressed confidence that if God granted him a hearing, his mouth would be filled with arguments. He was certain that God would not overwhelm him with his power. God would listen to a righteous man reason with him.[34] But God will not allow the righteous Job to argue his case before him. God will not allow his actions to be scrutinized by humans. While Job had grown increasingly heroic, vowing to confront God like a prince,[35] the reality is that he is a frail human, exhausted by his torment. He has experienced God as the *mysterium tremendum*. The theologian Rudolf Otto explains that God is an incomprehensible mystery whose awesome power provokes visceral terror.[36] One can approach such a deity only with fear and trembling. Silence is the only possible response. According to the tenth century Talmudic scholar, Saadya Gaon, Job's reply to God is equivocal: "When one interlocutor says to his partner, 'I can't answer you,' it may mean that he acquiesces in the other's position, equivalent to 'I can't gainsay the truth'; or it may mean he feels overborne by his partner, equivalent to 'How can I answer you when you have the upper hand?'"[37] Job is simply overpowered.

Bludgeoned by God's questions, Job submits before the numinous: "I am of small account. What shall I answer you? I lay my hand on my mouth." Since God considers him insignificant, no response from Job could satisfy him. But, ironically, Job is far from insignificant, for God has staked his honor on Job's faith. Job need not say anything more. He has submitted his solemn oath of innocence. His case against God complete, Job states emphatically: "I will proceed no further." Despite God's display of power, Job does not withdraw his lawsuit. The burden is upon God to present Job with the sins that justify his suffering. Job does not repent of any sin. Nor does he retract any words he uttered in defense of his integrity, words that he wished to have carved in stone for posterity. Above all, Job does not curse God to his face. But neither does he praise him.

Otto attempts to shed light on the silence of a human before the awesome majesty of God: "The truly 'mysterious' object is beyond our apprehension and comprehension, not only because our knowledge has certain irremovable limits, but because in it we come upon something inherently 'wholly other,' whose kind and character are incommensurable with our own, and before which we therefore recoil in a wonder that strikes us chill and numb."[38] Otto's description of the terrifying effect of experiencing God might explain Job's reluctance to speak. Overwhelmed by God, Job responds like any human. But the heroic Job does not capitulate. Neither will the poet allow Job to curse God directly to his face. Job's sole concern is not to retaliate against his divine abuser, but to vindicate his integrity. Besides, no curse could possibly harm God. The poet saw the need for a revised theology, but he did not wish to deliver a devastating blow to Israelite monotheism.

While conceding the obvious—his smallness compared to God—Job, sick and dying, sitting on the ash-heap, adheres to his integrity. Not even God can deny Job's integrity. He never claimed to be God's equal. He had affirmed God's omniscience and omnipotence. Job's creaturely status and lack of knowledge notwithstanding, he believes that he is still entitled to justice. While he had parodied the Eighth Psalm, he never repudiated its essential message: Although humans might seem insignificant compared to the majesty of the cosmos, God instilled them with dignity, making them "a little lower than the angels."[39] According to Genesis, humans are God's greatest creation. Yet God does not deign to mention the creation of humanity in his speech to Job.

## Chapter 40:6-14   God: How Dare Job Challenge My Justice?

DETERMINED TO DEMOLISH ALL TRACE OF RESISTANCE, God makes a second challenge to Job. The narrator again announces, "Yahweh answered Job out of the whirlwind." The second challenge repeats the words of the first: "Brace yourself like a man. I will question you, and you will answer me." God will not accept Job's noncommittal laconic reply. He wants Job's abject surrender. But could God continue to avoid the question of justice by re-directing Job's attention to the cosmos at large? Once again, Job is placed in the dock to be interrogated with a second battery of formidable rhetorical questions. God will put Job to the test as never before. Job's silence elicits another torrent of words from God.

God begins by acknowledging the issue raised by Job's lawsuit. After many verses of self-celebration, God finally refers to justice: "Will you even annul my judgment? Will you condemn me, that you may be justified?" Here lies the central conflict between Job and God, the conflict that drives the entire book. God is accusing Job of making his integrity more important than piety. Job's conscience had placed him in a dilemma: he could not affirm his integrity without accusing God of injustice. Bildad accused Job of wanting the moral order overturned so that he could escape divine justice.[40] In truth, God overturned the moral order when he afflicted Job unjustly. Job's visionary hope is that God will restore the moral order, bringing justice not only to himself but to countless innocent sufferers. God's accusatory questions echo the friends' belief that Job is self-righteous. God takes the side of the friends by denying that Job has the right to challenge him. According to the narrator, the friends stopped speaking to Job, "because he was righteous in his own eyes," and Elihu became infuriated with him because he "justified himself rather than God."[41]

God and Job are in opposing positions. In a lawsuit, the innocence of one party means the guilt of the other. As we have noted, if Job is innocent, God is unjust. If God is just, Job is not innocent, and deserves his suffering. Could Job's integrity be affirmed without denying God's integrity? As Job cried to his friends, "God has subverted me;" God has "taken away my right."[42] No more needed to be said. From the Prologue, we know that God is guilty and Job is innocent. Because God allowed the deaths of Job's ten children for no reason, God is guilty of injustice. Because God allowed Job's flocks to be stolen and his shepherds to be killed for no reason, God is guilty of injustice. Because God afflicted Job physically with painful sores from head to foot for no reason, God is guilty of injustice. The God who reveals himself in the Prologue to be the cause of such innocent suffering is neither good nor just.

Still on the offensive, God challenges Job by sarcastically inviting him to try to manage the universe. Having displayed his wisdom, God celebrates his infinite power. Can Job do what God does? Job is again battered with rhetorical questions, calling for the obvious negative replies: "Do you have an arm like God? Can you thunder with a voice like him?" To manage the universe, Job would have to possess God's infinite power. Can Job, like God, threaten with his thunder? Could Job, like Prometheus, dare attempt to usurp the role of a god? God mockingly invites Job to adorn himself with the regalia of the King of the universe: "Deck yourself with excellency and dignity. Array yourself with honor and majesty." Job has denounced God for permitting the wicked to prosper. God challenges the sick and dying Job to take over the moral government of the universe. Let Job destroy the wicked, since he thinks he is so wise. Let Job apply the retributive justice that is so important to him:

"Pour out the fury of your anger. Look at everyone who is proud, and bring him low. Crush the wicked in their place." Is God alluding to Job when he challenges him to vanquish the proud? Let Job's wrath destroy the proud and the wicked. "Hide them in the dust together. Bind their faces" in the grave below. If Job, assuming the reins of world government, could do all this, which God himself apparently has been unable to do completely, he will have earned God's admiration: "Then I myself will admit to you," God continues derisively, "that your own right hand can save you." If Job can vanquish the wicked, he will demonstrate that he has no need of God, for he can save himself. Having overthrown God, Job can then take over the moral management of the universe. If Job cannot do everything that God can do, he must submit to divine power and wisdom. Ironically, if Job could vanquish the proud and the wicked, he would be the just divinity that Yahweh is not.

## Chapter 40:15-24   God: Behold My Behemoth

CONTINUING HIS VERBAL ASSAULT, God proceeds to present a horror show featuring two beasts that Job is challenged to conquer: Behemoth and Leviathan. Each is an imaginary hybrid, combining the characteristics of a real animal with those of a mythological monster to make it appear more awesome. The absurdity is patent. God is oblivious to the fact that even if he wanted to, the dying Job is in no position to meet the divine challenges. Nevertheless, God has Job on the rack and will not relent until his victim surrenders. Both Behemoth and Leviathan, depicted by God in grandiloquent language, symbolize the evil and chaos that are part of the fabric of the world. Created by God himself, the beasts represent the deity's dark side. God can control them, but he cannot annihilate them without destroying a fundamental part of his nature. Behemoth is the most formidable land monster; Leviathan the most formidable sea monster. The implication is that for Job to manage the world morally better than the Creator, he would have to master both Behemoth and Leviathan.

Behemoth, derived from the Hebrew word for "beast," is traditionally associated with the enormous hippopotamus. But Behemoth is much more than a hippopotamus; he is similar to a prehistoric dinosaur. God allows Job to take a glimpse: "See now, Behemoth, which I made as well as you." God paints a loving portrait of Behemoth: "He eats grass as an ox.   Look now, his strength is in his thighs. His force is in the muscles of his belly. He moves his tail like a cedar. The sinews of his thighs are knit together. His bones are like tubes of brass. His limbs are like bars of iron." Job has never seen such a powerful and fearsome monster. Only God, its creator, can slay Behemoth, whose power and majesty are unrivalled among land creatures: "He is the chief of the ways of God." Only God could draw his sword and vanquish him. The herbivorous Behemoth feeds on plants, leaving wildlife unmolested: "The mountains produce food for him, where all the animals of the field play." He lurks in the swamp by rivers, "under the lotus trees, in the covert of the reed, and the marsh. The lotuses cover him with their shade. The willows of the brook surround him." Behemoth is such a powerful swimmer that "if a river overflows, he does not tremble. He is confident, though the Jordan swells even to his mouth." Behemoth is difficult to capture while submerged, its eyes and nose alone above the water: "Shall any take him when he is on the watch, or pierce through his nose with a snare?" God wants Job to understand that humans lack the power to capture such a monster as Behemoth. Since Job cannot control Behemoth, God's masterful creation, he dare not challenge God, infinitely more awesome and powerful than the beast.

## Chapter 41   God: Behold My Leviathan

NEXT IN GOD'S EXHIBIT OF HORRORS is Leviathan, a giant sea monster, traditionally associated with the crocodile of the Nile River. As with Behemoth, Leviathan's characteristics are mythically enhanced to make it even more formidable. Although God does not explicitly say that he created Leviathan, his speech implies that he did. According to the Psalmist, God filled the sea with innumerable creatures, including "Leviathan, whom you formed to play there."[43] Canaanite mythology depicts Leviathan as a giant sea dragon that personified primeval chaos. The Psalmist boasted that God "broke the heads of Leviathan in pieces. You gave him as food to people and desert creatures."[44] The first Isaiah prophesized that in the future God will deliver Israel by slaying with his sword the serpent Leviathan, monster of the sea.[45]

God's portrait of Leviathan is meant to be even more terrifying than Behemoth. God unleashes another round of rhetorical questions to show Job that Leviathan is so strong that all attempts by humans to capture it are futile: "Can you draw out Leviathan with a fish hook," God taunts Job, "or press down his tongue with a cord? Can you put a rope into his nose, or pierce his jaw through with a hook?" Only a fool would use such feeble implements to try to capture the indomitable Leviathan. God's next questions present a ridiculous scenario of what would happen if Job were to do the impossible and subdue Leviathan. Could Job imagine Leviathan begging for his life, using flattery to obtain its release, becoming a domesticated pet in Job's household, or agreeing to a life of perpetual servitude? "Will he make many petitions to you, or will he speak soft words to you? Will he make a covenant with you that you should take him for a servant forever? Will you play with him as with a bird? Or will you bind him for your girls?" Will traders barter for Leviathan, slicing him up "among the merchants?" These absurd questions obviously call for negative replies.

Having demeaned Job, God returns to the theme of the impossibility of any human capturing the invincible Leviathan. We recall Job's early desperate wish that Leviathan be roused to wipe the day of his birth from creation.[46] God interrogates his adversary: "Can you fill his skin with barbed irons, or his head with fish spears?" Leviathan is too large and powerful to succumb to such feeble weapons. Any person attempting the impossible will remember the struggle and "do so no more." Any hope of overcoming Leviathan is in vain: "Will not one be cast down even at the sight of him? None is so fierce that he dare stir him up." The awesome Leviathan attracted the literary imagination. Indeed, Herman Melville found in Leviathan the inspiration for his great white whale Moby Dick. As Melville's Ishmael declares: "Who wrote the first account of our Leviathan? Who but mighty Job!"[47] The monomaniacal Captain Ahab, for whom Moby Dick represents cosmic evil, perishes while trying to destroy it with a harpoon. Leviathan could easily crush Job.

God now arrives at the central subject. From the outset his aim is to compel Job to drop his lawsuit. No respectable God could permit a creature to accuse him in court. Unless Job is silenced, God might have to admit that he is not just and that Job suffers innocently. Job's evasive first response to the survey of the wonders of creation disturbed God. Shifting tactics, God presented Job with two ferocious beasts to intimidate him into submission. God's meaning is clear. Challenging him is more dangerous than rousing the fierce Leviathan. If Job cannot overcome Leviathan, jeers God, "who then is he who can stand before me?" How dare Job believe he can stand up to God in court? How dare Job presume that God owes him justice? "Who has first given to me, that I should repay him? Everything under the heavens is mine." Because all creation belongs to God, he does what he wishes, free from any obligation to humans. Hence, God is not bound by any covenant to reward the virtuous and punish the wicked.

If Job still hoped to present his claim against God, he now realizes the truth, confirming what he feared from the beginning. God claims sovereign immunity from prosecution. As ruler of the universe, he cannot be held responsible by humans. Because Job cannot conquer Behemoth or Leviathan, he cannot sue God for injustice. Nor can God be subject to a mediator. We have seen that fundamental to monotheism is the rejection of any standard higher than God. Hence, Job's lawsuit will be dismissed on the grounds that he lacks legal standing. He has no justifiable grievance. God is not obligated to reward Job for his righteousness or to publicly acknowledge his integrity. For God to concede that he abused his power in mistreating Job would jeopardize his divine authority and sanction resistance to his rule. But might is right only if the one in power is really right. Staying within the story of the Prologue, God, the cause of everything, is arguing that he may subject Job to horrible undeserved suffering merely to prove a point to the Satan.

To further overwhelm Job, God is anxious to provide a detailed physical description of Leviathan. The proud creator of the awesome monster proceeds: "I will not keep silence concerning his limbs, nor his mighty strength, nor his goodly frame." The Leviathan's natural armor of tough, tightly-packed scales makes it impregnable to attack by humans: "Who can strip off his outer garment? Who shall come within his jaws? Who can open the doors of his face? Around his teeth is terror. Strong scales are his pride, shut up together with a close seal. One is so near to another that no air can come between them. They are joined to one another. They stick together, so that they cannot be pulled apart." Amplifying the picture, God transforms Leviathan into the terrible fire-breathing dragon of myth, symbol of primordial chaos, far more formidable than the real crocodile: "His sneezing flashes out light. His eyes are like the eyelids of the morning. Out of his mouth go burning torches; sparks of fire leap out. Out of his nostrils a smoke goes, as of a boiling pot over a fire of reeds. His breath kindles coals. A flame goes out of his mouth." No creature can equal Leviathan's power: "There is strength in his neck. Terror dances before him. The flakes of his flesh are joined together. They are firm on him. They cannot be moved. His heart is as firm as a stone, firm as the millstone."

So powerful and well-armed is Leviathan, that it strikes terror in those humans who pursue it: "When he raises himself up, the mighty are afraid. They retreat before his thrashing." Weapons cannot penetrate giant Leviathan, who defies sword, spear, dart, javelin, arrows, sling stones, clubs and lances. He fears no conceivable weapon made by humans: "If one attacks him with a sword, it cannot prevail; nor the spear, the dart, not the pointed shaft." Hard iron and bronze weapons are ineffective: "He counts iron as straw and brass as rotten wood. The arrow cannot make him flee. Sling stones are like chaff to him. Clubs are counted as stubble. He laughs at the rushing of the javelin." Moving along the ground, Leviathan is like a juggernaut: "His undersides are like sharp potsherds, leaving a trail in the mud like a threshing sledge." Moving swiftly through the water, Leviathan "makes the deep to boil like a pot. He makes the sea like a pot of ointment." As it swims away, "he makes a path shine" in his wake, creating such a white foam that "one would think the deep had white hair." One can imagine Melville's Moby Dick, having sunk the ship of his whaler pursuers, swimming away in triumph.

Immensely proud of his ominous Leviathan, God concludes: "On earth there is not his equal, that is made without fear." God exalts both of his monsters: Behemoth "chief of the ways of God," and fearless Leviathan. But since God's speech closes with Leviathan, whose description is much longer and more detailed, the precedence must go to Leviathan. Why does God devote so much time to rhapsodizing Behemoth and Leviathan, describing them like a proud father, doting over his creations? They represent the evil that God instilled in the cosmos. God proclaimed through the second Isaiah, he creates light and darkness, prosperity and adversity, good and evil.[48] As with Behemoth, only God can control Leviathan. Evil is integral to the world, and suffering is a universal experience. With an obvious allusion to the rebel Job, God confronts him with the evil monster. Leviathan "sees everything that is high. He is king over all the sons of pride." The question is: Why does a God of supposed justice and goodness enjoy so much his vivid depiction of two creatures that personify evil?

Having shown that no human dare challenge the supremacy of either Behemoth or Leviathan, God rests his case. But taken literally, the portraits of Behemoth and Leviathan are ludicrous. Formidable as they appear, one imagines that Job in his prime could have assembled enough warriors to slay them both. Given enough whalers, even Melville's mighty Moby Dick could have been slain and transported back to Nantucket in pieces.

## Chapter 42   Job: Now My Eye Sees You

GOD HAS COMPLETED HIS LENGTHY HARANGUE. What can Job say in response? The elephant, having apparently vanquished the flea, orders the flea to respond. As we have seen, the poet frequently has Job parody established religious forms. Afflicted by the reputed God of absolute justice, Job had found no comfort in the customary platitudes of his friends. The speeches of God from the whirlwind are the poet's greatest parody. Whereas the traditional theophany consisted of a clear revelation from God, such as the Ten Commandments, or a manifestation of God's glory, the God of the Book of Job engages in a grand obfuscation. Speaking himself, not through prophets, God speaks at considerable length in the Book of Job, some 115 verses over three chapters. Yet he fails to communicate unequivocally. Given the opportunity to show compassion, God ignores Job's suffering. Instead, he overwhelms the frail Job with a boastful celebration of divine power. He bombards Job with over seventy rhetorical questions, but never addresses the central issue of divine justice. By objecting so vehemently to Job's challenge, God loses credibility. A critical reading of God's grandiloquent language leads to the conclusion that God indeed has something to hide. He becomes the proverbial character who protests too much. The poet's depiction of Yahweh as a self-centered megalomaniac, sublimely indifferent to human suffering, is the supreme blasphemy.

After God completes his second speech, the narrator intervenes: "Then Job answered Yahweh." Recovering his ability to speak, Job struggles to reply: "I know that you can do all things, and that no purpose of yours can be restrained." God's speeches were all about his power, not his justice or benevolence. Indeed, God is only concerned with delivering an auto-doxology, praising himself. His speeches, characterized by George Bernard Shaw as an "ignoble irrelevance," [49] are a turning point in which the plot fails to turn. God offers no credible answer for Job's undeserved suffering. As ruler of the universe, God can do whatever he wishes, including afflicting humans merely to test their faith. Job has always acknowledged God's power over the world he created. But God evades Job's questions about justice: Why am I suffering? Why do the innocent suffer? Why do the wicked prosper? Why did you murder my seven sons and three daughters? Why were you silent for so long? Is there a moral order in the universe? According to philosopher Ernest Bloch, "Yahweh's appearance and his words do everything to confirm Job's lack of faith in divine justice; far from being the theophany of the righteous God, they are like a divine atheism in regard to the (or rather paying no regard to) the moral order." [50]

Job has now experienced God's true nature. He responds by repeating God's initial challenge, which must have echoed in his mind. God had said to Job: "'Who is this who darkens counsel by words without knowledge?'" Since the question came from God, one would expect Job to quote the words verbatim. Instead, he makes a significant alteration:"'Who is this who hides counsel without knowledge?'" Job alters God's word "darkens" to "hides" counsel. This word change by the poet, a consummate artist, cannot be unintentional. Indeed, Job does darken counsel, casting a shadow on God's arbitrary and unjust character. But he has good reason to darken God's counsel with words, his only means to defend himself. God has hidden the truth from him and all humanity. God hides from Job the cause of innocent suffering. Having come to a new sobering awareness of God's dark side, Job exclaims: "I have uttered that which I did not understand, things too wonderful for me, which I did not know." Before experiencing the divine, Job did not know that God is not absolutely just or concerned with human suffering. Ignoring Job's suffering, God presented a wonderful panorama of creation, highlighting human insignificance in comparison. The vast universe elicits wonder, but it does not provide evidence of a just and compassionate God.

Job paraphrases God's second challenge, as it too echoes in his mind: "You [God] said 'Listen now and I will speak. I will question you and you will answer me.'" Job continues: "I had heard of you by the hearing of the ear, but now my eye sees you." God had reversed roles, making Job the defendant. Evading the question of justice, God had concentrated on the magnificent things he could comprehend and do that Job could not. But divine power and technical proficiency are not the equivalent of justice. Job was the beneficiary of a theophany, a rare privilege in the Hebrew Bible, in which his righteousness was not denied. In his early climactic speech, Job had expressed the desperate hope exclaiming: "In my flesh I shall see God" face-to-face before dying and be vindicated.[51] Job's experience was so vivid and immediate that hearing God, veiled by the whirlwind, was tantamount to seeing God. He has now "seen" God, but God is different than he had imagined: The God of hearsay was the God of Job and his friends, the deity of simplistic retribution theology, an absolutely just deity who automatically rewards the virtuous and punishes the wicked. Job had also heard of a God of love. But what Job experienced was a God devoid of compassion and justice, indifferent to human suffering.

We come to Job's final words. What does he conclude after "seeing" God? Read through the lens of translators determined to depict Job as a chastened rebel, repenting for challenging God, he is reduced to a groveling suppliant. The World English Bible translation, like many others, has Job declare in utter defeat: "Therefore I abhor myself, and repent in dust and ashes." But the Hebrew text allows more than one plausible translation. To translate is to interpret. First of all, the Hebrew word translated as "abhor," or "despise," can also be translated as "retract," "reject" or "recant." According to the Jewish Publication Society Bible, the New Jerusalem Bible and the New American Standard Bible, Job "retracts" or "recants." Secondly, the Hebrew verb lacks an object. Translators often infer the missing object, usually one that conforms to their overall interpretation of the book. Those who wish to see Job humbled before God, use "abhor" or "despise" as the verb, adding "myself" as the object. Hence, a repentant humiliated Job will declare, "I despise myself." Other translations leave the object unspecified. Thirdly, the word translated as "repent," may also be rendered as "change one's mind." Finally, the phrase "dust and ashes" is subject to differing interpretations. It might refer to Job's mortal status, created from the dust of the earth, and ultimately becoming ashes in death. Indeed, Abraham, after challenging God to act justly toward the city of Sodom, conceded that he was a fragile mortal, mere "dust and ashes." Hence, Job might be humbly admitting the obvious; compared to God he is mere "dust and ashes." We recall Job's lament that God violently brutalized him, reducing him to "dust and ashes."[52]

We maintain that the correct translation, true to the spirit of Job throughout dialogue, is: "I retract my lawsuit and change my mind about dust and ashes." In this case, the phrase "dust and ashes" refers to Job's condition as an abject mourner sitting amid his city's dirty refuse. But having confronted God face-to-face, Job has emerged victorious. He need not repent for sins he did not commit. No charges having been filed by God against him, Job can now withdraw his lawsuit.[53] He has been vindicated. The ash-heap, the place of Job's degradation, has been transformed into a place of triumph. Job can rise from this ash-heap and return to society,[54] confident that although betrayed by an unjust God, he maintained his integrity to the end.

Job's unwavering conviction of his integrity would not allow him to "abhor" or "despise" himself. This does not stem from arrogant pride, but from his righteous life. He is a person created in God's image, with inherent worth and an innate sense of right and wrong. Nor does Job repent. Not accused of sin by God, Job has nothing for which to ask forgiveness. If he were to repent, he would sanction the view of the friends that his torment is justified. Nor does Job retract his words challenging God's justice. Nevertheless, a lingering sense of mourning persists in the text. Job will carry irreparable losses into his new life. His greatest loss is the illusion of the God of absolute justice and goodness. Such a God would not cause innocent suffering. While Job survives his terrible ordeal and rises from the dust and ashes, he could never forget what God has done to him.

# EPILOGUE TO THE BOOK OF JOB

## Chapter 42:7-17   God: Job Spoke Right of Me

FOLLOWING JOB'S FINAL WORDS, we leave the realm of poetry and return to the prose narrative framework with which the book began. The story of Job concludes with stunning dramatic irony. Instead of continuing to rebuke Job, God rebukes the friends. They are now the objects of God's wrath. Job does not speak again. Neither do the friends. God is given the last words. He addresses Eliphaz, presumably because he is the oldest of the friends. The narrator explains: "After Yahweh had spoken these words to Job, Yahweh said to Eliphaz the Temanite, 'My wrath is kindled against you, and against your two friends; for you have not spoken of me the thing that is right, as my servant Job has.'" God is now referring to Job in the third person. Significantly, God ignores Elihu, perhaps to distance himself from his advocate's defense of divine justice. For the first time since the Prologue, God refers to Job as "my servant." Indeed, God calls Job "my servant" four times in three verses. No longer is Job the lowly creature whose cry for justice is ignored. He has regained the status of servant reserved for great biblical heroes such as Abraham, Moses, and Isaiah. Of course, this is the same "servant Job" whom God permitted to be unjustly afflicted in the Prologue.

To satisfy his wrath, God instructs the friends to have Job intercede on their behalf. Returning to the ancient ritualistic religion of the Prologue, where God demands animal sacrifices to atone for sin, Yahweh instructs the friends: "Take to yourselves seven bulls and seven rams, and go to my servant Job, and offer up for yourselves a burnt offering. My servant Job shall pray for you, for I will accept him and not deal with you according to your folly." God then repeats his judgment of Job and the friends: "You have not spoken of me the thing that is right, as my servant Job has." The significance of these words, affirming for the second time that Job has spoken what is right about God, should not be underestimated. God publicly acknowledges that Job has spoken the truth about him and that Job is indeed a person of integrity. These words affirming Job's integrity are the last God speaks in the Hebrew Bible.

What truth did Job speak about God? From the context, God is referring to the words Job spoke in the dialogue in opposition to the words of the friends. Ironically, God is corroborating Job's blasphemies against him. God does not deny the truth of Job's attack upon his justice. Throughout the dialogue, Job argued that God is unjust and that there is no moral order in the cosmos. Job's undeserved suffering made him realize that something had gone terribly awry. The world does not reflect divine retributive justice. Job lost his trust in God, but remained unwavering in his integrity. One's lot in life does not always reflect one's character.

What falsehood did the friends speak about God? They erred by insisting that God is absolutely just. Their arguments reflected the dying tradition of exact divine retribution. Despite the many exceptions offered by experience, the friends blindly adhered to the belief that God unerringly rewards the virtuous and punishes the wicked. But the Book of Job teaches that the doctrine of divine retribution is false. It must be supplanted by a theology that understands evil as integral to reality. God does not invariably reward the virtuous and punish the wicked. The righteous often suffer and the wicked often prosper. God either cannot alter, or chooses not to alter, this reality. The Book of Job sounds the death knell for the God of retributive justice.

The omniscient narrator who began the story of Job now brings it to a close: "So Eliphaz the Temanite and Bildad the Shuhite and Zophar the Naamathite went, and did what Yahweh commanded them, and Yahweh accepted Job." Ironically, the friends who had condemned Job in defense of God now depend on him to save them. Only Job's intercession can secure their pardon. Consistent with the virtuous life he outlined in his oath of innocence, Job shows compassion towards those who wronged him. The narrator continues: "When he prayed for his friends, Yahweh gave Job twice as much as he had before."

Having afflicted Job unjustly, God now rewards him by doubling everything he had prior to his innocent suffering. God apparently seeks to make amends for his reprehensible treatment of his righteous servant. Significantly, Job's restoration is a public affirmation of his integrity. Whether God's integrity remains intact is doubtful. Ironically, according to ancient Jewish law, a person caught stealing was obligated to repay his victim double what he had stolen.[1] No longer will Job be isolated, a pariah among his people. We imagine Job leaving the ash-heap and returning to his home. The graves of his ten children lay nearby.

No longer stigmatized as a great sinner, a hypocrite, and an enemy of God, Job is again accepted by his community: "Then came there to him all his brothers, and all his sisters, and all those who had been of his acquaintance before, and ate bread with him in his house." Where were these relatives and friends during Job's agony? As they ate together, they rejoiced in the return of Job's good fortune. Everyone knew that God had caused Job's suffering, but they did not know of God's betrayal of Job. Not privy to the fateful wager between God and the Satan, they did not question God's justice. We recall Job's anguished lament: "When I looked for good, then evil came."[2] But Job now received the sympathy and compassion denied him during his dark days: "They comforted him, and consoled him concerning all the evil that Yahweh had brought on him. Everyone also gave him a piece of money, and everyone a ring of gold."

God restored Job materially: "Yahweh blessed the latter end of Job more than his beginning. He had fourteen thousand sheep, six thousand camels, one thousand yoke of oxen, and one thousand female donkeys." Ignoring the atrocities he committed, God does not restore to life Job's ten children for whose death he is responsible. Nor does he bring Job's dead servants back to life. Instead, Job receives a new set of ten children as his wife, consigned to virtual invisibility throughout his ordeal, rejoins him: "He had also seven sons and three daughters." The daughters, unlike the sons, have names. He named the first Jemimah (Turtledove), the second, Keziah (Cinnamon), and the third, Keren Happuch (Eyeshadow)." Job could be proud of his daughters, for "in all the land were no women found so beautiful." Reflecting his devotion to his daughters, Job "gave them an inheritance among their brothers," unusual in the patriarchal culture of the ancient Near East. In Israel, daughters received an inheritance from their father only if there were no sons.[3] With his great wealth, the compassionate Job could afford to do the unusual. Completing Job's restoration, God doubles his lifespan, traditionally expected to be seventy years. Although the text does not say so, we assume that God heals Job of his loathsome skin disease, bringing him from the brink of death. Hence, Job enjoys the longevity of the great patriarchs of Israel— Abraham and Isaac— enabling him to see not only his grandchildren, but also succeeding generations of grand children: "Job lived one hundred forty years, and saw his sons, and his sons' sons, to four generations. Job died, being old and full of days."

Job had a long life, but was it a happy life?  While God's doubling what Job had possessed prior to his suffering reflects a kind of poetic justice, it nevertheless begs the question of God's justice. Even if compensated, innocent suffering is still evil. Ironically, in rewarding Job, God activates the retributive justice that the Book of Job is supposed to deny. This shows the arbitrary nature of God. Common sense demonstrates that not all innocent sufferers are restored. Indeed, they must bear their suffering while God remains hidden. No speeches from the whirlwind for them. Even though restored doubly by God in the end, how could Job view God in the same way as before? God had subjected him to senseless violent trauma. The poet was inspired to compose the dialogue, the core of the Book of Job, because the patient Job of the Prologue lacks psychological truth. But neither is the restored Job of the Epilogue credible. By the standards of his day, a happy life included material prosperity, many children, health, large flocks, riches, and a long life. The restored Job certainly had these, even greater than before his affliction. Job's passionate quest to vindicate himself was successful. But he could not forget what God had done to him. He has now "seen" God's dark demonic side, and the psychological scars caused by his suffering could not be erased. Unlike Job, we know that his suffering resulted not from God's transcendent wisdom, but from a gratuitous cruel test of Job's faith. Henceforth, Job could never feel safe in a world ruled by a capricious deity. Job's relationship with God had depended upon trust. Could Job continue to trust God? What would prevent God from subjecting him to another malicious test, another betrayal?

Can a child recover from his father's abuse? Can a human like Job ever recover from his divine father's abuse? God may have healed Job physically, but how could Job, or any human, accept another set of children to replace the dead ones? Dostoevsky's Father Zossima wondered how Job, remembering his dead children, could "be fully happy with those new ones, however dear the new ones might be? Zossima answers: "But he could, he could. It's the great mystery of human life that old grief passes gradually into quiet tender joy."[4] Only a person who has never lost a child could give such a mindless answer to what is every parent's greatest fear.

We recall that one of the possible meanings of the name Job is "where is my [Divine] father?" For Job, God was like a rich and powerful absentee father who permitted his virtuous son to be physically and emotionally abused to test his devotion. The son knows that his father is the ultimate cause of his suffering, but he does not know why. The son has done nothing to deserve the suffering. His desperate pleas for an explanation from his father go unheeded. When the father finally appears, the son anticipates learning why he suffers. But the father ignores his son's suffering, choosing instead to confront him with the wonders of the house he lives in: "Who designed this great house? Do you understand the complexities of architecture and engineering? Do you know how electricity works? Look at the variety of wonderful animals that populate the gardens. Everything is under my care. Come to the backyard and see the two ferocious animals I have confined in a cage. All this is part of my grand plan. My ways are not your ways. Can you understand what I understand? Can you do what I can do? Broaden your vision. Forget your suffering. It is insignificant from the perspective of the grand plan. Do not question your father." The son is speechless. Instead of admitting that his son was the victim of a foolish scheme, the father gloats over his superior power and knowledge and tries to compensate for his terrible injustice by doubling his son's inheritance. Who can defend a God who afflicts a righteous person in order to prove that he is a righteous person?

How could Job continue to live happily, knowing that God, the cause of all things, is responsible for the death of his children? How could Job believe in God's justice while so many suffer innocently? How many innocent sufferers could respect a God who took everything from them unjustly, even if they were restored doubly? Despite his restoration, Job was not happy. Jacob survives his wrestling with God, but he would limp for the rest of his life because of their encounter. Job also survives his wrestling with God, but he must have been emotionally scarred for the rest of his life. The best part of Job died on the ash-heap. The remaining Job, awakened to God's flawed nature, went on living. Søren Kierkegaard's narrator in *Fear and Trembling* imagines various scenarios of Abraham's reaction to God who tested him by commanding him to sacrifice his beloved son, Isaac. After God intervened to prevent the sacrifice, Abraham went home: "From that day on, Abraham became old. He could not forget that God had demanded this of him. Isaac strove as before; but Abraham's eye was darkened; he saw joy no more."[5] Like Job, Abraham was the victim of an insecure God, one who cruelly tested a righteous servant merely to prove his faith. If God would have lifted the veil for Job, permitting him to see the deity he worshipped manipulated so easily into afflicting him, we imagine that he would have been devastated.

So what are we to conclude about the wager between the Satan and God? We recall that the Satan challenged the purity of Job's faith. The Satan alleged that, deprived of his blessings, Job would show that his faith was not pure, but conditional. Indeed, the Satan declared that Job would respond by cursing God to his face. The Satan must be declared the winner of the wager. While it is true that Job did not curse God directly to his face, assuming this were possible, Job's arguments throughout the dialogue show that his faith was dependent upon God acting justly in accord with the doctrine of retribution. Once Job comprehended what God had done to him, he launched his heroic lawsuit to compel God to act justly. Had Job's piety been selfless, he would not have protested, but merely submitted as he did initially in the Prologue. Indeed, the issue of Job's faith raises the question whether pure, unconditional faith is possible for any person. Even the faith of Abraham, an inspiration to the three monotheistic religion – Judaism, Christianity, and Islam— was not disinterested. He abandoned his family and homeland in Mesopotamia and took the perilous journey to Canaan because God promised: "I will make of you a great nation. I will bless you and make your name great."[6] Moreover, the monotheistic religions of the world depend upon self-interested faith, the expectation that God will reward believers, either in this life or an afterlife.

Job's faith was conditioned upon God's recognition of his righteousness. The text indicates that Job was able to detach from his material wealth, even from his children, although he grieved for them, but never from his integrity.  For Job to deny his integrity would destroy his identity. Nevertheless, if Job's faith was not disinterested, the fault lies not with him, but with God. The overriding emotion towards God throughout the Book of Job is fear. Indeed, as noted, the God of the Hebrew Bible elicits terror. A tyrant cannot elicit disinterested piety. The text reveals that, from the very beginning fear, not love, played a significant role in Job's faith. The

Prologue shows Job so fearful that he offered sacrifices on behalf of his sons merely on the chance that they might have cursed God in their hearts.[7] We have seen that, once struck by terrible suffering, Job confessed that what he had always feared had come true.[8] He apparently did not trust God to always act justly, even towards him, his most loyal servant. We have seen that Job was almost overcome by terror when he contemplated the prospect of confronting God in court. We have also seen that when Job swore that he did not commit any of a litany of possible sins, he disclosed that he was motivated by fear of "calamity from God."[9] Were God really good and just, he would not want people to cower before him, but would honor a person of integrity like Job who heeds his conscience and speaks the truth. Yet the God of the Hebrew Bible is more interested in having his name and reputation exalted than showing compassion for his people.[10] Referring to God, the second Isaiah declares: "You led your people to make yourself a glorious name."[11] This is the same self-interested God who shows no compassion for the suffering Job.

# FROM AN IMMORAL TO AN AMORAL GOD

TO THE END, JOB REMAINS UNWAVERING in defense of his integrity. While God might be satisfied that Job endured innocent suffering without cursing him to his face, Job's courageous resistance is more noteworthy. God could no longer assume that all humans will approach him as patient sycophants. Indeed Job rebels. He rebels more forcefully than any other character in the Bible. God could no longer assume that all humans will accept injustice without protest, even injustice from God. Job attacks God's injustice. God did not anticipate Job's enormous courage, his willingness to risk his life and take his case to heaven to see justice done. Job is a person of conscience, justice and compassion. But God lacks the moral qualities of Job. The God who speaks from the whirlwind is the God of the Prologue— insecure, unreflecting and brutal. He never honestly confronts his guilt in causing Job's innocent suffering, nor does he show compassion. And when God declares that his servant Job spoke rightly of him, he concedes that Job's depiction of his injustice and cruelty are correct. God never directly accuses Job of blasphemy, for Job's angry words spoke the truth.

The silences in the Book of Job have their own eloquence. God hid his meaning in his silences, avoiding Job's probing questions about his justice. But Job's silences also bear implied meaning. Although he does not declare it explicitly, Job "sees" that retributive justice is not part of God's plan for the universe. The God that Job had heard about from tradition is different from the God he experiences. He is not a God of justice but of absolute power, arbitrary and unaccountable to humans. In fact, God was silent on the question of divine justice. The question of God's justice is central to the Book of Job. If God wished Job to understand that his justice is beyond human comprehension, he never expresses it. If

God wished humans to understand innocent suffering as a test of faith, why did he not say so? Would a benevolent God torment humans merely to test the sincerity of their faith? If God sends tribulation to humans as benevolent discipline, as Elihu argues, why did he not say so? Would a benevolent God allow horrendous suffering in order to strengthen human character?

If the poet intended to side with God, the book's conclusion would be the place for a stirring doxology from Job. Significantly, the poet refrains from having Job praise God as absolutely just or good. As Martin Buber, a devout Jew, lamented, "Dare we recommend to the survivors of Auschwitz, the Job of the gas chambers, to sing the praises of God's goodness and mercy."[1] Countless innocent sufferers over the centuries could declare the same. Asked in an interview whether Auschwitz proves the non-existence of God, Holocaust survivor Primo Levi replied: "There is Auschwitz, and so there cannot be God."[2] If God wanted a world without evil, Behemoth and Leviathan would not exist.

For those who expect the Book of Job to resolve the problem of innocent suffering, the speeches of God constitute one of the biggest anti-climaxes of world literature. With verse upon verse depicting unmitigated suffering, with God silent and hidden until the end, one expects some reprieve from a text suffused with pessimism. Nevertheless, the words composed for God by the poet demonstrate the power of rhetoric to seduce. Indeed, the speeches from the whirlwind have seduced generations of pious readers into believing that God puts Job's turmoil to rest. Did God wish to teach Job that, viewed from the divine perspective, his innocent suffering is not unjust, but bears a higher meaning? In the modern era, this view is reflected by Abraham Heschel, who refuses to apply human reason to the problem: "God writes straight in crooked lines, and man cannot evaluate them as he lives on one level and can see from only one perspective. We are not the final arbiters of meaning. What looks absurd within the limits of time may be luminous within the scope of eternity."[3] Similarly, Robert Gordis argues: "Just as there is order and harmony in the natural world, though imperfectly grasped by man, so there is order and meaning in the moral sphere, though often incomprehensible to man."[4] The views of Heschel and Gordis are echoed by many pious commentators. Many are honest in portraying Job's challenge to divine justice and goodness, but conclude by straining to salvage God's reputation by a leap of faith, unsupported by the text. Nevertheless, not all innocent sufferers of the world, many of them victims of horrendous evil, will surrender their human critical faculty. They do not believe that the crooked line is really straight or that order and harmony reside in a higher moral realm, even if incomprehensible to humans.

Like God in his speeches from the whirlwind, many pious interpreters wish to invalidate the theodicy question. They hold that God is not subject to human reason, ironically his greatest gift to humanity. Like Abraham and Job, humans must challenge God's justice. Law professor Alan Dershowitz offers a cogent defense of applying reason to God: "To accept the conclusion of the Book of Job that God's justice is not subject to human understanding, is to abdicate all human judgment of God's actions and to accept the injustices of our world....In the wake of the Holocaust, it is more difficult to shrug one's shoulders and sigh that God works in mysterious ways."[5]

Job might have been overwhelmed by God's speeches, he might have bowed before the majesty of God's creation, but there is no evidence in the text that he is satisfied with the divine response. Theologians who ignore the danger in faith without reason claim that even though Job receives from God no logical answer to his suffering, he rests content. The mere experience of God, they argue, is sufficient. Once he "saw" God, Job's questions dissolved. This view received its classic expression in the work of Rudolf Otto. In his famous book, *The Idea of the Holy*, Otto contends that the religious experience transcends human reason. According to Otto, God's response from the whirlwind is a "real theodicy," not only able to convince Job, "but utterly to still every inward doubt that assailed his soul." Having mystically experienced God as the *mysterium tremendum*, Job is no longer concerned with his suffering. Otto hails God's opening speech to Job as extraordinary: "In the 38th chapter of Job, we have the element of the mysterious displayed in rare purity and completeness, and this chapter may well rank among the most remarkable in the history of religion."[6]

God's response to Job is indeed remarkable, but not on the basis that Otto suggests. The text does not support his interpretation. Ironically, with prose as irrational as the non-rationality he claims to be the essence of religion, Otto holds that Job's experience of God "is at once an inward relaxing of his soul's anguish and an appeasement, an appeasement that would alone and in itself perfectly suffice as the solution to the problem of the Book of Job, even without Job's rehabilitation in chapter 42."[7] Such mystification is the last refuge of the religious apologist. Abdicating human reason, Otto holds that God's response provides a non-rational "theodicy of its own," leaving Job completely satisfied.[8] Otto follows the lead of Immanuel Kant who argued that God transcends human categories of reason. Like Kant, Otto would have us believe that somewhere in the transcendent realm, beyond human reason, lies God's answer to human suffering. Would that all victims of innocent suffering have the religious experience that Otto claims for Job.

We return full circle to the theodicy question. If God is omnipotent, absolutely good and just, why do the innocent suffer? With Job, we ask: Where can wisdom be found? The ancient Greek philosopher Epicurus (341-270 BCE) formulated the problem concisely: "Is God willing to prevent evil, but not able? Then he is not omnipotent. Is he able, but not willing? Then he is malevolent. Is he both able and willing? Then whence cometh evil? Is he neither able nor willing? Then why call him God?"[9] The question of God's goodness and justice looms over the Book of Job from the beginning, when God betrays the righteous Job, to the end, when God refuses to take responsibility for his evil acts. It is easier for some to accept a God whose power is limited rather than a God who permits evil and innocent suffering. Harold Kushner, in *When Bad Things Happen to Good People,* believes that God is good and just, but not omnipotent. Restricted by human free will and the unalterable laws of nature, God cannot prevent all evil and suffering in the world.[10] God could not intervene to prevent the innocent suffering and death of Kushner's young son. Along similar lines, the philosopher Hans Jonas also holds that God is not omnipotent. According to Jonas, "God was silent," failing to intervene in Auschwitz, "not because he chose not to, but because he *could* not."[11] This view that God is not omnipotent was also held by the philosophers John Stuart Mill and William James. Other modern thinkers, including J. L. Mackie and H. J. McCloskey, argue that horrendous evil simply proves that God does not exist.[12]

The God of the Book of Job is omnipotent, but not good or just. This God is obeyed not out of reverence but for the terror he instills. How can such a God be loved? The only way to justify God's treatment of Job is to deny that his suffering is innocent. The Prologue demonstrates that God unjustly afflicted Job, whom he affirmed was righteous. Commentators who deflect the blame from God to the Satan, God's agent, distort the text. Job believes that God is omnipotent and able to prevent his calamity. If God is able to prevent suffering but chooses not to do so, no human can conclude that God is good.

To enable God to escape human scrutiny, many resort to the argument from divine transcendence. Humans allegedly cannot fathom the wisdom of God, who has his reason for permitting the innocent to suffer and the wicked to prosper. When speaking through his prophet, the second Isaiah, God declared that he is beyond human standards of good and evil: "My thoughts are not your thoughts, and your ways are not my ways. For as the heavens are higher than the earth, so are my ways higher than your ways, and my thoughts higher than your thoughts."[13] The medieval Jewish philosopher, Moses Maimonides, echoes this thinking. In *The Guide of the Perplexed*, he claims that Job's protest stemmed from his lack of knowledge of God's providence. "We should not fall into the error," Maimonides insists, "of imagining His knowledge to be similar to ours, or His intention, providence, and rule similar to ours. When we know this, we shall find everything that may befall us easy to bear; mishap will create no doubts in our hearts concerning God, whether He knows our affairs or not, whether He provides for us or abandons us. On the contrary, our fate will increase our love of God."[14] Would Maimonides dare to say this to victims of the medieval pogroms, massacres of Jews, as they cried out to God for relief? Maimonides' theology merely evades the painful issue of God's justice and goodness. Responding to those who maintain that God transcends human moral standards, John Stuart Mill declared: "I will call no being good who is not what I mean when I apply that epithet to my fellow-creature; and if such a being will sentence me to hell for not calling him so to hell I will go."[15] To argue that God is above the moral law, beyond human conceptions of good and evil, makes everyone vulnerable to divine tyranny.

Humans have imposed upon God a moral responsibility he cannot bear. The Book of Job reveals that retributive justice is not part of God's plan for the universe. Humans have placed upon God the burden of absolute goodness and justice. Humans have assigned God the function of policing the world, justly distributing rewards and punishments. Perhaps God lacks the power to destroy all evil. Indeed, God challenges Job to try to control the evil that even he cannot annihilate. If God were relieved of the responsibility of enforcing strict retribution, he might be spared attacks from righteous humans like Job. Humans could then take full responsibility for their lives. They are accountable for both the moral good and evil in the world. The conception of God as the enforcer of absolute justice, intervening in the world, unfailingly rewarding the righteous and punishing the wicked, is illusory. Everyone knows that innocent people often suffer and evil people often prosper.

Jack Miles argues in his book, *God: A Biography,* that the character of God changes over the course of the Hebrew Bible. God undergoes a transformation within the Book of Job. The God of the Prologue is the God of retributive justice who behaves unjustly by afflicting Job. But God's speeches from the whirlwind at the end of the book reflect a paradigm shift. This God is not interested in justice or injustice. He sends rain upon the just and the unjust, the good and the evil alike. The God of retributive justice is dead.

But like the phoenix, God rises from the ashes, shorn of the moral categories that humans have imposed. The Book of Job implies a transition from an immoral God to an amoral God, beyond human conceptions of good and evil. The American writer Stephen Crane observed, "A man said to the universe: 'Sir I exist!' 'However,' replied the universe, 'The fact has not created in me a sense of obligation.'"[16] The American poet Robert Frost made an intriguing suggestion along these lines in *A Masque of Reason*. According to this poem, God and Job meet many years after their early experience together. Surprisingly, God credits Job with doing him a great service. God thanks the surprised Job "for the way you helped me establish once for all the principle there's no connection man can reason out between his just deserts and what he gets....My thanks are to you for releasing me from moral bondage to the human race. The only free will there at first was man's, who could do good or evil as he chose." God confesses that unless he wanted to "suffer loss of worship," he had to "prosper good and punish evil. You changed all that. You set me free to reign. You are the Emancipator of God."[17] Owing to Job, God is free to act according to his true nature.

We recall Job's lament that God ignored his desperate prayers: "Behold, I cry out of wrong, but I am not heard. I cry for help, but there is not justice."[18] Job's plea has been echoed by countless sufferers over the centuries. But God, detached from humans and the world he created, cannot be expected to answer prayers. Believers think that they can communicate with a personal God by means of prayer. They believe that God can intervene in the world, hearing requests and rectifying injustices. When by chance prayers are answered, God is given credit. When prayers go unanswered or innocent suffering happens, many accept it as God's will. But the God of the Prologue is not the same God at the end of the book. He can be neither credited nor blamed for what happens in the world. He created and sustains the cosmos with all of its marvels. But he does not intervene to prevent innocent suffering. An amoral God, he is not concerned with individual humans. Prayers of supplication assume that God will intervene to grant a petitioner's request. But he does not alter human affairs. If God does, why are the prayers of some innocent sufferers answered while the prayers of others, equally or more deserving, not answered? If God cannot be blamed, neither can God take credit for those who survive an earthquake or a tornado. Why should God allow some to survive and others to die? When evil persons exercise their moral freedom to murder others, God does not intervene. If he does, why are some saved while others perish? Prayers of thanksgiving assume that God bestows necessities or gifts upon humans. Why does God grant favors to some and deny the same favors to those equally or more deserving? Prayers glorifying God to curry favor for divine assistance are insincere. God should not require obsequious praise from suffering humans, unless he demands servile worship. The fact is that the amoral God at the conclusion of the Book of Job is divorced from the fate of humans and the world.

Significantly, after the Book of Job, God recedes from the world. In the remaining nine books of the Hebrew Bible he does not again intervene in human affairs.[19] Henceforth, he is closer to the God of eighteenth century deism, espoused by America's founders, Thomas Jefferson, Benjamin Franklin, and Thomas Paine. The standard defense of God is that innocent suffering is inevitable in a world of human freedom and unwavering natural laws. Were God to prevent evil, theists argue, human freedom would be destroyed and the natural order destabilized. But the God of deism is an impersonal deity who created the world but does not interfere with human freedom or the laws of nature. This God is the *deus otiosus,* the idle

God who chooses to be hidden. This God is not concerned with human morality and the processes of nature. Nor can he be blamed for not intervening to prevent moral evil and natural disasters. Humans exercise their freedom to act either morally or immorally and natural laws operate relentlessly. The God of deism is not concerned with the thoughts of humans. He does not demand worship. Nor is he interested in consigning to hell those who do not believe in him.

What does the Book of Job teach about the relationship between God and humanity? The Book of Job signals a radical transformation in the traditional conception of the deity. The Job poet is an unacknowledged Hebrew prophet, issuing a clarion call for a major revision in beliefs about the nature of God and his relation to the world. Transcendent and impersonal, the amoral God is not concerned with the questions of innocent sufferers or with comforting them in their anguish. Indeed, God's depiction of the wonders of the world that he created contains a startling omission. Except for a brief reference to the proud and the wicked,[20] human beings are absent from God's celebration of his works. The Book of Job undermines the anthropocentrism of Hebrew scripture. The God who demands reverence from human beings fails to show them proper reverence. According to Genesis, humans were created in God's image and given dominion over the earth. As the Psalmist proclaims, man was created "a little lower than the angels and crowned them with glory and honor."[21] The God of the prophets is sometimes concerned with human justice. Speaking through Amos, God enjoins: "Let justice roll on like rivers, and righteousness like a mighty stream."[22] But this vaunted God of justice fades into the background, replaced at the conclusion to the Book of Job by an amoral deity, indifferent to the human condition. Like Atlas, who carried the world upon his shoulders, God was burdened by the moral responsibility imposed upon him by humanity. With the Book of Job, God shrugs this responsibility, allowing it to fall upon human beings.

One marvels that the Book of Job is included in the Hebrew canon. Read critically, the book undermines the faith of ancient Israel. It demolishes the central tenet of monotheism—a God of absolute justice. The Job poet was Israel's great dissenter. He raised questions about the nature of God that few, if any, of his contemporaries dared to ask. He had the courage to show that the God of the Hebrew Bible might be omnipotent, but he is not perfectly good or just. Throughout the rest of the Hebrew canon, especially the Torah and the historical books, we find numerous examples of God's cruelty and injustice, but no Biblical character challenges God with the tenacity and power of Job. The early fifth-century Christian theologian Theodore of Mopsuestia attempted to remove the Book of Job from the canon because the blasphemous Job of the poetic dialogue contradicts the pious Job of the Prologue. Theodore did not succeed. His criticism of the Book of Job, among other charges, led to his posthumous condemnation for heresy. Perhaps the religious authorities could not exclude from the canon a book in which God speaks so much.

Nevertheless, over the centuries many must have had misgivings about the canonical status of the Book of Job. What kind of God is silent to innocent suffering, allowing evil to triumph and virtue to perish? Pious readers might wish the Book of Job's Prologue to have been different. The Prologue is the Achilles heel of all religious defenses of God. But the Prologue is consistent with ancient Hebrew theology: God causes suffering as well as prosperity, evil as well as good. Pious readers, holding every word of scripture to be the inspired word of God, ought to be shocked by the literal message of the Book of Job. Its canonical status induces them to evade or obfuscate issues that threaten their beliefs. Many might hold that the Prologue is only a story, not to be taken seriously. But if the Prologue is considered fiction, so must the rest of the book. God alone, not personal sin, caused Job's unjust suffering. The cruel test of Job says much more about God than the purity of Job's faith. The God of the biblical Book of Job is the same God who wiped out the world with the Great Flood, killing countless men, women, children, animals, and plant life. Throughout the Hebrew Bible, the God depicted is tyrannical, unjust and arbitrary.

The word integrity best captures the character of Job. Although a bleak tone pervades the text, it is redeemed by the shining light of Job's courage. For Job, his horrific suffering is virtually inconsequential compared to what matters most in his life, his integrity. Job refuses to speak or act in any way contrary to his fundamental values. Centuries of readers upon opening the book's Prologue have been greeted by the omniscient narrator's declaration that Job is "blameless and upright."[23] God himself affirms Job's integrity. After betraying Job by afflicting him unjustly, we recall, God declares to the Satan: "He still maintains his integrity, although you incited me against him, to ruin him without cause."[24] Abandoned by God and his friends, the suffering Job utters a defiant battle cry directed at the heavens: "Until I die, I will not put away my integrity from me. I hold fast to my righteousness, and will not let it go."[25] Job takes his rightful place with Noah and Daniel, hailed by the prophet Ezekiel for their righteousness.[26] Job wished that his words be preserved in stone so that the knowledge of his righteous life would never die. While Job's words have not been preserved in stone, the poet has memorialized them for all time. Job, hurling his accusatory words against God, represents the triumph of the human spirit over tyranny and injustice. The Book of Job honors a noble hero of conscience, steadfast in his integrity, who dared to wrestle with God.

# NOTES

## Explanation of Citations to the *Book of Job*

Unless otherwise indicated, biblical references are taken from the *World English Bible* (WEB), a public domain translation available online at www.biblegateway.com. Our analysis follows strictly the order of the Book of Job. Readers consulting the WEB translation, or any other translation, can easily find the chapters and verses discussed. Citations to other books of the Bible and cross-references to the Book of Job will be found in the notes below.

---

## INTRODUCTION: A REVOLUTIONARY BOOK

[1] Søren Kierkegaard, *Repetition*, in *Fear and Trembling/Repetition*, (1983), 204.

[2] Franz Kafka, "To Oscar Pollak," January 27, 1904, in Franz Kafka, *Letters to Friends, Family and Editor*, translated by Richard and Clara Winston, (New York: Schocken Books, 1977), 16.

[3] Primo Levi, *The Search for Roots: A Personal Anthology*, translated and with an introduction by Peter Forbes, (Chicago: Ivan R. Dee, Publisher, 1997), 11.

[4] Virginia Woolf, *The Letters of Virginia Woolf*, Volume II, 1912-1922, edited by Nigel Nicolson and Joanne Trautmann, (New York: Harcourt, Brace and Jovanovich, 1976), 585.

[5] Karl Jaspers, *The Origin and Goal of History*, (1953); Karen Armstrong, *The Great Transformation: The Beginning of Our Religious Traditions,* (2008).

[6] *Habakkuk* 1:13.

[7] *Job* 12:9.

[8] Ernest Renan, *The Book of Job*, (n.d.), xl.

[9] *Exodus* 22: 28; 1 *Kings* 21:10.

[10] *Leviticus* 24:10-16; also *Exodus* 22:28 and 1 *Kings* 21:10.

[11] Robert Alter, *The Art of Biblical Narrative*, (1983), 182.

[12] Samuel Terrien, "Job: Introduction and Exegesis," in *Interpreter's Bible*, edited by G.A. Buttrick, 12 volumes, vol. 3, (Nashville: Abingdon, 1954), 892.

[13] Harold Bloom, *The Shadow of a Rock: A Literary Appreciation of the King James Bible,* (2011); Jack Miles, *God: A Biography*, (1995).

[14] Jack Kahn, *Job's Illness: Loss, Grief and Integration. A Psychological Interpretation,* (1975).

## PROLOGUE TO THE BOOK OF JOB

[1] *Ezekiel* 14:14, 20
[2] Kierkegaard, "The Lord Gave, and the Lord Hath Taken Away, Blessed be the Name of the Lord," in *Edifying Discourses*, (1958), 84-86.
[3] M. Weiss, *The Story of Job's Beginning: Job 1-2,* (1983), 37.
[4] *Deuteronomy* 28:35.
[5] Thomas Aquinas, *The Literal Exposition on Job*, (1989), 84.
[6] Marvin H. Pope, (1973), 22.
[7] Weiss, *The Story of Job's Beginning*, (1983), 71.
[8] Robert Sutherland, *Putting God on Trial: The Biblical Book of Job*, (2004), 43.
[9] *Job* 7:3.
[10] *Genesis* 50:10; *Ezekiel* 3:15.
[11] *Deuteronomy* 30 & 28; *Leviticus* 26.
[12] A. B. Davidson, *The Book of Job*, (1951), 31; Buchanan Blake, *The Book of Job and the Problem of Suffering*, (1911), 150, 223.
[13] *Isaiah* 45:5, 7. In this book we apply the modern practice of distinguishing three different authors for the *Book of Isaiah*: "First Isaiah," chaps. 1-39; "Second Isaiah," chaps. 40-55; and "Third Isaiah," chaps. 56-66.
[14] *Amos* 3:6.
[15] *Lamentations* 3: 38.
[16] *Job* 2:10.
[17] Elisabeth Kübler-Ross, *On Death and Dying*, (1969).
[18] *Job* 2:6.
[19] *Psalms* 22:1.
[20] Elie Wiesel, *Night*, (1982), 32.

## JOB'S LAMENT

[1] Yeats, "The Second Coming" (1920).
[2] *Jeremiah* 20:14-18.
[3] *Genesis* 1:3-4.
[4] *Ecclesiastes* 1:2.
[5] *Job* 1:10.
[6] *Exodus* 4:24.
[7] Norman Whybray, " 'Shall Not the Judge of All the Earth Do What Is Just?' God's Oppression of the Innocent in the Old Testament," in *Shall Not the Judge of All the Earth Do What Is Right? Studies on the Nature of God in Tribute to James L. Crenshaw*, edited by David Penchansky and Paul L. Redditt, (Winona Lake, Indiana: Eisenbrauns, 2000), 2.
[8] Katherine Dell, *The Book of Job as Sceptical Literature*, (1991), 125-133; Carol A. Newsom, "The Book of Job: Introduction, Commentary, and Reflections," in *The New Interpreter's Bible*, vol. 4, (1996), 397-398, 430-432.

## FIRST CYCLE OF SPEECHES

[1] Walther Eichrodt, *Theology of the Old Testament*, vol. II, (1967), 394-395.
[2] *Numbers* 12:8.
[3] *Genesis* 22:1-19.
[4] *1 Kings* 19:12.
[5] Terrien, *Job: Poet of Existence*, (1957),75.
[6] *Deuteronomy* 13:1-5; *Jeremiah* 23:25-32.
[7] *Genesis* 8:21.
[8] *Proverbs* 3:11-13.
[9] Kübler-Ross, *On Death and Dying*, (1969), 44.
[10] *Job* 5:2.
[11] *Letter of James* 5:11.
[12] *Job* 5:8.
[13] Pascal, *Memorial*, a brief note found on Pascal after his death, published posthumously in 1670.
[14] *Deuteronomy* 32:23, 42; *Psalms* 7:13; 38:1-2; *Lamentations* 3:12-13; *Ezekiel* 5:16.
[15] *Job* 5:17-18.
[16] Pope, *Job*, 318.
[17] *Isaiah* 43:3, 14-15.
[18] Kierkegaard, *Repetition*, (1983), 197.
[19] *Psalm* 8:4-5 (New International Version).
[20] *Deuteronomy* 32:10.
[21] Carl Jung, *Answer to Job*, (1955), 141.
[22] *Job* 4:17.
[23] *Job* 8:3.
[24] *Job* 5:8.
[25] *Job* 1:22.
[26] *Jeremiah* 12:1.
[27] Commentators who discuss the legal aspects of Job's confrontation with God include: Habel (1985), 54-57; Dick (1983, 1992); Magdalene (2007); Scholnick (1975), (1992); and Sutherland (2004).
[28] *Genesis* 6:5-7.
[29] Erich Fromm, *You Shall Be As Gods: A Radical Interpretation of the Old Testament and Its Tradition*, (1966), 22-26.
[30] *Exodus* 33:20.
[31] Rudolf Otto, *The Idea of the Holy: An Inquiry into the Non-Rational Factor in the Idea of the Divine and Its Relation to the Rational*, (1950).
[32] *Job* 5:8-16.
[33] *Job* 2:3.

[34] *Job* 4:7; 8:20.

[35] *Job* 2:10.

[36] *Genesis* 18:25.

[37] *Job* 5:1.

[38] *Babylonian Talmud*, Baba Bathra 16a.

[39] *Euthyphro* 10a.

[40] Yehezkel Kaufmann, *The Religion of Israel: From Its Beginnings to the Babylonian Exile*, (1960), 21-24.

[41] Abraham Heschel, *The Prophets*, (1962), 217-218.

[42] John Milton, *Paradise Lost* I:25-26.

[43] *Epistle to the Romans* 8:18 (The Jerusalem Bible).

[44] *Daniel* 12.

[45] Fyodor Dostoevsky, *The Brothers Karamazov*, translated by Constance Garnett, (New York: The Modern Library, Random House, Inc., 1995), 271-272.

[46] Richard L. Rubenstein, *After Auschwitz: Radical Theology and Contemporary Judaism*, (1966), x, 153.

[47] Avivah Gottlieb Zornberg, *Genesis: The Beginning of* Desire, (Philadelphia: The Jewish Publication Society, 1995), 18.

[48] *Isaiah* 64:8.

[49] For more on the distinction between shame and guilt, see James A. Colaiaco, *Socrates against Athens: Philosophy on Trial*, (New York: Routledge, 2001), 91-94.

[50] *Job* 8:2.

[51] *Proverbs* 10:19.

[52] *Job* 9:21.

[53] *Job* 10:7.

[54] *Job* 6:28.

[55] *Job* 10:21-22.

[56] *Genesis* 22:1-19.

[57] *Job* 11:7.

[58] *Job* 9:22.

[59] Immanuel Kant, "On the Failure of All Attempted Philosophical Theodicies" (1791) in *Kant on History and Religion*, (1973), 292.

[60] *Exodus* 20:16.

[61] Victor E. Reichert, *Job*, Hebrew Text & English Translation and Commentary, (1946), 85.

[62] Martin Buber, "Job," in *On the Bible: Eighteen Studies by Martin Buber,* (1968), 192. Emphasis in original.

[63] *Psalm* 14:1.

[64] Elie Wiesel, *Night, (1982),42.*

[65] Elie Wiesel, *All Rivers Run to the Sea: Memoirs*, (1995), 84.

[66] Martin Buber, "The Dialogue between Heaven and Earth," in *On Judaism by Martin Buber*, (1967), 224.

[67] *Exodus* 3:1-6.

[68] *Exodus* 33:20.

[69] *Genesis* 18:25.

[70] Northrop Frye, *The Great Code: The Bible and Literature*, (New York: Harcourt Brace Jovanovich, Publishers, 1982), 195.

[71] Weiss, *The Story of Job's Beginning*, (1983), 20.

[72] *King Lear*, IV, Scene 1: 36-37.

[73] Martin Luther, "Preface to the Book of Job," (1524) in *Works of Martin Luther*, With Introduction and Notes, The Philadelphia Edition, vol. six, (Philadelphia: Muhlenberg Press, 1932), 383.

[74] *Macbeth*, Act V, Scene 5: 23-28.

[75] *Isaiah* 54: 8.

[76] *Genesis* 8:1.

[77] *Psalm* 23:1-4.

## SECOND CYCLE OF SPEECHES

[1] *Matthew* 23:65.

[2] *Proverbs* 8:25.

[3] *Jeremiah* 23:18.

[4] *Job* 12:3.

[5] C.S. Lewis, *A Grief Observed*, (2009), 37.

[6] Søren Kierkegaard, *Edifying Discourses, A Selection*, (New York: Harper & Brothers, 1958), 85-86.

[7] *Job* 4:3-4.

[8] Gerhard von Rad, *Wisdom in Israel*, (1972), 217.

[9] *Exodus* 15:21.

[10] Eichrodt, *Theology of the Old Testament*, I, (1961), 228-230.

[11] *Psalm* 24:8.

[12] *Numbers* 21:2; 31:17-18; *Deuteronomy* 2:34; 3:6; 7:1-2, 16, 23-24; 9:3; 11:22-25; 12:29-30; 13:15; 20:10-18; *Joshua* 6:17-19, 21; 8:24-27; 10:1, 28, 32-40; 11:11-14; 16-23; 1 Samuel 15:3, 18; 16:7; 27:9. The annihilation of people to honor God for making victory over enemies possible was common in ancient biblical times. While archaeological evidence has led many scholars to conclude that the extent of the practice of extermination, called "coming under *herem*," is exaggerated, even fictional, it is nevertheless disturbing that the authors of the Bible celebrated such horrendous violence. On the *herem*, see Bernhard W. Anderson, *Understanding the Old Testament*, 3rd ed., (Englewood Cliffs, NJ: Prentice-Hall, Inc., 1975), 172-173; Norman K. Gottwald, *A Light to the Nations: An Introduction to the Old Testament*, (New York: Harper & Row, Publishers, 1959), 158-159; Christine Hayes, *Introduction to the Bible,* (New Haven: Yale University Press, 2012), 190, 410-411; Yehezkel Kaufmann, *The Religion of Israel*, 75, 254; Eric A. Seibert, *The Violence of Scripture: Overcoming the Old Testament's Troubling Legacy,* (Minneapolis: Fortress Press, 2012), 95-98.

[13] *Numbers* 16:49.

[14] *Exodus* 12:29.

[15] *Exodus* 31:14-15.

[16] *Exodus* 22:20.

[17] *Leviticus* 24:16.

[18] Thomas Paine, *The Age of Reason,* Part 1 (1794), chap. VII, "Examination of the Old Testament," in *Paine: Political Writings,* edited by Bruce Kuklick, (Cambridge: Cambridge University Press, 2000), 278.

[19] *Genesis* 4:10.

[20] *Job* 5:1.

[21] Commentators who argue correctly that Job's witness is not God include: Balentine (2006), 259; Clines (1989), 389-390; Habel (1985), 274-275; Pope (1973), 125; Terrien (1954), 1026; and Seow (2012),738.

[22] *Job* 15:8.

[23] Pope, *Job,* 76.

[24] Commentators who misidentify Job's witness as God include: Alden (1993), 187; Andersen (1976), 182-183; Davidson (1862), 146; Dhorme (1967), 239; Driver and Gray (1921), 148; Gordis (1978), 187; Anthony and Miriam Hanson (1953), 50, 57, 59; Hartley (1988), 264; Konkel (2006), 119-120; Peake (1904), 168-169; Rowley (1970), 120-121; Strahan (1914), 155; and Whybray (1998), 91.

[25] *Psalm* 119:121-122.

[26] Pascal, *Pensées* (1670), #423. Louis Lafuma edition.

[27] *Job* 11:17-18.

[28] *Job* 8:2.

[29] *Job* 12:7-8.

[30] *Job* 16:9.

[31] *Psalms* 13:9; 20:20; 24:20.

[32] *Job* 3.

[33] *Job* 18:2.

[34] *Job* 8:3.

[35] *Job* 18:3.

[36] *Habakkuk* 1:2.

[37] *Job* 1:11-12; 2:4.

[38] *Job* 14:21.

[39] Commentators who misidentify Job's redeemer or vindicator as God include: Andersen (1976), 194; Davidson & Lanchester (1951), 167; Delitzsch (1949), vol. I, 354; Driver & Gray (1921), vol. I, 163, 171; Gordis (1978), 206; Gutierrez (1987), 65; Hanson & Hanson (1953), 69; Kissane (1946), 119; Longman (2012), 263; Peake (1904), 192; Rowley (1970), 137-138; Strahan (1914), 170; Whybray (1998), 102; and Wilson (2007), 208.

[40] *Exodus* 6:6; 15:13; *Psalms* 74:2; 77:16; 103:4; *Isaiah* 41:14; 43:14; 44:6.

[41] Commentators who argue correctly that Job's redeemer or vindicator is not God include: Balentine (2006), 297; Clines (1989), 459; Habel (1985), 305-306;

Newsom (1996), 478; Pope (1973), 146; Seow (2012), 804; and Terrien (1954), 1052.
[42] *Leviticus* 25:47-5.
[43] *Leviticus* 25:25-28; *Jeremiah* 32:6-15.
[44] *Ruth* 2:20; 3:12; 4:1-6.
[45] *Numbers* 35:19-28; *Deuteronomy* 19:6-12; *2 Samuel* 14:7, 11.
[46] *Deuteronomy* 19:16; *Isaiah* 19:21; *Psalm* 27:12.
[47] *Job* 13:15.
[48] *Job* 7:9; 10:21; 14:10, 12.
[49] *Psalm* 11:7.
[50] *Job* 19:25-27 (New English Bible).
[51] Norman C. Habel, *The Book of Job, (1985),* 314-315.
[52] *Job* 15:25.
[53] *Job* 16:12-14.
[54] *Job* 1:16.
[55] *Job* 16:18-19.
[56] *Job* 19:25.
[57] *Job* 15:11.
[58] *Job* 16:2.
[59] *Jeremiah* 12:1.
[60] *Ecclesiastes* 8:14.
[61] *Job* 15:17-35; 18:15-21; 20:6-29.
[62] *Job* 20:11.
[63] *Job* 18:19.
[64] *Job* 15:20-22.
[65] *Job* 9:24.
[66] *Job* 18:5.
[67] *Job* 20:28.
[68] *Psalm* 1:4.
[69] *Exodus* 34:7.
[70] *Lamentations* 5:7.On inherited guilt, see also *Exodus* 20:5 and *Numbers* 14:18.
[71] Job reflects the evolution in moral thinking in the Hebrew Bible from inherited guilt to individual responsibility, expressed by the prophets. Jeremiah 31:29-30 and Ezekiel 18:19-20.
[72] Aquinas, *The Literal Exposition on Job,* (1989), 680.
[73] *Job* 15:28, 34; 18:15-21; 20:26-28.
[74] *Job* 18:13-21; 20:20-29.
[75] *Job* 18:17.
[76] *Job* 1:8; 2:3.

## THIRD CYCLE OF SPEECHES

[1] *Job* 18:8-10.
[2] *Psalm* 73:11.
[3] *Proverbs* 10:9.
[4] *Job* 21:14.
[5] *Job* 21:16.
[6] *Psalm* 58:10.
[7] *Job* 15:11.
[8] *Job* 9:33; 16:19; 19:25.
[9] *Job* 9:14-18.
[10] Buber, *On The Bible* ,(1968), 193. Emphasis in original.
[11] *Psalm* 42:3.
[12] *Job* 22:15.
[13] *Psalm* 17:5.
[14] *Job* 6:10.
[15] *Job* 9:12.
[16] Gutierrez, *On Job*, (1987), 32.
[17] *Exodus* 22:22.
[18] *Psalm* 44:23-24.
[19] *Exodus* 3:7-8.
[20] *Psalm* 22:1, 4-5.
[21] *Job* 24:18-24.
[22] Gordis, *The Book of God and Man*, (1965), 269.
[23] Commentators who treat chapter 24, lines 18-24, as the words of Job include: Hartley (1988), 353-353; and Newsom (1996), 511-512.
[24] Hartley (1988), 352; Longman (2012), 304, 314; and Wilson (2007), 278-279.
[25] Andersen (1976), 213.
[26] *Job* 9:22.
[27] *Job* 23:13-15.
[28] *Job* 9:2.
[29] *Psalm* 8:4-6 (New International Version).
[30] *Job* 4:17.
[31] *Job* 9:4-7, 12-13; 12:13-25.
[32] *Job* 9:5-13.
[33] 2 *Samuel* 22:9.
[34] *Psalm* 18:7; also *Isaiah* 2:19, 21; 13:13.
[35] Habel, *The Book of Job*, (1985), 379-380.
[36] *Koran* (Qu'ran), Sura 9:119.
[37] *Job* 2:3, 9.
[38] Wiesel, *Messengers of God,* (1976), 208.
[39] *Job* 19:28-29.
[40] *Job* 13:16.

[41] *Deuteronomy* 19:16-21.
[42] *Job* 22:24.
[43] *Job* 24:18-25.
[44] *Jeremiah* 18:17; *Proverbs* 1:27.
[45] *Jeremiah* 49:17; *Lamentations* 2:15.
[46] *Psalm* 145:18.

## HYMN TO WISDOM

[1] G. K. Chesterton, Introduction to *The Book of Job* (London, 1916), in Glatzer, *The Dimensions of Job* (1969), 230.
[2] Commentators who treat the "Hymn to Wisdom" as the words of Job, integral to the book, include: Childs (1979), 542-543; Good (1990), 290-293; Janzen (1985), 187-188; Alison Lo (2003); and Whybray (1998), 15, 31.
[3] *Job* 9:4; 12:13; 26:14.
[4] *Proverbs* 1:2; 4:5, 7; 9:10; 16:16.
[5] *Genesis* 7:11; 49:25.
[6] *Proverbs* 8:22-23.
[7] *Proverbs* 3:19.
[8] Walton, *Job* (2012), 292.
[9] *Job* 11:6.
[10] *Ecclesiastes* 12:13; also *Proverbs* 1:7; 3:7; *Psalm* 111:10.
[11] *Job* 1:8.

## JOB'S SUMMATION

[1] 2 *Samuel* 22:29.
[2] *Job* 10:14; 13:27.
[3] *Ruth* 4:1-12; *Deuteronomy* 21:19.
[4] *Job* 22:6-9.
[5] *Proverbs* 21:21.
[6] *Job* 29:2.
[7] *Job* 1:3.
[8] *Job* 29:25.
[9] *Job* 19:14.
[10] C.S. Lewis, *A Grief Observed,* (2009), 18-19.
[11] *Job* 27:5.
[12] M. B. Dick, "The Legal Metaphor in Job 31," in *Sitting with Job* (1992), edited by Zuck, 331.
[13] *Exodus* 22:7-8, 10-11.
[14] Gordis, *The Book of Job* (1978), 339; Fohrer, "The Righteous Man in Job 31," in *Essays on Old Testament Ethics* (1974), edited by Crenshaw and Willis, 14, 19.
[15] *Job* 1:5.

[16] *Leviticus* 20:10; *Deuteronomy* 22:22.

[17] *Exodus* 21:23-25.

[18] *Matthew* 5:27.

[19] *Deuteronomy* 32:22.

[20] *Exodus* 23:6.

[21] *Exodus* 21:1-11; *Deuteronomy* 15:12-18.

[22] *Proverbs* 22:2.

[23] *Job* 24:6-9.

[24] *Job* 30:26.

[25] *The Babylonian Talmud,* Sotah 27b.

[26] 1 *Kings* 19:18; *Hosea* 13:2.

[27] *Deuteronomy* 17:2-7.

[28] *Jewish Study Bible* (2004), 1545.

[29] *Job* 27:7.

[30] *Job* 42:7-9.

[31] *Job* 13:24-25.

[32] *Job* 13:25.

[33] *Job* 19:9.

[34] *Job* 23:10.

[35] Gutierrez, *On Job,* (1987), 42.

[36] Kübler-Ross, *On Death and Dying,* (1969), 99.

[37] Nietzche, *Twilight of the Idols*, "Maxims and Arrows," 12.

[38] Nietzche, *Beyond Good and Evil: Prelude to a Philosophy of the Future,* edited by Rolf-Peter Horstmann and Judith Norman, tr. Judith Norman, (Cambridge: Cambridge University Press, 2002), Part 9, section 270, page 166.

[39] Kierkegaard, *Repetition* (1983), 207-208.

## ELIHU SPEAKS

[1] *Proverbs* 3:7.

[2] Magdalene, *On the Scales of Righteousness,* (2007), 225-246.

[3] C. L. Seow, *Job 1-21,* (2012), 33.

[4] *Jeremiah* 20:9.

[5] *Job* 13:7-8.

[6] *Job* 9:34; 13:21.

[7] *Job* 9:21; 10:7; 16:17; 23:7, 10-12; 27:6; ch. 31.

[8] *Job* 13:24, 27; 19:11.

[9] *Job* 7:21; 13:26; 14:17.

[10] *Job* 16:17.

[11] *Job* 9:32.

[12] *Job* 9:1-20, 32; 12:13-25; 13:13-25.

[13] *Job* 7:14.

[14] *Job* 5:18.

[15] *Psalm* 119:67, 71.

[16] C. S. Lewis, *The Problem of Pain* (1996), 91.

[17] Hick, *Evil and the God of Love* (1977), 211-215; 253-256.

[18] *Job* 9:32-35; 16:19; 19:25.

[19] *Job* 19:25-27.

[20] *Psalm* 11:7.

[21] *Haggai* 1:13; *Malachi* 2:7.

[22] *Job* 27:6.

[23] *Job* 19:6-8; 27:2.

[24] *Job* 27:4.

[25] *Job* 15:16.

[26] *Job* 8:3.

[27] *Job* 31:4.

[28] *Job* 24:13-17.

[29] *Job* 24:10.

[30] *Job* 18:4.

[31] Thomas Aquinas, *The Literal Exposition on Job* (1989), 390. Emphasis in original.

[32] *Malachi* 3:14.

[33] *Job* 7:17-19.

[34] *Job* 7:20.

[35] *Job* 24:1-17.

[36] *Psalm* 42:8; also *Psalm* 32:7.

[37] Victor E. Reichert, *Job* (1946), 185.

[38] *Job* 37:16.

[39] *Job* 7:17-21.

[40] *Psalms* 18:19; 23:5.

[41] *Exodus* 19-20.

[42] Eichrodt, *Theology of the Old Testament*, vol. II (1967), 16.

[43] *Job* 36:4.

[44] *Job* 31:35-7.

[45] *Ezekiel* 1:4.

## YAHWEH SPEAKS FROM THE WHIRLWIND

[1] *Job* 2:10.

[2] John T. Wilcox, *The Bitterness of Job* (1989). Wilcox recognizes that Job curses God repeatedly (ch. 4, pp. 51-70). But Wilcox does not show that Job never fulfills the Satan's prediction that he would go so far as to curse God directly and explicitly in a face-to-face encounter.

[3] *Job* 9:32.

[4] *Job* 6:28.

[5] *Job* 13:15.

[6] Leonard W. Levy, *Treason Against God* (1981), 21.

[7] *Deuteronomy* 34:10.

[8] Gordis (1965), 126. On *Genesis* 18:25.

[9] *Exodus* 20:18-21.

[10] *Job* 2:3.

[11] Robert Alter, *The Wisdom Books* (2010), 158, note 2.

[12] *Job* 10:7.

[13] *Job* 10:13.

[14] *Job* 13:18.

[15] *Job* 19:6.

[16] 1 *Kings* 18:46; *Isaiah* 5:27.

[17] Cyrus H. Gordon, "Belt-Wrestling in the Bible World," in 23 Hebrew Union College Annual (1950-51), 131-136, at 136.

[18] Terrien, *The Iconography of Job Through the Centuries* (1996), 37-40.

[19] *Job* 7:12.

[20] *Exodus* 20:2-3.

[21] *Isaiah* 44:8.

[22] *Job* 31:35.

[23] *Job* 13:22.

[24] *Ezra* 3:10-11.

[25] 2 *Chronicles* 5:13.

[26] *Genesis* 1:9.

[27] *Genesis* 1:3-5.

[28] *Exodus* 9:22-26.

[29] *Joshua* 10:11.

[30] *Genesis* 1:28.

[31] *Job* 31:35.

[32] *Exodus* 33:11.

[33] *Job* 9:15, 17.

[34] *Job* 23:4-7.

[35] *Job* 31:37.

[36] Otto, *The Idea of the Holy* (1958).

[37] Moshe Greenberg, "Job," in *The Literary Guide to the Bible*, edited by Alter and Kermode, 298.

[38] Otto, *The Idea of the Holy*, (1950), 28.

[39] *Psalm* 8:5 (New International Version).

[40] *Job* 18:40.

[41] *Job* 32:1-2.

[42] *Job* 19:6; 27:2.

[43] *Psalm* 104:26.

[44] *Psalm* 74:14.

[45] *Isaiah* 27:1.

[46] *Job* 3:8.

[47] Melville, *Moby Dick*, chap. 24, "The Advocate."

[48] *Isaiah* 45:7.

[49] George Bernard Shaw, *Treatise on Parents and Children,* (1910), "The Bible."

[50] Ernst Bloch, *Atheism in Christianity* (1972), 118.

[51] *Job* 19:26-27.

[52] *Job* 30:19.

[53] Clines, *Job 38-42* (2011), 1218; Habel, *The Book of Job* (1985), 579, 582-583; Sutherland, *Putting God on Trial* (2004), 130-131.

[54] Donald Capps, *Reframing* (1990), 158-159; Habel, *The Book of Job* (1985), 576, 583; Dale Patrick, "The Translation of Job XLII 6," 26 *Vetus Testamentum* (1976), 369-371.

## EPILOGUE TO THE BOOK OF JOB

[1] *Exodus* 27:4.

[2] *Job* 30:26.

[3] *Numbers* 27:8.

[4] Fyodor Dostoevsky, *The Brothers Karamazov*, translated by Constance Garnett, (New York: The Modern Library, Random House, Inc., 1995), 325.

[5] Kierkegaard, *Fear and Trembling*, translated with an introduction by Alastair Hannay, (1985), 46.

[6] *Genesis* 12:2.

[7] *Job* 1:5.

[8] *Job* 3:24.

[9] *Job* 31:22.

[10] See, for example, *Exodus* 9:16; 11:9; 14:18; 18:11.

[11] *Isaiah* 63:14.

## FROM AN IMMORAL TO AN AMORAL GOD

[1] Buber, "The Dialogue between Heaven and Earth," in *On Judaism by Martin Buber* (1967), 224.

[2] Ferdinando Camon, *Conversations with Primo Levi*, translated by John Shepley, (Marlboro, Vermont: The Marlboro Press, 1989), 68.

[3] Abraham Joshua Heschel, *A Passion for Truth* (1995), 301.

[4] Gordis, *The Book of God and Man,* (1965), 133.

[5] Alan M. Dershowitz, *The Genesis of Justice* (2000), 80.

[6] Otto, *The Idea of the Holy* (1950), 77.

[7] Otto, (1950), 78.

[8] Otto (1950), 78.

[9] John Hospers, *An Introduction to Philosophical Analysis*, 3rd edition, (New York: Routledge, 1990), 310.

[10] Harold Kushner, *When Bad Things Happen to Good People* (1981), chapters 7 and 8.

[11] Hans Jonas, "The Concept of God after Auschwitz," (1987), 10. Emphasis in original.

[12] J. L. Mackie (1955); H. J. McCloskey (1960).

[13] *Isaiah*, 55:8-9.

[14] Maimonides, *The Guide of the Perplexed*, (1904), Part III, chapter XXIII, 111.

[15] John Paterson, *The Book is Alive* (1954), 113.

[16] Stephen Crane,  "War Is Kind and Other Lines," (1899), XXI.

[17] Robert Frost,  "A Masque of Reason," in *The Poetry of Robert Frost*, edited by Edward Connery Latham, (New York: Holt Rinehart and Winston, 1969), 475-476.

[18] *Job* 19:7.

[19] Jack Miles, *God: A Biography,* (1995), 11.

[20] *Job* 40:11-12.

[21] *Psalm* 8:5 (New International Version).

[22] *Amos* 5:24.

[23] *Job* 1:1.

[24] *Job* 1:8; 2:3.

[25] *Job* 27:5-6.

[26] *Ezekiel* 14:14, 20.

# SELECTED BIBLIOGRAPHY

Aitken, James. *The Book of Job.* Edinburgh: T & T Clark, 1905.

Alden, Robert L. *Job.* The New American Commentary. Nashville: Broadman & Holman, 1993.

Alter, Robert. *The Art of Biblical Narrative.* New York: Basic Books, 1983.

_____ *The Art of Biblical* Poetry. New York: Basic Books, 1985.

_____ *The Wisdom Books: Job, Proverbs, and Ecclesiastes.* New York: W.W. Norton & Co., 2010.

Armstrong, Karen. *The Great Transformation: The Beginning of Our Religious Traditions.* New York: Alfred A. Knopf, 2006.

Andersen, Francis I. *Job: An Introduction and Commentary.* Tyndale Old Testament Commentaries. Downers Grove, Illinois: Inter-Varsity Press, 1976.

Aquinas, Saint Thomas. *The Literal Exposition on Job: A Scriptural Commentary Concerning Providence.* Tr. Anthony Damico. Martin D. Yaffe, Interpretive Essay and Notes. Atlanta, Georgia: Scholars Press, 1989.

Atkinson, David. *The Message of Job: Suffering and Grace.* Downers Grove, Illinois: Inter-Varsity Press, 1991.

Balentine, Samuel E. *Job.* Smyth & Helwys Bible Commentary. Macon, Georgia: Smyth & Helwys, 2006.

Barnes, Albert. *Notes on the Old* Testament. 2 vols. London: Blackie & Son, 1847.

Bartholomew, Craig G. and Ryan P. O' Dowd. *Old Testament Wisdom Literature: A Theological Introduction.* Downers Grove, Illinois: Inter-Varsity Press, 2011.

Barton, George A. *Commentary on the Book of Job.* New York: Macmillan Co. 1911.

Bennett, T. Miles. *When Human Wisdom Fails: An Exposition of the Book of Job.* Grand Rapids, Michigan: Baker Book House, 1971.

Bergant, Dianne. *Job, Ecclesiastes.* Wilmington, Delaware: Michael Glazier, 1982.

Blake, Buchanan. *The Book of Job and the Problem of Suffering.* London: Hodder and Stoughton, 1911.

Blank, S. "The Curse, Blasphemy, the Spell, and the Oath." *Hebrew Union College Annual* 23 (1950-51): 73-95.

Bloch, Ernst. *Atheism in Christianity: The Religion of the Exodus and the Kingdom*. Tr. J. T. Swann. New York: Herder and Herder, 1972.

Bloom, Harold. Ed. *The Book of Job*. New York: Chelsea House, 1988.

_____ *The Shadow of a Rock: A Literary Appreciation of the King James Bible*. New Haven: Yale University Press, 2011.

Blumenthal, David R. *Facing the Abusing God: A Theology of Protest*. Louisville, Kentucky: Westminster John Knox Press, 1993.

Bode, William. *The Book of Job and the Solution of the Problem of Suffering it Offers*. Grand Rapids, Michigan: Eeerdmans-Sevensma Co., 1914.

Boss, Jeffrey. *Human Consciousness of God in the Book of Job: A Theological And Psychological Commentary*. London: T & T Clark International, 2010.

Bradley, George Granwille. *Lectures on the Book of Job*. Oxford: Clarendon Press, 1887.

Brenner, Athalya. "God's Answer to Job." *Vetus Testamentum* 31 (1981): 129-137.

Brown, Charles Reynolds Brown. *The Strange Ways of God: A Study in the Book of Job*. Boston: The Pilgrim Press, 1908.

Brown, William P. "The Deformation of Character: Job 1-31;" "The Reformation of Character: Job 32-42." In *Character in Crisis: A Fresh Approach to the Wisdom Literature of the Old Testament*, 50-119. Grand Rapids, Michigan: Eerdmans, 1996.

Brueggemann, Walter. "The Book of Job." In *An Introduction to the Old Testament: The Canon and Christian Imagination*, 293-303. Louisville: Westminster John Knox Press, 2003.

_____ "The Formfulness of Grief." *Interpretation* 31 (1977): 263-275.

Buber, Martin. "Job." In *On the Bible: Eighteen Studies by Martin Buber*, edited by Nahum N. Glatzer, 188-198. New York: Schocken Books, 1968.

_____ "The Dialogue between Heaven and Earth." In *On Judaism by Martin Buber*, edited by Nahum N. Glazer, 214-225. New York: Schocken Books, 1967.

Bullock, C. Hassell. "The Book of Job," in *An Introduction to the Old Testament Poetic Books*. Revised and Expanded, 79-129. Chicago: Moody Publishers, 1988.

Buttenwieser, Moses. *The Book of Job*. New York: Macmillan, 1922.

Capps, Donald. *Reframing: A New Method in Pastoral Care*. Minneapolis, Minnesota: Fortress Press, 1990.

Carstensen, Roger N. *Job: Defense of Honor*. New York: Abingdon Press, 1963.

Chase, Steven. *Job*. Belief: A Theological Commentary on the Bible. Louisville, Kentucky: John Knox Press, 2013.

Cheyne, T. K. *Job and Solomon*. London: Kegan Paul, Tranch & Co, 1887.

Childs, Brevard S. *Introduction to the Old Testament as Scripture*. Philadelphia: Fortress Press, 1979.

Clasby, Nancy Tenfelde. "Job." In *God, The Bible ,and Human Consciousness*, 115-132. New York: Palgrave Macmillan, 2008.

Clifford, Richard J. "The Book of Job." In *The Wisdom Literature*, 69-96. Nashville,Tennessee: Abingdon Press, 1998.

Clines, David J. *Job 1-20*. Word Biblical Commentary 17. Nashville: Thomas Nelson, 1989.

_____ *Job 21-37*. Word Biblical Commentary 18a. Nashville: Thomas Nelson, 2006.

_____ *Job 38-42*. Word Biblical Commentary 18b. Nashville: Thomas Nelson, 2011.

_____ "Job." In *New International Bible Commentary*. Based on the NIV [New International Version], edited by F. F. Bruce, 520-551. Grand Rapids, Michigan: Zondervan, 1979.

_____ "Job's Fifth Friend: An Ethical Critique of the Book of Job." *Biblical Interpretation* 12 (2004): 233-250.

_____ "Why Is There a Book of Job and What Does It Do to You if You Read It?" In *The Book of Job*, edited by W.A.M. Beuken, 1-20. Leuven, Belgium: Leuven University Press, 1994.

Constable, Thomas L. "Notes on Job." In *Notes on the Bible*, Vol. III, 7-56. Fort Worth, TX: Tyndale Seminary Press, 2012.

Cox, Samuel. *A Commentary on the Book of Job*. With a Translation. 2nd ed. London: Kegan Paul, Trench & Co. 1885.

Crenshaw, James L. *Defending God: Biblical Responses to the Problem of Evil*. Oxford: Oxford University Press, 2005.

_____ "Job." In *The Oxford Bible Commentary*, edited by John Barton and John Muddiman, 331-355. Oxford: Oxford University Press, 2001.

_____ *Reading Job: A Literary and Theological Commentary*. Macon, Georgia: Smyth & Helwys, 2011.

_____ "The Search for Divine Presence: Job." In *Old Testament Wisdom: An Introduction*, 97-126. Louisville, Kentucky: Westminster John Knox Press, 2010.

_____ *A Whirlpool of Torment: Israelite Traditions of God as an Oppressive Presence*. Overtures to Biblical Theology. Philadelphia: Fortress Press, 1984.

Curtis, John Briggs, "On Job's Response to Yahweh." *Journal of Biblical Literature* 98 (1979): 497-511.

_____"On Job's Witness in Heaven," *Journal of Biblical Literature 102 (1983): 549-562.*

Daiches, David. "The Book of Job: God Under Attack." In *God and the Poets.* The Gifford Lecture, 1983, 1-25. Oxford: Clarendon Press, 1984.

Davidson, A. B. *The Book of Job.* A Commentary, Grammatical and Exegetical, with a Translation. Vol. 1. Edinburgh: Williams and Norgate, 1862.

_____*The Book of Job: With Notes, Introduction and Appendix* Adapted to the text of the Revised Version with some supplementary notes by H. C. O. Lanchester. Cambridge: Cambridge University Press, 1951.

Davison, W. T. "The Book of Job." In *The Wisdom Literature of the Old Testament*, 20-105. London: Charles H. Kelly, 1900.

Delitzsch, F. *Biblical Commentary on the Book of Job.* Tr. F. Bolton, 2 vols. Grand Rapids, Michigan: Eerdmans, 1949.

Dell, Katherine. *The Book of Job as Sceptical Literature.* Beihefte zur Zeitschrift fur die Alttestamentliche Wissenschaft 197. Berlin: de Gruyter, 1991.

_____*Shaking a Fist At God: Struggling with the Mystery of Underserved Suffering.* Liguori, Missouri: Triumph Books, 1995.

_____*Job: Where Shall Wisdom be Found?* Sheffield: Sheffield Phoenix Press, 2013.

Dershowitz, Alan M. *The Genesis of Justice: Ten Stories of Biblical Injustice that Led to the Ten Commandments and Modern Law.* New York: Warner Books, 2000.

Dhorme, Édouard. *A Commentary on the Book of Job.* Tr. Harold Knight. New York: Thomas Nelson & Sons, 1967.

Dick, M. B. "The Legal Metaphor in Job 31." In *Sitting with Job: Selected Studies on the Book of Job,* edited by Roy B. Zuck, 321-334. Grand Rapids, Michigan: Baker Academic, 1992.

_____ "Job 31, The Oath of Innocence, and the Sage." *Zeitschrift fur die Alttestamentliche Wissenschaft* 95 (1983): 31-53.

Dillon, E. J. "The Poem of Job." In *The Sceptics of the Old Testament,* 1-53. London: Isbister and Co. Ltd., 1895.

Driver, S. R. "Book of Job." In *An Introduction to the Literature of the Old Testament*, 408-435. Gloucester, Mass.: Peter Smith, 1972.

Driver, S. R. *The Book of Job in the Revised Version.* With Introductions and  Brief Annotations. Oxford: The Clarendon Press, 1908.

Driver, S. R. and G. B. Gray. *The Book of Job.* International Critical Commentary. Two Volumes. Edinburgh: T. & T. Clark, 1921.

Duquoc, Christian, and Casiano Floristan, eds. *Job and the Silence of God.* New York: Seabury, 1983.

Eichrodt, Walther. *Theology of the Old Testament.* Tr. J. A. Baker. Two Volumes. Philadelphia: The Westminster Press, 1961, 1967.

*The English Bible: King James Version.* Volume One: The Old Testament, edited by Herbert Marks. Norton Critical Edition. New York: W. W. Norton & Co., 2012.

*English Standard Version [ESV] Study Bible,* edited by Lane T. Dennis and Wayne Grudem. Wheaton, Illinois: Crossway, 2008.

Erhman, Bart D. *God's Problem: How the Bible Fails to Answer Our Most Important Question—Why We Suffer.* New York: Harper Collins, 2008.

Estes, Daniel J. *Handbook on the Wisdom Books and Psalms.* Grand Rapids, Michigan: Baker Academic, 2005.

_____ *Job.* In Teach the Text Capital Commentary Series. Mark L. Strauss and John H. Walton, general editors. Grand Rapids, Michigan: Baker Goods, 2013.

Ewald, G. H. A. *Commentary on the Book of Job.* With Translation. Tr. J. Smith. London: Williams and Norgate, 1882.

Fingarette, Herbert. "The Meaning of Law in the Book of Job." *The Hastings Law Journal.* 29 (1978): 1581-1617.

Fohrer, Georg. "The Righteous Man in Job 31." In *Essays on Old Testament Ethics,* edited by James L. Crenshaw and John T. Willis, 1-22. New York: KTAV Publishing House, Inc., 1974.

Frankl,Viktor E. *Man's Search for Meaning.* Boston: Beacon Press, 2006.

Freehof, Solomon B. *The Book of Job: A Commentary.* New York: Union of American Hebrew Congregations, 1958.

Fromm, Erich. *You Shall Be As Gods: A Radical Interpretation of the Old Testament and Its Tradition.* New York: Holt, Rinehart and Winston, 1966.

Frost, Robert. "A Masque of Reason." In *The Poetry of Robert Frost,* edited by Edward Connery Latham, 473-490. New York: Holt, Rinehart and Winston, 1969.

Froude, James Anthony. "The Book of Job." In *Short Studies on Great Subjects*, Volume I, 244-293. New York: Charles Scribner's Sons, 1908.

Genung, John F. *The Epic of the Inner Life Being the Book of Job.* Translated Anew, and Accompanied with Notes and an Introductory Study. Boston: Houghton, Mifflin and Co., 1891.

Gerber, Israel J. *Job on Trial: A Book for Our Time.* Gastonia, North Carolina: E. P. Press, Inc, 1982.

Gibson, Edgar C. S. *The Book of Job.* With Introduction and Notes. London: Methuen and Company, 1899.

Gibson, John C. J. *Job.* Philadelphia: The Westminster Press, 1985.

Gill, John. *An Exposition of the Old Testament.* Volume III. "Job," 187-523. London: Mathews and Leigh, 1810.

Glatzer, Nahum N. editor. *The Dimensions of Job: A Study and Selected Readings.* New York: Schocken Books, 1969.

Goldberg, David. "Providence and the Problem of Evil in Jewish Thought." In *Evil and the Response of World Religion,* edited by William Cenkner, 32- 42. St. Paul, Minnesota: Paragon House, 1997.

Good, Edwin M. *In Turns of Tempest: A Reading of Job with a Translation.* Stanford, Calif.: Stanford University Press, 1990.

_____ "Job." In *Harper's Bible Commentary.* James L. Mays, general editor, 407-423. San Francisco: Harper & Row, Publishers, 1988.

Gordis, Robert, *The Book of God and Man: A Study of Job.* Chicago: University of Chicago Press, 1965.

_____ *The Book of Job: Commentary and New Translation, and Special Studies.* New York: Jewish Theological Seminary of America, 1978.

_____ "The Conflict of Tradition and Experience (The Book of Job)." In *Great Moral Dilemmas In Literature, Past and Present,* edited by R. M. MacIver, 155-178. New York: Harper & Brothers, 1956.

Gordon, Cyrus H. "Belt-Wrestling in the Bible World." 23 *Hebrew Union College Annual* (1950-1951): 131-136.

Green, William Henry. *The Argument of the Book of Job Unfolded.* New York: Robert Carter and Brothers, 1874.

Greenberg, Moshe. "Job." In *The Literary Guide to the Bible,* edited by Robert Alter and Frank Kermode, 283-304. Cambridge: Harvard University Press, 1987.

Gutierrez, Gustavo, *On Job: God-Talk and the Suffering of the Innocent.* Tr. M. J. O'Connell. Maryknoll, N. Y.: Orbis, 1987.

Habel, Norman C. *The Book of Job:* A Commentary. Old Testament Library. Philadelphia: Westminster John Knox, 1985.

Hanson, Anthony and Miriam. T*he Book of Job: Introduction and Commentary.* London: SCM Press, 1953.

Hartley, John E. *The Book of Job.* New International Commentary on the Old Testament. Grand Rapids, Michigan: Eerdmans, 1988.

Hayes, Christine. *Introduction to the Bible.* New Haven: Yale University Press, 2012.

Heschel, Abraham Joshua. "The Kotzker and Job." In *A Passion for Truth*. Reprint, 261- 303. Woodstock, Vermont: Jewish Lights Publishing 1995.
____*The Prophets*. Philadelphia: The Jewish Publication Society of America, 1962.
Hick, John. *Evil and the God of Love*. Revised edition. San Francisco: Harper Collins, 1977.
Holbert, John C. *Preaching Job*. St. Louis: Chalice, 1999.
*The Holy Scriptures According to the Masoretic Text*. Philadelphia: The Jewish Publication Society of America, 1917.
Humphreys, W. Lee. "The Tragic Vision and the Book of Job." In *The Tragic Vision and the Hebrew Tradition*, 94-123. Philadelphia: The Fortress Press, 1985.
Irwin, W. A. "Job." In *Peake's Commentary on the Bible*, edited by M. Black and H. H. Rowley, 391-408. London: Thomas Nelson & Sons, 1962,
Janzen, J. Gerald. *Job*. Interpretation. A Bible Commentary for Teaching and Preaching. Atlanta: Westminster John Knox, 1985.
Jaspers, Karl. *The Origin and Goal of History*. Tr. Michael Bullock. New Haven: Yale University Press, 1953.
Jastrow, Morris, Jr. *The Book of Job: Its Origin, Growth and Interpretation. Together with a New Translation Based on a Revised Text*. Philadelphia: J. B. Lippincott Co. 1920.
*Jewish Study Bible*, edited by Adele Berlin and Marc Zvi Brettler. Jewish Publication Society. Tanakh Translation. Oxford: Oxford University Press, 2004.
Jonas, Hans. "The Concept of God after Auschwitz." *The Journal of Religion* 67 (1987): 1-13.
Jones, Edgar. *The Triumph of Job*. London: SCM Press, 1966.
Jung, Carl Gustav. *Answer to Job*. Tr. R. F. C. Hull. New York: Pastoral Psychology, 1955.
Kahn, Jack. *Job's Illness: Loss, Grief and Integration. A Psychological Interpretation*. Oxford: Pergamon Press, 1975.
Kallen, H. *The Book of Job as a Greek Tragedy*. New York: Moffat, Yard & Co., 1918.
Kant, Immanuel."On the Failure of All Attempted Philosophical Theodicies." (1791) In *Kant on History and Religion*. Tr. Michel Despland, 283-297. Montreal: McGill-Queens University Press, 1973.
Kaufmann, Walter. "Suffering and the Bible." In *The Faith of a Heretic*. Anchor Books, 137-169. New York: Doubleday & Company, Inc., 1963.

Kaufmann, Yehezkel. The Religion of Israel: From Its Beginnings to the Babylonian Exile. Tr. and abridged by Moshe Greenberg. Chicago: University of Chicago Press, 1960.

Kelly, Balmer H. "Job." The Layman's Bible Commentary. Richmond, Virginia: John Knox Press, 1962.

Kent, H. Harold. Job, Our Contemporary. Grand Rapids, Michigan: William B. Eerdmans Publishing Co., 1967.

Kepnes, Stephen. "Job and Post-Holocaust Theodicy." In Strange Fire: Reading the Bible after the Holocaust, edited by Tod Linafelt, 252-266. New York: New York University Press, 2000.

_____ "Rereading Job as Textual Theodicy." In Suffering Religion, edited by Robert Gibbs and Elliot R. Wolfson, 36-55. London and New York: Routledge, 2002.

Kidner, Derek. The Wisdom of Proverbs, Job and Ecclesiastes. Downers Grove, Illinois: Inter-Varsity, 1985.

Kierkegaard, Søren. Fear and Trembling, translated with an introduction by Alastair Hannay. London: Penguin Books, 1985.

_____ "The Lord Gave, and the Lord Hath Taken Away, Blessed be the Name of the Lord." In Edifying Discourses. A Selection Edited with an Introduction by Paul L. Halmer. Tr. David F. and Lillian Marvin Swenson, 67-86. Harper Torchbooks. New York: Harper & Brothers, 1958.

_____ Repetition. In Fear and Trembling/ Repetition. Edited and translated by Howard V. and Edna H. Hong, 125-231. Princeton: Princeton University Press, 1983.

Kissane, E. The Book of Job. Translated from a Critically Revised Hebrew Text with Commentary. New York: Sheed & Ward, 1946.

Konkel, A. H. "Job." In Job, Ecclesiastes, Song of Songs, edited by P. W. Comfort, 1-249. Cornerstone Biblical Commentary. Carol Stream, IL: Tyndale House, 2006.

Kraeling, Emil G. The Book of the Ways of God. New York: Charles Scribner's Sons, 1938.

Kübler-Ross, Elisabeth, On Death and Dying. Collier Books. New York: Macmillan Publishing Company, 1969.

_____ On Grief and Grieving: Finding the Meaning of Grief Through the Five Stages of Loss. New York: Scribner, 2005.

Kushner, Harold S. The Book of Job: When Bad Things Happened to a Good Person. New York: Schocken Books, 2012.

_____ When Bad Things Happen to Good People. With a New Preface by the Author. New York: Schocken Books, 1981, 2001.

Larrimore, Mark. *The Book of Job: A Biography.* Princeton: Princeton University Press, 2013.

Laytner, Anson. *Arguing with God: A Jewish Tradition.* Northvale, New Jersey: Jason Aronson Inc., 1990.

Leaman, Oliver. "Job." In *Evil and Suffering in Jewish Philosophy,* 19-32 Cambridge: Cambridge University Press, 1995.

Levy, Leonard W. *Treason Against God: A History of the Offense of Blasphemy.* NewYork: Schocken Books,1981.

Lewis, C.S. *A Grief Observed.* New York: Harper Collins Publishers, 2009.

_____ *The Problem of Pain.* New York: Harper Collins Publishers, 1996.

Lo, Alison. *Job 28 as Rhetoric: An Analysis of Job 28 in the Context of Job 22-31.* Supplement to Vetus Testamentum 97. Leiden: Brill, 2003.

Long, Gary. "Job." In *The Baker Illustrated Bible Commentary,* edited by Gary M. Burge and Andrew E. Hill, 453-493, Grand Rapids, Michigan: Baker Books, 2012.

Longman, Tremper, III. *Job.* Grand Rapids, Michigan: Baker Academic, 2012.

MacKenzie, R. A. F. and Roland E. Murphy. "Job." In *The New Jerome Biblical Commentary,* edited by Raymond E. Brown, Joseph A. Fitzmyer, and Roland E. Murphy, 466-488, Englewood Cliffs, New Jersey: Prentice Hall, 1990.

Mackie, J. L. "Evil and Omnipotence." *Mind* 64 (1955): 200-212.

Magdalene, F. R. *On the Scales of Righteousness: Neo-Babylonian Trial Law and the Book of Job.* Brown Judaic Studies 348. Providence: Brown Judaic Studies, 2007.

Maimonides, Moses. *The Guide of the Perplexed.* Translated from the Original and Annotated by M. Friedlander. New York: Hebrew Publishing Company, 1904.

Marshall, J. T. *The Book of Job.* Philadelphia: American Baptist Publication Society, 1904.

_____ *Job and His Comforters.* London: James Clarke & Co, 1905.

McCloskey, H. J. "God and Evil." *Philosophical Quarterly* 10 (1960): 97-114.

McFadyen, John Edgar. *The Problem of Pain: A Study in the Book of Job.* London: James Clarke & Co, 1910.

McKechnie, James. *Job: Moral Hero, Religious Egoist and Mystic.* New York: George H. Doran Co. 1927.

McKenna, David L. *Job: The Communicator's Commentary.* Waco Texas: Word Books, 1986.

Mettinger, Tryggve N. "The God of Job: Avenger, Tyrant, or Victor." In *The Voice from the Whirlwind: Interpreting the Book of Job,* edited by Perdue, L. G. and W. C. Gilpin, 39-49 Nashville: Abingdon, 1992.

Miles, Jack. *God: A Biography.* New York: Alfred A. Knopf, 1995.

Mitchell, Stephen. *The Book of Job.* San Francisco: North Point, 1987.

Morrow, William. "Consolation, Rejection, and Repentance in Job 42:6." *Journal of Biblical Literature* 105 (1986): 211-225.

Moulton, Richard G. *The Book of Job,* edited with an Introduction and Notes. New York: The Macmillan Co., 1922.

Murphy, Roland E. "Job the Steadfast." In *The Tree of Life: An Exploration of Biblical Wisdom Literature*, 33-48. New York: Doubleday, 1990.

_____ *The Book of Job: A Short Reading.* New York: Paulist, 1999.

_____ *Wisdom Literature: Job, Proverbs, Ruth, Canticles, Ecclesiastes, and Esther.* Forms of the Old Testament Literature 13. Grand Rapids, Michigan: Eerdmans, 1981.

Neher, André. *The Exile of the Word: From the Silence of the Bible to the Silence of Auschwitz.* Tr. David Maisel. Philadelphia: The Jewish Publication Society of America, 1981.

*New English Bible.* With the Apocrypha. Samuel Sandmel, general editor. New York: Oxford University Press, 1972.

*New International Version [NIV] Study Bible.* Kenneth L. Barker, general editor. Grand Rapids, Michigan: Zondervan, 2011.

*The New Interpreter's Study Bible.* New Revised Standard Version with the Apocrypha. Walter J. Harrelson, general editor. Nashville, Tennessee: Abingdon Press, 2003.

*New King James Version [NKJV] Study Bible.* Second edition. Ronald B. Allen, Old Testament editor. Nashville, Tennessee: Thomas Nelson, 2007.

*New Oxford Annotated Bible.* Containing the Old and New Testaments. New Revised Standard Version, edited by Bruce M. Metzger and Roland E. Murphy. New York: Oxford University Press, 1994.

*New Oxford Annotated Bible.* New Revised Standard Version with the Apocrypha, edited by Michael D. Coogan. Oxford: Oxford University Press, 2010.

Newsom, Carol A. "The Book of Job: Introduction, Commentary, and Reflections." In *The New Interpreter's Bible ,* edited by Leander E. Keck. Vol. 4, 319-637. Nashville, Tennessee: Abingdon, 1996.

Nimmo, Peter W. "Sin, Evil and Job: Monotheism as a Psychological and Pastoral Problem." *Pastoral Psychology (1994): 427-438.*

Noyes, George R. *The Book of Job*. A New Translation with an
Introduction, and Notes Chiefly Explanatory. Boston: James Munroe and
Co., 1861.

O'Connor, Kathleen M. *Job*. New Collegeville Bible Commentary.
Collegeville, Minnesota: Liturgical Press, 2012.

_____ "Job and the Collapse of Relationship." In *The Wisdom Literature*,
86-113. Collegeville, Minnesota: The Liturgical Press, 1990.

Otto, Rudolf. *The Idea of the Holy: An Inquiry into the Non-Rational Factor
in the Idea of the Divine and Its Relation to the Rational.* 2nd edition. Tr.
John W. Harvey. London: Oxford University Press, 1950.

Ozick, Cynthia. Preface. *The Book of Job*. Vintage Spiritual Classics. New
York: Vintage Books, 1998.

Parsons, Gregory W. "The Structure and Purpose of the Book of Job." In
*Sitting with Job: Selected Studies on the Book of Job*, edited by Roy B.
Zuck, 17-33. Grand Rapids, Michigan: Baker Academic, 1992.

_____ "Literary Features of the Book of Job." In *Sitting with Job: Selected
Studies on the Book of Job*, edited by Roy B. Zuck, 35-49. Grand
Rapids, Michigan: Baker Academic, 1992.

Paterson, John. *The Book of Alive: Studies on Old Testament Life and
Thought as Set Forth by the Hebrew Sages.* New York: Charles Scribner's
Sons, 1954.

Patrick, D., "The Translation of Job 42:6." Vetus Testamentum 26 (1976):
369-371.

Peake, A. S. *Job*. The Century Bible. London: T. C. & E. C. Jack, 1904.

_____ *The Problem of Suffering in the Old Testament*. 1904. London: The
Epworth Press, 1947.

Penchansky, David. *The Betrayal of God: Ideological Conflict in Job.*
Louisville: Westminster John Knox, 1991.

_____ "The Meaning of the Book of Job." In *Understanding Wisdom
Literature: Conflict and Dissonance in the Hebrew Text*, 35-49. Grand
Rapids, Michigan: William B. Eerdmans Publishing Co., 2012

Perdue, L. G. and W. C. Gilpin, eds. *The Voice from the Whirlwind:
Interpreting the Book of Job.* Nashville: Abingdon, 1992.

Pfeiffer, Robert H. *Introduction to the Old Testament.* New York: Harper &
Brothers Publishers, 1948.

Pope, Marvin. H. *Job*. 3rd ed. Anchor Bible. Garden City, N Y: Doubleday,
1973.

Preminger, Alex and Edward L. Greenstein, eds. *The Hebrew Bible in
Literary Criticism.* New York: Ungar Publishing Co., 1986.

*The Pulpit Commentary,* edited by H.D. M. Spence and Joseph S. Exell. Volume 7: Ezra, Nehemiah, Esther & Job. "Job." Exposition by G. Rawlinson, Homiletics by T. Whitelaw. Pp. i-xxii; 1-684. Grand Rapids, Michigan: Eerdmans Publishing Co., 1977.

Reichert, Victor E. *Job.* Hebrew Text & English Translation with an Introduction and Commentary. London: The Soncino Press, 1946.

Renan, Ernest. *The Book of Job*. Translated from the Hebrew, with a Study upon the Age and Character of the Poem, 1859. Rendered into English by A.F.G. and W.M.T. London: W.M. Thomson, Marlborough House, Ludgate  Hill, n.d.

Reyburn, William D. *A Handbook on the Book of Job.* USB Handbook Series, N. Y. United Bible Societies, 1992.

Roberts, J. J. M. "Job's Summons to Yahweh: The Exploitation of the Legal Metaphor." *Restoration Quarterly.* 16 (1973): 159-165.

Robertson, D., "The Book of Job." In *The Old Testament and the Literary Critic,* 33-54. Philadelphia: Fortress Press, 1977.

Robinson, T. H. *Job and His Friends.* London: SCM Press LTD., 1954.

Robinson, Thomas. *Homiletical Commentary on the Book of Job.* London: Richard D. Dickinson, 1876.

Rowley, H. H. "The Book of Job and Its Meaning." In *From Moses to Qumran: Studies in the Old Testament*, 141-183. New York: Association Press, 1963.

_____ *Job.* New Century Bible, Thomas Nelson & Sons, 1970.

Roy, Arlin. "The Book of Job: A Grief and Human Development Interpretation." *Journal of Religion and Health.* 30 (1991): 149-159.

Rubenstein, Richard L. *After Auschwitz: Radical Theology and Contemporary Judaism.* Indianapolis: Bobbs-Merrill Co., Inc., 1966.

_____ "Job and Auschwitz." In *Strange Fire: Reading the Bible after the Holocaust*, edited by Tod Linafelt, 233-251, New York: New York University Press, 2000.

Safire, William. *The First Dissident: The Book of Job in Today's Politics.* New York: Random House, 1992.

Sanders, Paul. ed. *Twentieth Century Interpretations of the Book of Job: A Collection of Critical Essays.* Englewood Cliffs, NJ: Prentice-Hall, 1968.

Scheindlin Raymond P. *The Book of Job.* Translation, Introduction, and Notes. New York: W. W. Norton & Company, 1998.

Scholnick, S. H. *Lawsuit Drama in the Book of Job.* Ph. D. dissertation, Brandeis University, 1975.

_____ "The Meaning of *mispat* in the Book of Job." In *Sitting with Job: Selected Studies on the Book of Job*, edited by Roy B. Zuck, 349-358. Grand Rapids, Michigan: Baker Academic, 1992.

Seeskin, Kenneth. "Job and the Problem of Evil." *Philosophy and Literature*. 11 (1987): 226-241.

Seow, C. L.. *Job 1-21*. Grand Rapids, Michigan: Eerdmans, 2012.

Simundson, Daniel J. *The Message of Job*. Lima, Ohio: Academic Renewal Press, 2001.

Singer, Richard E. *Job's Encounter*. New York: Bookman Associates, Inc., 1963.

Smick, Elmer B. and Tremper Longman III (reviser). "Job." In *The Expositor's Bible Commentary*, revised edition, Vol. 4, edited by Tremper Longman III, 675-921 Grand Rapids, Michigan: Zondervan, 2010.

Steinberg, Milton. "Job Answers God: Being the Religious Perplexities of an Obscure Pharisee." *The Journal of Religion* 12 (1932):159-176.

Stevenson, William Barron. *Critical Notes on the Hebrew Text of The Poem of Job*. Aberdeen, Scotland: Aberdeen University Press, 1951.

Strahan, James. *The Book of Job Interpreted*. 2nd ed. Edinburgh: T. & T. Clarke, 1914.

Surin, Kenneth. "Theodicy?" *Harvard Theological Review* 76 (1983): 225-247.

Sutherland, Robert. *Putting God on Trial: The Biblical Book of Job*. Victoria, B. C., Canada: Trafford Publishing, 2004.

Swindoll, Charles R. *Job: A Man of Heroic Endurance*. Nashville, Tennessee: W. Publishing Group, a Division of Thomas Nelson Publishers, 2004.

Terrien, Samuel. *The Iconography of Job Through the Centuries. Artists and Biblical Interpreters*. University Park, Pennsylvania: Pennsylvania State University Press, 1996.

_____ "Job: Introduction and Exegesis." In *The Interpreter's Bible,* edited by G. A. Buttrick. 12 vols. Volume 3, 877-1198. Nashville: Abingdon, 1954.

_____ *Job: Poet of Existence*. Indianapolis: Bobbs-Merrill, 1957.

Thomason, Bill. *God on Trial: The Book of Job and Human Suffering*. Collegewille, Minnesota: The Liturgical Press, 1977.

Tilley, Terrence W. "God and the Silencing of Job." *Modern Theology* 5 (1989): 257-270.

Tur-Sinai, N. H. *The Book of Job: A New Commentary*. Revised Edition. Jerusalem: Kiryat Sefer, 1957

Tsevat, Matitiahu. "The Meaning of the Book of Job." In *Sitting with Job: Selected Studies on the Book of Job*, edited by Roy B. Zuck, 189-218. Grand Rapids, Michigan: Baker Academic, 1992.

Vawter, Bruce. *Job and Jonah: Questioning the Hidden God.* New York: Paulist Press, 1983.

Von Rad, Gerhard. *Wisdom in Israel.* Tr. J. D. Martin. Nashville: Abingdon, 1972.

Walton, John H. *Job.* The NIV Applicaton Commentary.  Grand Rapids, Michigan: Zondervan, 2012.

Watson, Robert A. *The Book of Job.* London: Hodder and Stoughton, 1892.

Weiss, M. *The Story of Job's Beginning: Job 1-2, A Literary Analysis.* Jerusalem: Magnes, 1983.

Westermann, C. *The Structure of the Book of Job: A Form-Critical Analysis.* Tr. Charles A. Muenchow. Philadelphia: Fortress, 1981.

Wharton, James A. *Job.* Westminster Bible Companion. Louisville, Kentucky: Westminster John Knox Press, 1999.

Whybray, Norman. *Job.* Readings: A New Biblical Commentary. Sheffield: Sheffield Academic Press, 1998.

_____ "Shall Not the Judge of All the Earth Do What is Just?" God's Oppression of the Innocent in the Old Testament. In *Shall Not the Judge of All the Earth Do What is Right? Studies on the Nature of God In Tribute to James L. Crenshaw.* Edited by David Penshansky and Paul L. Redditt. 1-19. Winona Lake, Indiana: Eisenbrauns, 2000.

Wiesel, Elie. *All Rivers Run to the Sea: Memoirs.* New York: Alfred A. Knopf,  1995.

_____ "Job." In *Peace, In Deed.* Essays in Honor of Harry James Cargas, edited by Zev Garber and Richard Libowitz, 119-134. Atlanta, Georgia: Scholars Press, 1998.

_____ "Job our Contemporary." In *Messengers of God: Biblical Portraits and Legends.* Tr. Marilyn Wiesel, 187-208. New York: Random House, 1976.

_____ *Night.* Tr. Stella Rodway. New York: Bantam Books, 1982.

Wilcox, J. T. *The Bitterness of Job: A Philosophical Reading.* Ann Arbor: University of Michigan Press, 1989.

Wilson, Gerald H. *Job.* New International Biblical Commentary. Peabody, MA: Hendrickson, 2007.

*World English Bible.* Biblegateway.com.

Wood, James. *Job and the Human Situation.* London: Geoffrey Bles, 1966

Zuck, Roy B. ed. *Sitting with Job: Selected Studies on the Book of Job.* Grand Rapids, Michigan: Baker Academic, 1992.

Zuckerman, B. *Job the Silent, A Study in Historical Counterpoint.* Oxford: Oxford University Press, 1991.

Made in the USA
Middletown, DE
19 November 2015